Governing

Issues and Applications from the Front Lines of Government

Edited by Alan Ehrenhalt

SECOND EDITION

CQ PRESS

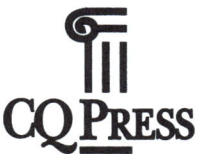

A Division of Congressional Quarterly Inc., Washington, D.C.

CQ Press
1255 22nd Street, N.W., Suite 400
Washington, D.C. 20037

(202) 729-1900; toll-free, 1-866-4CQ-PRESS (1-866-427-7737)
www.cqpress.com

Copyright © 2005 by CQ Press, a division of Congressional Quarterly Inc.

All rights reserved. No part of this publication may be reproduced or transmitted in any form or by any means, electronic or mechanical, including photocopy, recording, or any information storage and retrieval system, without permission in writing from the publisher.

♾ The paper used in this publication exceeds the requirements of the American National Standard for Information Sciences—Permanence of Paper for Printed Library Materials, ANSI Z39.48-1992.

Printed and bound in the United States of America

09 08 07 06 05   5 4 3 2 1

Cover illustration by Bill Cigliano
Cover design by TGD Communications, Alexandria, Va.

Library of Congress Cataloging-in-Publication Data

Governing : issues and applications from the front lines of government / edited by Alan Ehrenhalt.— 2nd ed.
   p. cm.
 Articles previously published in Governing.
 Includes index.
 ISBN 1-56802-995-0 (alk. paper)
 1. State governments—United States. 2. Local government—United States. 3. Federal government—United States. I. Ehrenhalt, Alan, 1947- II. Governing. III. Title.

JK2443.G68 2005
351.73—dc22

2004029190

Contents

INTRODUCTION   xi

STRUCTURE

1 Are City Councils a Relic of the Past?   1
One of America's oldest political institutions isn't adapting very well to 21st-century urban life.
Rob Gurwitt

2 Anatomy of a Merger   7
Greater Louisville is about to be born. How much greater will it be?
Alan Greenblatt

3 In Search of the Ideal Legislature   13
A new look at how state legislatures have changed.
Alan Ehrenhalt

4 The Phantom of New York   16
Quasi-governmental authorities spend billions of dollars of Empire State taxpayers' money every year. They don't have to answer many questions about it.
Christopher Swope

MONEY

5 The Great GASB   21
States and localities now have to account for the real value of everything from city halls to drainage systems.
Michele Mariani

6 Insufficient Funds   24
Half of the states are embroiled in lawsuits charging that school spending is inadequate. How much money is enough—and where will it come from?
Dennis Farney

7 The Well That Dried Up   29
Pittsburgh has weathered some tough economic times and there are encouraging signs. If only the government weren't broke.
Anya Sostek

8 Risky Ventures   33
Private investors are pushing a complex venture-capital scheme that involves big risks and uncertain rewards for states.
Christopher Swope

HUMAN RESOURCES

9 Worth the Money?   39
The competition for top talent is producing a cadre of highly paid public executives.
Jonathan Walters

10 Going Outside   44
The push to privatize is expanding beyond service delivery into the areas of policy making and program design.
Jonathan Walters

iii

CONTENTS

11 Payout Planning   49
   As older workers retire, state pension funds are finding they've made more promises than they can keep.
   Christopher Swope

12 Civil Service Tsunami   52
   Florida's radical overhaul of its personnel system is making big political waves.
   Jonathan Walters

TECHNOLOGY

13 The Dot-Bomb's Silver Lining   57
   In the wake of the tech sector's tumble, governments are finding it easier to fill IT positions.
   Ellen Perlman

14 Legislators Who Get IT   60
   Politicians hold the purse strings for big technology projects. But few are interested in or informed about IT issues.
   Ellen Perlman

15 Dealing in Data   64
   Forget about building a big all-purpose database. There are other ways to integrate state and local information.
   Ellen Perlman

16 Honey, I Shrunk the Deficit!   68
   Computer games offer citizens the chance to see how government works and the trade-offs involved in policy making.
   Christopher Conte

REGULATION

17 Trading for Clean Water   73
   States and localities are intrigued by proposals to create market mechanisms for solving intractable water-pollution problems.
   Tom Arrandale

18 The E-mail Mess   76
   A new federal law is riding roughshod over tough state efforts to stop unwanted—and often indecent—spam.
   Ellen Perlman

19 Who's Afraid of the DMV?   79
   For most people, motor vehicle offices are the face of government. It's not a pretty face.
   Jonathan Walters

20 Unscrambling the City   83
   Archaic zoning laws lock cities into growth patterns that hardly anybody wants. Changing the rules can help set them free.
   Christopher Swope

POLICY

CRIME

21 Murder Mystery   87
   In the 1990s, New York and Boston achieved dramatic decreases in homicide. One of them is still improving. The other is getting worse again. Why?
   John Buntin

22 Revising Sentences   93
   State budget problems have sparked pragmatic, bipartisan debates about alternatives to incarceration.
   Christopher Swope

HEALTH

23 Deadly Strains   96
   SARS, West Nile virus and bioterrorism are the big scares. But the greater threat is the gradual erosion of public health services.
   Christopher Conte

24 Maine's Medical Gamble   101
   Can broader insurance coverage bring health care costs under control? One state is betting on it.
   Penelope Lemov

EDUCATION

25 The Left Behind Syndrome   105
   The federal government is telling school systems exactly what they must accomplish. It isn't doing much to help them accomplish it.
   Alan Greenblatt

CONTENTS

26 Edge-ucation — 110
What compels communities to build schools in the middle of nowhere?
Rob Gurwitt

HOMELAND SECURITY

27 Politics and Promises — 116
Rhetoric meets the reality of a slowdown in homeland security funding.
Christopher Logan

28 Breaking and Entering — 121
Protecting government networks against terrorists requires being relentlessly vigilant.
Ellen Perlman

FEDERALISM

29 Enemies of the State — 125
State-versus-local tension is getting worse. Locals fear state budgets will be balanced at their expense. They may be right.
Alan Greenblatt

30 Made in Sacramento — 130
California is using its clout to fill what officials there view as a national policy void on key issues. Is the state overstepping its boundaries?
Christopher Swope

31 Squeezing the Federal Turnip — 135
This isn't the easiest time for localities to get money out of Washington. But they aren't about to quit asking.
Alan Greenblatt

32 HUD the Unlovable — 139
The federal housing agency changes its focus every couple of years. The only constant is local frustration.
Christopher Swope

ETHICS

33 The Avengers General — 144
State AGs have accumulated an enormous amount of power. Too much, some people think.
Alan Greenblatt

34 That Clean-All-Over Feeling — 148
Maine's reformers believe they are washing the special interest money out of state politics. But critics say they are just laundering it.
Alan Greenblatt

35 Addicted to Corruption — 152
San Bernardino has been crooked for years. It will take years to clean it up.
William Fulton and Paul Shigley

36 The Soft-Money Crackdown — 157
There's a lot that state political parties still don't know about the new campaign finance law. They need to learn fast.
Alan Greenblatt

LEADERSHIP

37 Sugar Daddy Government — 162
A new generation of billionaires is remaking American cities. The cities are better off; the democratic process sometimes suffers.
John Buntin

38 How to Win Friends and Repair a City — 167
Atlanta needs all the help it can get. Luckily, it has a mayor who knows where to get it.
Rob Gurwitt

39 Capital Gains — 172
The District of Columbia, once the nation's poster child for managerial incompetence, is staging a comeback.
Jonathan Walters

40 Huge Turnover in Hard Times — 177
A bumper crop of new state leaders will move in next January. Some may soon wonder why they wanted the job.
Alan Greenblatt

INDEX — 181

Contributors

Tom Arrandale is a Livingston, Montana, freelance writer who focuses primarily on government pollution control and resource management policy. He writes a regular *Governing* magazine column on state and local environmental issues in addition to occasional feature articles. He holds a bachelor of arts in history from Dartmouth College and a master of arts in journalism from the University of Missouri.

John Buntin is a staff correspondent for *Governing* magazine. A graduate of Princeton University's Woodrow Wilson School of Public and International Affairs, he previously wrote about government institutions and policy issues as a case writer at Harvard University's John F. Kennedy School of Government. He is the coauthor with Kevin S. Smith and Alan Greenblatt of *Governing States and Localities* (CQ Press, 2005).

Christopher Conte is a freelance writer based in Washington, D.C. As a staff correspondent for *Governing* magazine, he has written on a wide range of social and economic policy issues, including public health, telecommunications, welfare reform and urban sprawl. He has written and edited articles and reports for many organizations, including AARP and the World Bank. For 16 years, Conte covered economic policy and the White House, among other topics, for the Washington bureau of the *Wall Street Journal*. He has also worked as a reporter for Congressional Quarterly and the *Rutland Herald* and *Barre Times-Argus* in Vermont. He holds a bachelor of arts from Harvard University.

CONTRIBUTORS

Alan Ehrenhalt is the executive editor of *Governing* magazine. Before he joined *Governing*, his professional career included stints with the Associated Press, *Washington Star* and Congressional Quarterly. He is the author of *Democracy in the Mirror* (CQ Press, 1998), *The Lost City* (1995) and *The United States of Ambition* (1991). He served as editor of the first four editions (1982–1998) of *Politics in America*, a biennial reference book that profiles all 535 members of Congress and their districts. Ehrenhalt is a member of *USA Today*'s board of contributors, and he has written frequently for the *New York Times*, *Washington Post Book World* and *New Republic*. In 2000 he was the winner of the American Political Science Association's Carey McWilliams award for distinguished contributions to the field of political science by a journalist.

Dennis Farney is a retired *Wall Street Journal* political reporter. He has covered the White House, Congress and national politics and was a finalist for the Pulitzer Prize in 1993. He lives in Kansas City, Missouri.

William Fulton is president of the Solimar Research Group, a California-based public policy firm, and the author of four books on economic development and land-use planning, including *The Reluctant Metropolis* (2001) and *Guide to California Planning* (1991). He has been *Governing*'s economic development columnist since 1994.

Alan Greenblatt has been writing about politics and government in Washington, D.C., and the states for more than a decade. As a reporter at Congressional Quarterly, he won the National Press Club's Sandy Hume award for political journalism. Since joining the staff of *Governing* magazine, he has covered issues of concern to state and local governments, including budgets, taxes and higher education. Along the way, he has written about politics and culture for numerous publications, including the *Washington Post* and the *San Francisco Chronicle*. He is the coauthor with Kevin S. Smith and John Buntin of *Governing States and Localities* (CQ Press, 2005).

Rob Gurwitt has written for *Governing* since it debuted in 1987. He is currently a freelance writer concentrating on how communities grapple with change. His articles have appeared in *Mother Jones, Preservation, DoubleTake* and *Wilson Quarterly*. He graduated from Swarthmore College with a bachelor of arts in political science and lives in Vermont.

Penelope Lemov is the associate editor of *Governing* magazine. As a reporter for *Governing*, she has been covering municipal finance and health issues for 14 years. As associate editor, she is in charge of the business of government section of the magazine, which includes news coverage of state and local government activities in finance, transportation, economic development, technology, management, health and environment. She is also the magazine's health columnist. Before joining *Governing*, she was business editor of *Builder* magazine.

Christopher Logan is deputy editor of CQ Homeland Security.

Michele Mariani is a senior editor at *Builder* magazine, which covers the residential home building and real estate industries. As senior editor, she directs the magazine's business coverage, including such topics as the mortgage market, home building finance and general business management techniques. Prior to joining *Builder*, Mariani served as senior special project reporter at *Governing* magazine, where she co-reported and co-wrote four editions of the Government Performance Project, a study of state and local government management. Mariani earned a bachelor's degree in magazine journalism and public policy from Syracuse University.

Ellen Perlman has been a reporter with *Governing* magazine for more than 10 years, and before that she spent six years as a reporter for *City & State* magazine, a publication for state and local government officials that has since been incorporated into *Governing*. Her focus is on technology, and she covers such trends as state and local government outsourcing and governments' move to the Internet. She has a graduate degree in journalism from Northwestern University and has won several awards for her work, including a National Press Club award for Washington correspondence.

Paul Shigley is editor of *California Planning & Development Report*, the only independent statewide trade publication for land use planners, developers and attorneys in California. A former newspaper reporter and editor, Shigley is an occasional contributor to *Governing* and *Planning* magazines, as well as the op-ed pages of the *Los Angeles Times,* the *Sacramento Bee* and the *Bakersfield Californian.* He lives in the Shasta County, California, community of Centerville.

Anya Sostek is an editorial writer for the *Pittsburgh Post-Gazette.* She previously wrote for *Governing* magazine for four years, focusing on voting, homeland security and pensions. Sostek has also freelanced for the *Washington Post, St. Petersburg Times* and *Teachers* magazine. She is a graduate of Duke University.

Christopher Swope is a *Governing* magazine staff writer. In seven years with the magazine, he has covered housing, economic development, management and other state and local public policy issues. Before joining *Governing,* Swope was a researcher with *Congressional Quarterly Weekly Report.* He studied journalism and political science at American University.

Jonathan Walters is a staff correspondent for *Governing* magazine and the author of *Measuring Up! Governing's Guide to Performance Measurement for Geniuses and Other Public Managers (1998).*

Introduction

It is often argued that the history of the American governmental system is a saga of inexorably increasing federal power and gradual state and local decline. Before the New Deal years of the 1930s, historians agree, the national government in Washington did relatively little, and states and cities were the dominant governmental force. Then the federal government began to intervene in one area after another—health care, education, provision for old age. The federal share of the public policy agenda has grown larger with every passing decade, and the state and local portion of the agenda has steadily eroded in consequence.

So the argument goes. In many ways, it is difficult to dispute. Once the federal government begins to regulate or police something, the chances that it will withdraw voluntarily are next to nil. Whenever a new federal agency is created to monitor what was previously a state or local responsibility—as happened with the environment, for example, in the 1970s—the momentum is all but impossible to reverse.

It is a valid argument, but it is incomplete. For any student of American federalism willing to take the long view, the process is more accurately perceived as a roller coaster than an unbroken downhill slide. When it comes to influence, creativity and political capacity, states and localities are up one decade, down the next. At times in the past couple of decades, federal encroachments notwithstanding, devolution has been a popular idea. The creativity, enthusiasm and resources to create change have mostly been on the state and local side, and the major initiatives on critical social and economic problems have tended to emanate from there. That was true for much of the 1980s, and for a period in the late 1990s as well.

Not only did state governments take the lead in wrestling with such fundamental problems as health care and utility regulation, but the Supreme Court encouraged them by siding with the states in most of the important federalism-related cases.

Then the mood turns, and seemingly overnight all the action appears to be in Washington. Congress and the president make the rules, and those at the further reaches of the federal system would seem to have few options other than to go along and make the best of it. That is how many would describe the political arrangement at the close of 2004, following President Bush's reelection to a second term.

Some of the reasons are obvious. In the years that have passed since the September 11 terrorist attacks, more and more Americans have come to see centralization of government as the best route to future security. The USA Patriot Act, passed by Congress in 2002, has brought increased federal involvement in what used to be considered routine state and local law enforcement responsibilities. Color-coded homeland security alerts have rewritten the duties and increased the costs of ground-level civil authorities all over the country. Concern for security has brought proposals to federalize dozens of additional state and local activities, both major and minor—including, in the most recent session of Congress, the provision of drivers' licenses.

Even beyond security-related issues, however, the first half of the current decade has seen an unusual amount of aggressive federal intervention. The No Child Left Behind Act, signed into law in 2002, imposes strict federal penalties on local school systems in which pupils are unable to pass standardized tests. The Medicare reform act of 2003 created a new federal prescription drug entitlement—over the opposition of most state and local health care officials, who lost much of the authority leverage they had in enacting their own drug coverage programs.

Remarkably, these and other centralizing federal initiatives have been launched by a conservative Republican president and Congress whose previous rhetoric tended to support devolution and states' rights as a hedge against unbridled federal power. "The ardor for devolution and federalism among Republicans has cooled considerably," Michael Greve of the American Enterprise Institute observed in late 2004. "People don't even pay lip service to it any more."

Does the centralization trend of the past several years represent one more step in a gradual descent of states and localities toward dependency and sideshow status? Or is it seen more accurately as a dip in the roller coaster, an interlude of reduced influence following a period of expansion?

Some recent events suggest that the roller-coaster theory is in fact the more convincing one. On the day that President Bush was reelected, voters in California approved $3 billion in spending on stem cell research, reclaiming state stewardship of an important issue over which Congress has long been deadlocked. In the wake of the California vote, several additional states moved ahead with their own stem cell programs—and Congress made it clear that it had no plans to act on the subject in the near future. State governments all over the country are embarking on experimental programs in fields that range from long-term health care to criminal sentencing to environmental trading markets—all critical topics on which Congress has taken little significant action.

Perhaps most significantly, more than forty states have ratified and are preparing to implement a uniform sales tax system, making it possible in the near future for financially pressed state treasuries to collect taxes on electronic sales, which represent a large and growing sector of economic activity everywhere in the country. Some tax specialists have argued plausibly that the uniform state sales tax project is the beginning of a reform effort that could result in a national sales tax being imposed in place of the existing federal income tax.

The sales tax project reveals a pattern that is increasingly common in current state and federal relations: the states take up a subject, begin writing legislation on and regulating it and then Congress comes along later and passes a national law weakening some of the stronger state initiatives but building on the numerous state enactments. This is what happened successfully in 2003 with the federal "Do Not Call" list restricting telemarketers; it is what happened, a little less successfully, when it came to the anti-spam Internet regulations that became law in 2004. It may be what takes place, in a different form, on the sales tax front. A national sales tax would likely represent a preemption of state taxing prerogatives by the federal legislative authority. But it would also represent an acceptance of the state-level efforts that formed the prelude to federal action.

The contents of this book, drawn from articles that appeared in *Governing* magazine between the start of 2002 and the end of 2004, chronicle the work of government in states and localities all over America during what looked very much like a time of partial state and local eclipse. These articles document the expanded federal role in such broad areas as education and homeland security, giving students—current and future practitioners—a real taste of how the changing character of federal power affects everything from budgetary constraints and windfalls to the everyday realities of policy implementation and evaluation. But these articles also report on the public policy creativity that has emanated from frontline managers in states and localities. The readings not only showcase managerial innovation at the state and local levels, but also underscore the importance of understanding the political context within which it takes place. If the roller-coaster theory holds true, how can managers best ride the peaks and dips? Navigating such turns of fortune is critical to the policy success stories we see in the pages of *Governing* on a regular basis—health care reforms in Maine, moves toward metropolitan government in Kentucky and the growing influence of state attorneys general in prosecuting regulatory abuses in every section of the country.

Each of the forty articles is about government officials trying to deal with a bewildering array of new problems and challenges in the first decade of the twenty-first century. Taken together, they draw a picture of the complexities of the job on the front lines and of a political system during a difficult and unusual period in American history. They also, we believe, make good reading, providing lessons about how to effectively manage and govern and about where public policy in America will be heading in the years to come.

1

Are City Councils a Relic of the Past?

Rob Gurwitt

One of America's oldest political institutions isn't adapting very well to 21st-century urban life.

You notice two things right off about the 19th Ward in St. Louis. The first is that pretty much everywhere there's construction, there's also a large sign reading, "Assistance for the project provided by Michael McMillan, Alderman." The second is just how limited Alderman McMillan's domain happens to be. Walk a few minutes in any direction, and you're out of his ward. You don't see the signs anymore. You also don't see as much construction.

Within the friendly confines of the 19th, St. Louis looks like a city busily reviving. There are new high schools being built, scattered apartments and loft projects underway, efforts to rejuvenate the historic arts and entertainment district, and a HOPE VI retrofit of an enormous public housing facility. While all this activity has some powerful people behind it, just one person has had a hand in all of it, and that is McMillan himself. Only 31, he has been on the St. Louis Board of Aldermen for six years, and in that time has made it clear that his ambitions for his ward—and by extension, himself—are high. "I don't have other obligations," he says. "I'm not married, I have no kids, I have no other job. It's one of my competitive edges."

Cross the ward boundary, and you find out what "competitive edge" means in St. Louis politics. North of the 19th, and for some distance to the east, stretch a series of neglected, depopulated neighborhoods that do not in any way suggest urban revival. This is, in part, a consequence of private market decisions: These neighborhoods don't have much clout within the corporate suites where such decisions are made. But equally important, they don't have much clout in local government, either—at least not when it comes to large-scale development projects.

From *Governing*, April 2003.

That's because in St. Louis, each of the 28 ward aldermen is the gatekeeper of development in his or her little slice of the city. If they're shrewd and well connected, like Michael McMillan, the ward does fine. If they're inattentive, or maladroit at cutting deals, or on the outs with local developers, or just plain picky, which is the case in more than a few wards, hardly anything gets done. "You don't see a Mike McMillan coming out of some of these devastated wards," says one City Hall insider. "They have a voice, but if it's weak, what do they really get?"

To be sure, even the weak aldermen in St. Louis have their uses. They get potholes filled and streetlights fixed, offer advice on how to handle code violations or deal with housing court, and see that garbage gets picked up in alleyways where contractors dump it illegally. This hands-on attention is hardly a bad thing. In the words of Jim Shrewsbury, who as president of the Board of Aldermen runs at large and is its 29th member, the city's deeply entrenched system of political micromanagement "protects neighborhoods and gives people a sense of influence." As members of a democratic institution, that's what city councilmen are supposed to do. But when that's about *all* many of them do, in a city that is struggling to emerge from years of economic debility, even Shrewsbury agrees that something is wrong. The system, he says, "creates a sense of parochialism and feudalism. We become the Balkans."

FEUDING AND HOT AIR

The concept of balkanization could be applied these days to councils and boards of aldermen in many of America's biggest cities—perhaps most of them. Look around the country and you can quickly compile a dossier of dysfunction.

Sometimes it is a case of pursuing tangents, as the Baltimore City Council likes to do. In a recent commentary about what it called "the hot-air council," the Baltimore *Sun* suggested that frequent resolutions on foreign affairs, hearings on the differences between telephone exchanges, and debate about counteracting "the negative images of Baltimore, as portrayed in 'real-crime' fiction, TV dramas and movies" suggested that the members didn't have enough real work to do.

Other councils become so embroiled in internal maneuvering that they lose their relevance. In Philadelphia, where a former mayor once referred to the city council as "the worst legislative body in the free world," there was a brief period of council influence in the mid-1990s, when John Street was council president and worked closely with Mayor Ed Rendell. Now, however, Street is mayor and finds himself in regular tangles with various council factions. "It's like an opera where everybody has a different libretto," says Mark Alan Hughes, an urban affairs professor at the University of Pennsylvania and columnist for the *Philadelphia Daily News*. "The melodrama is clear, it's just the meaning that's completely obscure."

There are councils where bickering and infighting are so intense that the entire body acquires an image of irresponsible flakiness. In Detroit recently, one member charged that supporters of the city's mayor had sabotaged the electric massager in her desk chair to give her a jolt when she used it. Not surprisingly, the public's response was disdainful—what most people saw was a group of elected officials engaged in sabotaging its own reputation.

There are places where, if you want to find the future of the city being pondered, the council chamber is the last place you'd look. "What you have," says a close watcher of civic affairs in Pittsburgh, "is a group of people who primarily deal with very mundane, housekeeping things in their districts. That's what they do, it's what they're interested in, and it's the way they see their power." The real power lies in the mayor's office and with the city's still-strong civic and corporate leadership.

Finally, there are councils whose problem has not been an absence of energy but a hyperactive compulsion to argue over everyday management decisions and prevent important decisions from being made. In Hartford, Connecticut, the city charter for years gave most of the political power to the council, but the council had a long history of intervening in the day-to-day administration of city services and tying itself up in petty squabbles corrosive to the morale of residents, as well as city employees. In the 1990s, the council essentially torpedoed the program of Mayor Mike Peters, who appeared to have broad voter support for his economic reform and revival ideas. Small surprise that when they were finally given a straightforward chance last November to change things, the city's voters opted to create a new form of government that strengthened the mayor at the council's expense.

None of this is to say that councils in large cities never tackle important issues or play a key role in crafting policy. Council members in Los Angeles, for instance, have a great deal to say about basic infrastructure issues, in their districts and across the city. And for all its infighting, the Philadelphia City Council did help to re-shape Street's ambitious urban renewal program, the Neighborhood Transformation Initiative, to be more responsive to neighborhood concerns.

But in all too many large cities these days, the power of councils is, at most, the power to stop things. The wellsprings of citywide innovation and progress lie elsewhere. It is telling that until this past year, neither of the two major national organizations speaking for cities addressed the specific concerns of big-city councils. The National League of Cities is dominated by small- and medium-sized jurisdictions; the U.S. Conference of Mayors, which focuses on larger cities, doesn't address council members at all. "We're literally locked out of the one national group that deals with big cities," observes Nick Licata, a Seattle council member.

Licata, who was struck by the dearth of representation from places like his when he first attended a League of Cities meeting, has put together a new "Central Cities Council" at the League, for council members in the 100 or so largest cities to share information and strategies on common issues. "We're not communicating on a regular basis, we're not exchanging information on local programs we can learn from, and on the national level, when we should be lobbying, we don't have our act together," he says. "This should help us link up."

Still, the sense of floundering one often gets watching big-city councils isn't really a surprise. Over the years, as mayors have moved to get a handle on crime, economic development and even school management, and as semi-private institutions—redevelopment authorities, stadium authorities, transit authorities, convention center authorities, tax increment finance districts—have proliferated,

> *"I think city councils have been neutered in most cases. They are engaging in the most trival aspects of urban government, rather than the most important aspects."*
>
> Dennis Judd, Urban Affairs Specialist at the University of Illinois-Chicago

the role of councils in the most critical issues of urban governance has atrophied. Individual council members, the Michael McMillans of the country, may still have a share of power and influence, but the bodies on which many of them serve have lost their identity. "I think city councils have been neutered in most cases," says Dennis Judd, an urban affairs specialist at the University of Illinois-Chicago. "They are engaging in the most trivial aspects of urban government, rather than the most important aspects."

Under these circumstances, it is hard not to wonder whether city councils are becoming relics of the political past, poorly adapted to making the decisions of 21st-century urban life. In all too many cases, they seem in danger of becoming the dinosaurs of American local government.

OUT OF THE LOOP

There was a moment not long ago when the St. Louis Board of Aldermen managed to command national attention, but it's one local politicians would rather forget. In the midst of a tense and racially charged ward redistricting debate in 2001, Alderman Irene Smith was conducting a filibuster when she asked whether she could go to the bathroom. Told by Board President Shrewsbury that the rules required her to yield the floor to do so, she summoned her supporters, who brought in a trash can and surrounded her with improvised drapes while she appeared to urinate into the can. "I was mortified," says a St. Louis politician who happened to be watching on cable television at the time. "If you've been in the aldermanic chambers, they call to mind a time when the city was a powerful city, a grand place. To think of her staging that in there! The stock of the entire board of aldermen went down." Smith was later indicted on charges of public indecency but was acquitted in January on the reasoning that no one could know for sure whether she was actually urinating or simply pretending to do so.

To those who spend their time in City Hall, the incident was puzzling, because Smith, a lawyer and former judge, is generally seen as one of the more careful and thoughtful members of the board. "She's bright, she knows how to read the law, she asks tough questions in committee hearings," says one aldermanic insider. But to many in the city at large, there was little question about how to interpret her outburst: Not even its own members accord the board much respect any longer.

The fact is, for all the opportunities that ambitious aldermen have to promote development within their own neighborhoods, it's been a while since the board has played a significant role in shaping matters of vital interest to St. Louis as a whole. One of the biggest issues on the plate of Mayor Francis Slay—himself a former board president—is a new stadium for the St. Louis Cardinals baseball team, and while pieces of the complex deal he has put together will require aldermanic approval, the board itself has had very little role in constructing it.

"When I was in City Hall," says a former aide to one of Slay's recent predecessors, "I only went to the board if I absolutely had to. The truth is, I never felt the need to involve people there on the front end in order to get something passed on the back end. In the 1970s or '80s, if a mayor had a stadium project, he'd have had to line up five or six people on the board before he even went public with it." Because that didn't happen in the current situation, the aide argues, this stadium deal is just a stadium deal—it is not part of any broader city commitment to, say, refurbishing public sports facilities or community centers in the neighborhoods.

There are any number of theories about what has led the board of aldermen to its diminished citywide import, and many of them focus on its size. The 28 wards were created in 1914, when St. Louis had 680,000 people. They remained in place when the city reached its peak of 850,000 in 1950. And they're still there, half a century later, when it's down to 340,000. This means that each alderman represents about 12,500 people. Chicago's 50-member city council, which is one of the largest in the country, would have to grow to 200 members if its wards were the same size as those in St. Louis.

If all you expect of an alderman is close attention to garbage pickup and street repairs, of course, small wards are just fine. But they have a cost, as well. For one thing, they form a low barrier to political entry. In some wards, a politician needs as few as 800 votes to get elected.

When the city was larger, says former Mayor Freeman Bosley Jr., "you had to be a real leader to get on the board, someone who could put together thousands and thousands of votes. That plays into your ability to . . . put people together and pull them in a direction. So as the years have gone by, the number of go-to people has diminished."

To be sure, it's possible to overstate the case. "Just because we were once a city of 800,000 people doesn't mean we had rocket scientists serving on the board of aldermen," notes Jim Shrewsbury. "I don't think someone makes a decision between running a corporation and being an alderman." But it's equally true that city councils are, in essence, a political proving ground—former U.S. House Minority Leader Richard Gephardt, for instance, got his start on the St. Louis Board of Aldermen. The less skill and vision they demand of their members, the poorer a city's civic life is likely to be.

"If you can make the council a place where young people who are interested in public policy think they ought to be, then it serves as a farm system to create people who understand how local government works and who have sympathy for it," says Mike Jones, a former alderman who now runs the regional Empowerment Zone. "Because the real question is, Where do you get local leadership from? On a city council where you've got to work hard to get elected, it takes good political instincts and hones them into political and policy-making skills."

IRONCLAD PRIVILEGE

Over time, the small size of the constituencies and the rules of the institution itself have combined to make the lure of parochialism more and more irresistible. In the 1950s, following passage of the federal Urban Renewal Act of 1949, aldermen in St. Louis suddenly found themselves with real power in their neighborhoods as the arbiters of development. That law, says Lana Stein, a University of Missouri-St. Louis historian, "brought a huge pot of money, and the aldermen had to pass bills authorizing urban renewal projects and highway projects. They were courted by Civic Progress [the group of corporate movers and shakers at the time] and by the mayor. Even though there were working-class people and saloon keepers elected to the board, they became a much bigger deal because of what they were voting on."

But if the urban renewal money brought the board instant influence, it also led inexorably to parochialism. As requests grew for new housing or redevelopment in the wards, they ran into the ironclad principle of aldermanic privilege—the notion that no member of the board would interfere in matters affecting another member's ward.

Fifty years later, developers still need help from the city, and that usually means a vote from the aldermen, supporting a "blighting" provision or providing a tax abatement or creating a tax-increment financing district. If you happen to live in a ward with an active, responsive alderman who knows how to put together development deals, you're fortunate. But there's scarcely anyone left on the board looking at what makes sense for the city as a whole. Aldermen rarely feel any right or responsibility to look closely at deals being made in others' wards.

When a group of downtown residents recently challenged plans backed by their alderman to demolish a historic, marble-fronted building to make way for a parking garage, the board deferred to the alderman's wishes by essentially ignoring the protest. The demolition plans were backed by the mayor and by his allies, and the developers insisted that the garage was vital to their plans, even though there are underused garages within a block's walk.

The local residents, part of a small but growing group of loft dwellers who form one of the few tangible signs of hope for St. Louis' downtown, attended the one aldermanic hearing on the matter and found no one to talk to. "It was a farce," says Margie Newman, one of their leaders. "There was no opportunity to make our case. Literally, there was an alderman with the Sunday comics held up in front of his face, and of the six on the committee, three were wandering in and out. Remember, this was at our one opportunity to bring our case."

Indeed, confirms Matt Villa, a young alderman who represents the city's far southeast, there is little incentive on the board to pay attention to what others are doing when you don't have to. "In our neighborhood," he says, "there's a neighborhood association and a housing corporation, and we sit down to plan the next five years and never take into consideration what other wards are doing. I don't even know how a citywide plan would be embraced by 28 aldermen."

And because the board itself doesn't have an independent capacity to look carefully at measures that come before it—it has very few staff members, and those who want help, such as Michael McMillan, raise funds on the side to pay for an assistant—it often approves important decisions with scarcely any scrutiny at all. "We give pay raises and pension raises and things like that," Villa says, "without really knowing the fiscal impact. The alderman who's sponsored it explains, we pass it, and years later it turns out it wasn't a $5 million impact, it was a $50 million impact."

CHARTER CHANGES

If there's anyone unhappy with this state of affairs, it's Jim Shrewsbury, who as president would like the board to become more independent and active. "The truth is, most legislation and ideas originate with the administration," he says. "The vast majority of bills are administration-sponsored bills; they have the resources and the interest and the concentration. Sometimes, I wish we were more careful and would scrutinize them more carefully. And I wish there were more innovation, that more legislation originated here." But he is also quick to point out that in the calculus of the 28 politicians who serve alongside him, that may be more of a risk than they want to take. "I know that on Election Day, the one

Bodies Large and Small

Size of selected city councils

City	Number of Districts	Average Size of District
Los Angeles	15	246,000
Phoenix	8	165,000
New York	51	157,000
Kansas City	6	74,000
Memphis*	9	72,000
San Francisco**	11	71,000
Milwaukee	17	35,000
Minneapolis	13	29,000
Richmond	9	22,000
St. Louis	28	12,000

*Two districts have three members each, the others each have one, for a total of 13 members

**City/county supervisors

Source: Governing research

thousand people who hate me will be there," he explains. "I don't know how many of the thousands who like me will be. I'm prepared to lose my office for something that was in *Profiles in Courage*. If it's not, you start to wonder whether it's worth getting involved."

Yet it's possible that change will come to the St. Louis Board of Aldermen anyway. Although St. Louis is technically a "strong mayor" city, the political reality is that the mayor is constitutionally among the weakest in the country for a city this size. Power has to be shared with a half-dozen other elected officials; the state controls the police through a board on which the mayor has only his own seat; budget decisions and city contracts have to be approved by two of the three members of the Board of Estimate and Apportionment, which is made up of the mayor, comptroller and aldermanic president. "St. Louis is probably the nation's best case of an unreformed government," says the University of Illinois' Dennis Judd, referring to the nationwide movement early in the last century to give mayors enhanced authority. "It's as if it never was touched by the reformers."

Like the board's awkward size, all of this is a result of the 1914 city charter, which is still in effect. But last November, voters statewide approved a home-rule provision for St. Louis that will allow it to take up charter change. Although most of the attention is likely to go to placing more power in the hands of the mayor, there is plenty of sentiment among civic leaders for shrinking the size of the board of aldermen.

This is happening in other big cities with similar problems. Contraction is on the docket in Milwaukee, where some aldermen themselves have proposed shrinking the Common Council from 17 to 15 members, and in Baltimore, where voters last November approved trimming the city council from 19 to 15. Baltimore's initiative, backed by a coalition of labor unions and community organizations, was opposed by most of the city's elected leadership, but it passed overwhelmingly.

It's unclear how much impact tinkering with council size will really have, in St. Louis or anywhere else. But it's clear that some fundamental changes will have to take place for city councils such as these to maintain any real relevance at all in coming years.

By any standard, there is still important work for these bodies to do. Cities need robust political institutions, and by all rights, city councils ought to be among them—they are, after all, the one institution designed to serve as the collective voice of residents and communities, whether their members are elected in districts or at large. But when little is expected of them, because a city's most important decisions are made elsewhere, it's no surprise that over time the ambitions of their members shrink to take in smaller and smaller patches of turf.

There are undeniable benefits to this. Two decades ago, voters in St. Louis overwhelmingly turned down an initiative to cut the number of wards. They felt, says Shrewsbury, "that government had gotten so complicated and big, the only way their voice could be heard was having an alderman who paid close attention." It may be that all most people really want from their city council is the kind of personal stroking that is often hard to come by elsewhere in a big city. But it's also hard to escape the feeling that, as Judd puts it, "when citizens are consulted these days, it's about things that are less and less consequential. What we're seeing is the slow strangulation of local democracy."

2

Anatomy of a Merger

Alan Greenblatt

Greater Louisville is about to be born. How much greater will it be?

In 1938, some of Louisville's bourbon distillers decided they didn't want their South End neighborhood to be annexed by the city, because that would force them to pay higher taxes. They persuaded the Kentucky legislature to allow small cities veto power over annexation and then quickly created a new jurisdiction called Shively, as a kind of tax shelter. The idea soon spread and before long every subdivision in Jefferson County that wanted lower taxes or its own one-man police force chose to incorporate. By the 1970s, the county had more than 80 municipalities. Their proliferation was a source of frustration for everyone, from engineers laying down sewer lines to developers trying to figure out which building codes applied where.

Worse still, the region had a mayor running Louisville and a judge-executive in charge of Jefferson County, more often than not with wildly different agendas. Business leaders complained that trying to get the two levels of government to agree on anything made them feel like children trying to wheedle a joint decision out of parents who refuse to talk to one another. "When you think about trying to make deals with companies," says Bill Summers, a former Louisville deputy mayor now with the local economic development agency, "you often spent more time negotiating with the two governments, trying to get them to agree on what we wanted to offer, and who was going to take credit and how they were going to take it, than actually negotiating with companies to get them here."

Next month, however, the days of duplication and rivalry will end. As a result of a ballot initiative passed two years ago, Louisville and Jefferson County will be combined into one metropolitan government, implementing a merger of a size that no city in America

From *Governing*, December 2002.

has pulled off since Indianapolis did it in 1970. Already, scout ants from Memphis, Milwaukee, Rochester, Buffalo, Cedar Rapids and Fresno have come sniffing around, hunting for strategies they can use in their own nascent moves toward merger. "The model of what Louisville is doing would be ideal for us," says Fresno councilman Brian Calhoun.

Despite all the interest and attention, the architects of Louisville-Jefferson Metro Government, as the new entity will be officially known, are trying to avoid promising too much. They are not claiming that the merger will be an economic development panacea, that Louisville will become America's new hot city, a Seattle or Austin that spawns trendy industries, or an engine of growth along the lines of Atlanta.

People in Louisville tend to regard their city realistically, as a comfortable, solid, unspectacular place. Louisville and Jefferson County still contain two-thirds of the people and 80 percent of the jobs in the seven-county metropolitan area—job suburbanization has taken place largely within the Jefferson County lines—but the trend is that both jobs and people are moving farther out. If the merger can help Louisville maintain a decent mix of jobs and industries, while preserving the importance of the merged city in the larger area, that will be triumph enough.

THE BORN CLOSER

One of the important aspects of the Louisville merger that may not be easily duplicated elsewhere involves a cult of personality. Jerry Abramson, who served as mayor of the "old" Louisville for a dozen years before he was term-limited out in 1999, won the newly created office of metro mayor last month with 74 percent of the vote against three opponents. Abramson is the closest thing Louisville has to a resident rock star. Steve Higdon, president of Greater Louisville Inc., the local chamber and economic development agency, says "there's not one better person on the planet" to lead the area politically. That kind of hyperbole isn't uncommon. "I would not underestimate the urge to throne him again," says Mike Herrald, regional president of PNC Bank. "People had the belief, rightly or wrongly, that if only he were in charge of the whole thing it would be better."

The 56-year-old Abramson is a legendary salesman, a "born closer," in the words of one associate, who can drive around his city and point with pride to all the successful projects built during his previous tenure: the minor league baseball field; the riverfront reclaimed and revitalized east of downtown; and the 1,400-unit public housing disaster that was remade into a New Urbanist mixed-income neighborhood. Abramson is also a true policy wonk who likes to hold Clintonesque bull sessions with his staff and can discuss drainage problems in the far corners of the city without notes.

Abramson is taking an almost Mussolini-like approach to the details of the merger, devoting himself to making sure that all of the managerial trains run on time. Ask him what he plans to do once he takes office, and rather than revealing any grand blueprint, he talks about changing the radio systems of the city police and county sheriff's departments so that officers in the combined jurisdiction can actually talk to one another. He'll go on at length in public forums about the $400,000 software package he wants to buy for county human resources personnel so they can team up easily with their city counterparts.

Abramson understands that the merger will not be a hit with the public unless the trash is carted away on the usual day and citizens can connect with the right person when they call to get a stray dog picked up. But simply providing the accustomed level of services without a tax increase will be a challenge in itself: As a result of city and county tax code differences, the new Louisville government faces an immediate shortfall of at least $44 million. "There's a good reason why people aren't lined up to be the first mayor of the new city," Abramson says. "There'll be a cavalry charge to be the second."

A TOUGH SELL

Discussions of regional governance generally take two forms nowadays. In areas that have experienced rapid growth, such as Denver and California's Silicon Valley, political leaders—generally prompted by local business interests—are recognizing that issues such as transportation and the environment don't honor political boundaries. This leads to a kind of ad hoc approach in which regional solutions are discussed for individual problems—water management, for example—but the idea of actually merging governments is barely a blip.

Serious merger discussions usually happen in less vibrant areas, where metropolitan government is viewed as a way of shaking things up and cutting down on costs.

If matters are difficult, the urge toward a grand solution is stronger. But merging governments is always a tough sell. While regionalism is often portrayed as the cure to a lot of urban ills, from traffic congestion to wasteful duplication of resources, few localities are eager to sacrifice their autonomy merely in the hope that it might lead to a more efficient combined water district. Municipalities, even small and inefficient ones, like to be able to provide their own services without having to be dependent on someone else.

Merger is an especially tough sell in declining areas where fights over diminishing resources have, perversely, made cooperation more difficult. In Milwaukee County, for example, where consolidation is being pushed by a local economic development agency, there is great distrust between the city of Milwaukee and the suburbs, growing out of a decade-long fight over who would pay for court-ordered city sewer improvements. The city won that fight, but may have lost the war when it comes to looking for further help from its neighbors.

Suburbanites want to maintain their friendly local police and fire departments, and don't want their tax dollars sent to prop up ailing downtowns. Cities might cry that the suburbs should help finance the urban amenities that their residents enjoy, but suburbs like to complain that cities talk to them only when they need money. When Fresno's Brian Calhoun put a resolution before the city council calling for a commission to study merger ideas, it passed unanimously, only to be shelved by the county board of supervisors. "The pressure was coming from all these smaller communities that somehow thought big bad Fresno would step on their turf," Calhoun says. Memphis Mayor Willie Herenton has been pushing for a referendum on merger, but polling indicates the idea has a long way to go before residents of surrounding Shelby County will embrace it. "Does the phrase 'D.O.A.' mean anything?" asks John Ryder, Republican National Committeeman from Shelby County.

In Erie County, New York, County Executive Joel Giambra has backed away from his earlier calls to fold the city of Buffalo into the county, which has about 60 separate governments. "There are not many people in the suburbs who have much confidence in the city government," Giambra admits. Having no hope of a full-scale merger, Giambra has been taking an "inch by inch" approach, setting up agreements for the county to share purchasing, assessing and water management with some of the municipalities, and facilitating shared services, such as law enforcement, between neighboring towns and villages. With several of Erie's smaller governments having raised tax rates by double-digit percentages in recent weeks, Giambra hopes his call for abolishing duplication will take on greater urgency. Even in Milwaukee County, savings from merged fire districts in smaller North Shore communities have kept hope of merger alive.

> *With a single public-sector agenda, 'we should be able to make economic development decisions faster.'*
>
> Jerry Abramson,
> Louisville Mayor

FALLING BEHIND

As dramatic as Louisville's move may seem, the truth is that consolidation has been happening on a piecemeal basis between the city and Jefferson County for years. The water and sewer authority has answered to both jurisdictions since shortly after World War II, and the school systems merged in 1975. In the early 1980s, Abramson negotiated a deal with the county that combined administration of the park, zoo and library systems, and put an end to annexation wars by establishing a permanent proportional split of occupational tax revenues. This year, Jefferson County will write a check to Louisville for $11 million to keep the county at its codified 58 percent of the occupational tax take.

Even so, proposals to merge Louisville and Jefferson County failed three times, in 1956, 1982 and 1983, before finally winning approval in 2000. This was in large part because they spelled out too much of the detail in advance. Plans to abolish local fire districts, for example, drew plenty of fire themselves. This time, merger proponents were careful to give voters few specifics to worry about. The ballot measure simply provided that the city and county would become a single unit, with a metro mayor taking over the responsibilities of the previous city mayor and county executive, and one metro council replacing the board of aldermen and the county's fiscal court. Beyond changing the nature of these elected offices, nothing was settled as to whether agencies or even administrative functions of the city and county would be consolidated. All those 80-odd municipalities within the county and the 21 fire districts outside the city of Louisville could remain intact (although a dozen or so of the smaller cities have chosen to merge with each other in recent months to have more of a voice in metropolitan affairs).

For most proponents, the reason to merge this time was more economic than political. Louisville has a relatively stable employment base, headed by manufacturing companies (among them Ford and General Electric) which still account for about 20 percent of the jobs. The city and county are home to a growing health services sector. The airport is the overnight hub for United Parcel Service, Kentucky's largest private employer, which recently completed a billion-dollar expansion of its facilities. And Louisville has long been a fast-food paradise, spawning Kentucky Fried Chicken, Papa John's pizza, Rally's, Chi Chi's, Long John Silver and several other chains. The mix of junk food, tobacco and bourbon leads locals to joke that they don't engage in healthy living but "happy living."

Still, the national economic boom of the 1990s largely passed Louisville by. Young people have been leaving steadily for the past 30 years—a net loss of 35,000 people in the current 25- to 34-year-old age group since 1970. Elderly residents comprise 14 percent of Louisville's population, among the highest proportions of seniors in the country. Academic studies place the region at the bottom of the list of technology-friendly metropolitan areas. "Ultimately," says Steve Higdon, the president of Greater Louisville Inc., "what is at stake for any community is whether you can attract and retain the brightest people. And we have not done well at that at all for decades."

Louisville boosters never tire of trumpeting the fact that merger will vault their city from the 64th largest in the country to the 16th largest, the highest ranking it has held in more than a century. Greater Louisville Inc. recently launched a quarter-million-dollar public relations campaign to get that word out nationally. "From an economic development standpoint," says Higdon, "perception is reality. Period."

When companies look for a "Top 20" city, or one that's home to more than 500,000 people—which many of them do—Louisville will now make the cut. Higdon and other business leaders believe that the city-county merger will end 40 stagnant years by creating the sense that the city finally has regained some ambition. If Louisville can change the entire government structure for 700,000 people, this line of thinking goes, it can shake off its historic complacency and insularity. "We are now looked at as a community that's ready to embrace change," says Rebecca Jackson, Jefferson County's outgoing judge-executive.

READY FOR CHANGE

During nearly a decade as county clerk, Jackson watched as a succession of mayors and county judge-executives pursued conflicting agendas and maneuvered for power. She herself voted against merger in the 1980s but ran for judge-executive in 1998, she says now, in order to make merger happen. She was a major public face of the 2000 campaign, posing for pictures with Louisville Mayor Dave Armstrong, who had hoped to run for the new metro mayor job himself. (He eventually bowed out in favor of Abramson.)

Organizers of the "unity" campaign, as the merger supporters called themselves, also managed to shepherd every living person who had held the mayor or county judge-executive position onto a single stage for a news conference announcing their unanimous support. All this symbolism and political theater were important, because the earlier merger attempts were widely perceived to have foundered in part because they were driven strictly by the business establishment.

Even with so many stars in alignment for merger, however, the key factor was Abramson. Polling—done by consultants hired from both major parties—showed that Abramson's regular public appearances and starring role in television ads made the difference. The new city has a strong-mayor structure, and voters seemed reassured by the near-certainty that Abramson would be the mayor, lending his experience and political skill to the newly elected 26-member metro council, which will be made up overwhelmingly of political novices.

Because his election was a foregone conclusion, Abramson has been planning the transition for months, meeting with citizens in each of the 26 new council districts and strategizing with key decision-makers such as Greater Louisville Inc. and the Louisville *Courier-Journal* editorial board. Weeks before the November election, outgoing Jefferson County Commissioner Dolores Delehanty said, "People are now talking about 'WWJD'—What would Jerry do? People immediately think, how is this going to fly with Jerry?"

But what does Abramson actually want to do with his home city, now that it has nearly tripled in size and abolished some of its longstanding habits of institutionalized parochialism? Abramson says that the merged city-county governments of the 1960s and '70s—Nashville, Indianapolis, Charlotte, Jacksonville and nearby Lexington, Kentucky—offer little guidance in putting together Greater Louisville. Those mergers took place before the modern era of information technology and under different public employee union contracts. Suburban growth wasn't as advanced as it is now, meaning issues of drainage, sewer lines and permits are quite different.

A more useful and up-to-date model, Abramson says, comes from corporate mergers. He jokes about meeting with an alphabet soup of CEOs, CFOs and COOs who talked with him about their mergers, how they had done months of preparation and due diligence and when they switched on the lights the first day, it was all a big mess anyway. But their failures were mostly private affairs. Abramson knows he'll make plenty of mistakes, and he knows that each will be treated as breaking news.

TRUCKS AND SQUAD CARS

Still, the city and county seem far closer to being ready for this merger than even supporters of the idea dared hope two years ago. Only a few technical issues, regarding such matters as Social Security and bank forms, actually have to be taken care of the first day, January 6, but city and county departments have proven surprisingly cooperative in planning for the new world they're about to enter, and the public works, information technology, human resources and finance departments are preparing to consolidate as of day one.

Final decisions about the shape and scope of larger government changes will have to wait for the mayor and council to be sworn in, but the outlines of many of those are clear as well. There had been a lot of debate in Louisville whether to follow the Indianapolis model, under which the city and county public safety agencies remain separate, three decades after consolidation, but a police-sheriff merger in Louisville/Jefferson County appears all but inevitable. The current arguments focus on what color the squad cars should be.

But Abramson and the council will have plenty of difficult questions to cope with, such as balancing city-run versus county-privatized emergency medical services, reconciling different pay scales for everyone from custodians and secretaries on up, and negotiating with the different unions that represent public works employees. Abramson always got a laugh during the campaign by comparing the different ways the city and county classify trucks. The city, he says, has 12 separate truck classifications, while the county has only two—big and little. "I like two," he says.

In the beginning, city, suburbs and unincorporated areas will receive essentially the same services they are receiving now. The old city will retain its boundaries as an "urban service district," with higher taxes and more services. Whether people outside the former city limits will come to expect more services, and will be willing to pay more in taxes for them, remains to be seen.

Kentucky's legislature has given the new government five years to work out differences between pre-existing city and county statutes. After that, laws that haven't been rec-

Bigger and Better?

Louisville before and after the merger

	Before	After
Area in square miles	60	386
Population	256,231	693,784
White	64%	79%
African American	34%	19.5%
Hispanic	2%	2%
High school graduates	76%	82%
Bachelor's degree	21%	25%
Graduate degree	9%	10%
Median household income	$28,843	$39,457
Median home price	$82,300	$103,000
Homeownership rate	52.5%	64.9%
Median age	35.8	36.7
Unemployment rate	7.4%	5%

Source: U.S. Census Bureau, 2000

onciled will simply expire. In the meantime, the rules are that if both the county and the old city have a law addressing a given topic, the county law prevails. Where the city has a law and the county doesn't, such as a curfew ordinance, the city law takes effect throughout the county.

In some cases, the differences aren't worth much bother. In September, a Louisville alderman dropped his plan to ban roosters from the city when he realized a county ordinance would soon make his bill redundant. But other differences will matter a great deal, from inconsistencies in tax rates to the fact that the much weaker county housing code, meant for a rural area, will suddenly apply in the city. "The first year is going to be fair chaos," says Mike Herrald, the bank executive, "but the person who goes to the zoo, the person who goes to the library, the person who calls the police with a fender bender, they aren't going to notice the change and, God knows, that's the object."

Even while trying to make good on Herrald's premise, though, and preventing any disruption in core functions, Abramson wants ultimately to bring about real restructuring. When he built the downtown baseball park, during one of his earlier terms as mayor, he visited parks in five other cities and stole the best design elements from each of them. He hopes to do the same thing with ideas for delivering services, combining and experimenting wherever it makes sense to try something new. Abramson told one audience recently that, if the city has 20 garbage trucks and the county has 20 garbage trucks, "and we merge them and have 40 garbage trucks and call it consolidation, we will have missed that opportunity to remake local government."

Driving past the ballpark, Abramson still sounds a little bitter about the trouble he had raising money to build it. He raised millions from private sources, but it took him forever to score the last $3 million he needed because county officials wanted no part of the deal—even though their constituents would take advantage of the new park, just as they were prime users of a $4 million swimming complex and other facilities that the city of Louisville had built. "I could have built that park a year and a half earlier," the mayor recalls, if it had not been for the jurisdictional rivalry.

After January 6, Abramson will no longer have to wait to get the county to sign off on his favored projects. "We'll have a single public-sector agenda," he says. "We should be able to make economic development decisions faster. That's the hope, anyway."

3

In Search of the Ideal Legislature

Alan Ehrenhalt

A new look at how state legislatures have changed.

You and I might not agree on the best American governors of recent years, but we would probably agree on what makes a governor effective. Mostly, it's a matter of having a coherent program and finding ways to get it enacted. Similarly, it's not too hard to define the qualities of an outstanding legislator. This is somebody with the brains to understand complex problems, the creativity to frame solutions, and the personal skill to build majorities in favor of the things he proposes. However people may differ on the elements of wise policy, they tend toward consensus on who's good at getting the job done.

But broaden the subject of the inquiry from individuals to institutions, and the consensus all but disappears. What's a good legislature? For that matter, what's an effective one? That's about as slippery a question as you can find anywhere in the textbooks of political science. Those who believe in tax reduction and limited government tend to think the Republican-managed state legislatures of the past decade have generally acted in the public interest. Those more interested in maintaining high levels of social service spending come to an opposite conclusion. At the institutional level, good performance is very difficult to disentangle from ideology.

But if students of legislative life have been a little bit befuddled in their search for the good, they have historically been rather confident that at least they knew a really bad legislature when they saw one. A bad legislature is unable to attract talented members, is lacking in staff and resources, succumbs to the pressures and personal favors of lobbyists, meets only infrequently and allows the governor to treat it like a doormat. A bad legislature is one pretty much like those found in most American states in the 1950s and '60s.

From *Governing*, September 2004.

It was in the late 1960s that the Ford Foundation, subscribing to this view, funded one of the most influential crusades in modern American government—to improve the quality of state legislative practice. Over a period of several years, Ford subsidized a long series of detailed reports, a widely circulated paperback book, called *The Sometime Governments,* and a much-publicized ranking of every legislature in the country, from 1st to 50th, on categories labeled functionality, accountability, informedness, independence and representativeness. The majority of legislatures did poorly in virtually every one of the categories.

There was, however, one shining model for states to copy. It was California, which under the leadership of Speaker Jesse Unruh had transformed itself from corruption and ineptness—"I am the governor of the legislature," liquor lobbyist Artie Samish had proclaimed just a few years earlier—into a condition of admirable capability. California's legislature, researchers reported, was stocked with talent, impressively staffed, resistant to old-fashioned lobbying pressures and strong enough to challenge governors.

And so, backed by mountains of surveys and scholarly research, legislatures throughout the country began to reposition themselves in the direction of Sacramento. They sought to professionalize. Not all of them moved equally far in this direction, of course—some small states scarcely moved at all—but on balance, it is fair to say that state legislatures transformed themselves dramatically in a relatively short period of time.

Three decades after the reform project completed its work, there is no question that state legislatures as an institution possess more resources, more information and a higher degree of independence than virtually any of them did in the bad-old pre-reform days. But are they better? That remains an elusive question.

Its elusiveness can be demonstrated by a brief look at two of the states that took reform most seriously. Both Minnesota and Wisconsin moved expeditiously from part-time, poorly staffed institutions to ones that remain in session for a good part of the year and provide members with abundant personal and informational support. For a decade or so, this looked like a highly positive development. More recently, it hasn't looked so good.

In the 1990s, the Minnesota and Wisconsin legislatures fell into a culture of partisanship and incivility that made it difficult for them to handle the most basic governmental tasks. By the end of the decade, voter disgust with the infighting among Democrats and Republicans in Minnesota helped contribute to the upset gubernatorial victory of third-party insurgent Jesse Ventura. But the situation didn't change during Ventura's four years in office, and it hasn't changed since his departure. This year, partisan bickering was so intense in Minnesota that lawmakers adjourned in May without coming close to passing a budget, and the House Speaker declared the session the least productive of his 25-year career.

Wisconsin's legislature, with a century-long tradition of honest politics and public-spirited reform measures, professionalized to the point where the two parties became electoral war machines willing to go to virtually any lengths in the battle for control. Leaders became consumed with campaigns and fund-raising. As I write this, half a dozen longtime members, including the former Speaker and the former Senate majority leader, are under indictment on charges that range from extorting contributions to misusing state funds for political purposes.

Meanwhile, the legislature in California, so recently a model for what such bodies ought to be like, has become a model for what they should not be like. Famously unable to take any serious action against the state's multibillion-dollar budget shortfall, it has largely abdicated its fiscal authority to Governor Arnold Schwarzenegger, whose fulminations against legislative politics were in part responsible for his election last fall.

What are we to make of all this? Not that professionalization was a mistake, I think, but simply that legislatures can fail in more than one way. The poorly equipped, lobbyist-dominated institutions of the 1960s were inadequate and needed to change; the reforms of the 1970s largely took care of that. But solving one set of problems doesn't preclude the emergence of new ones. A cynic might simply say that all we've managed to do over the past 30 years is trade one kind of "bad" legislature for another.

Alan Rosenthal, who may know more about American legislatures than anyone, doesn't take the cynical position. Rosenthal was involved in the reform efforts of the 1970s as a young political scientist and has been studying the legislative process ever since. He has spent much of his time stalking state capitol corridors, buttonholing the members and the lobbyists, forging personal relationships with the leaders. Through all those years, half a dozen scholarly books and countless essays, he has pondered not only the negative side of the issue—How do legislatures get in trouble?—but also the opposite and much more difficult side: What makes a good legislature?

Rosenthal's newest book, *Heavy Lifting: The Job of the American Legislature,* is in large measure an effort to sum up his life work by answering the latter question. He starts by citing a couple of criteria that, in his view, shouldn't be used to determine whether a legislature is good or not.

One is the product. That's a matter of political values and personal taste. I might think a legislature that grows the state budget is a model of performance. I have a right to my opinion. But you have a right to the opposite opinion. As Rosenthal says, "it's probably not possible to agree on a product that is indispensable to a 'good' legislature. It may not even be worth the search."

Then there's structure. The legislatures of the 1960s lacked the staff, physical facilities and communications apparatus to serve the public interest. But, as the past two decades have shown, all the equipment in the world doesn't guarantee virtue. The essence of a "good" legislature lies somewhere else.

At that point, Rosenthal suspends the inquiry and takes the reader on a 200-page discursive tour of legislatures and leaders he has known, especially those he has watched in recent years. When the tour is over, he does his best to answer the question. Legislative excellence is all about balance and harmony. There are three major functions of the modern legislature: representation, lawmaking and dealing with the executive branch. The ideal legislature does all of them well, and keeps them in proper proportion. Currently, Rosenthal argues, legislatures are performing the representative function extremely well. Members are listening to constituents, and solving people's problems. The lawmaking function isn't quite as strong, and the executive-relations function is the weakest of the three.

It's nice and symmetrical, anyway. It almost sounds like Plato's Republic. Does it have any practical value? Actually, it does have some. If the lawmaking side needs improvement, it might be a good idea to increase the power of the committee system. Committees are where most lawmaking actually gets done. If legislatures are finding themselves overmatched by governors, one might want to reexamine term limits. Term limits have deprived legislative bodies of the senior members who can wrestle with the executive on an equal basis. And when leaders come and go every couple of years, nobody has sufficient clout to keep the fragile components of the institution in sufficient balance.

I confess that, even when I had finished reading about life in Rosenthal's Republic, I still didn't have a clear idea of what a "good" legislature would look like up close. Quite likely I never will. But then, on this subject as with many fields of inquiry, it may not be the answers that matter most. What's important is that we keep asking the questions. Judged by that standard, Alan Rosenthal has performed an admirable service to American government.

> *The poorly equipped, lobbyist-dominated institutions of the 1960s were inadequate and needed to change; the reforms of the 1970s largely took care of that. But solving one set of problems doesn't preclude the emergence of new ones.*

4

The Phantom of New York

Christopher Swope

Quasi-governmental authorities spend billions of dollars of Empire State taxpayers' money every year. They don't have to answer many questions about it.

Every politico in New York State is familiar with the story of Robert Moses, even if few have finished reading all 1,100 pages of Robert Caro's biography of him. Moses, back in the 1930s, '40s and '50s, amassed the power to build roads, bridges, parks and housing projects in New York City and all over the state, pretty much however and wherever he wished, through his domination of public authorities—quasi-governmental agencies of which he controlled more than a dozen. Using the authorities, he could issue bonds to pay for public works and collect tolls or fees, all without seeking permission from any formal legislative body. He was able to exercise vast discretion with virtually no accountability at all.

Public authorities aren't quite as powerful today as they used to be, due in part to the backlash against Moses' abuse of them. But they remain very crucial, if little-noticed, institutions not just in New York but across the country. They manage an impressive array of America's infrastructure: airports, stadiums, convention centers, transit systems, turnpikes, bridges, tunnels, cargo facilities, sewer and water systems, public housing and even parking garages. These are critical functions. So it seemed like a reasonable request, given the authorities' significance and their checkered past, when Alan Hevesi, the comptroller of New York State, recently asked for a list of all of the state's public authorities. Surely a complete list must exist somewhere, Hevesi thought.

It didn't. So Hevesi's staff went on a public authority hunt. Flipping back and forth through volumes of state statutes, they recorded the names of hundreds of bureaucracies. Some were familiar to citizens, such as the New York State Thruway Authority and the Port Authority of New York and New Jersey. But many were

From *Governing*, November 2004.

obscure entities that few have ever heard of: the Industrial Exhibit Authority; the Islip Resource Recovery Authority; the Overcoat Development Corp. The list went on and on. This past February, in a report that likened these bodies to a "secret government," Hevesi put the tally of state and local public authorities in New York at 640. Since then, his staff has "discovered" 70 more. They're still not sure they've found them all.

At the very least, it is a sign of weak oversight if a state government doesn't even know how many public authorities are acting in its behalf. But lately there have been other signs of poor management and questionable contracting. The Metropolitan Transit Authority, which runs the subways, buses and commuter trains in the New York City area, was accused of lying about its budget numbers in order to justify a fare hike. In another case, a subsidiary of the Thruway Authority known as the Canal Corp. offered lucrative development rights along the Erie Canal to a campaign contributor of Governor George Pataki's—for a paltry $30,000. Attorney General Eliot Spitzer put it bluntly when he said that "public authorities are becoming to New York what off-balance-sheet partnerships were to Enron."

A consensus is building that something about public authorities is broken in the Empire State—even if Pataki, Spitzer, Hevesi and the legislature don't agree on what to do about it. At the same time that the authorities are being attacked, however, more of them are being created. For example, a new state-local authority was just established to build a convention center in Albany. Discussions are underway to create an entertainment authority to manage sports and arts facilities in Greater Binghamton.

The biggest new entry, however, would be in the Big Apple, where the city and state are talking about forming a development corporation to redevelop the west side of Manhattan. "Public officials can cluck their tongues and say authorities are out of control," notes Steve Malanga, a senior fellow at the Manhattan Institute, a conservative think tank. "But when an issue comes up that they think can't win with the voters, they go back to using authorities."

ONE STEP REMOVED

Public authorities have been around since the 1920s, when good-government reformers suggested that quasi-independent agencies might perform certain tasks more efficiently than government could. There were good reasons to believe that, and there still are today. "Public authorities are pretty darned useful," says Kathryn Foster, a planning professor at SUNY Buffalo.

The original argument was essentially that authorities could remove politics from the delivery of basic services. Take sewers. If every rate hike had to go to a public referendum, long-term maintenance might never get done. Authorities are meant to circumvent such political messiness. They're typically set up one step removed from city, county or state government. They're supposed to enjoy the managerial freedoms of the private sector, while retaining some of the accountability that is so important in the public sector.

It's not easy to generalize about authorities. Not only do they perform vastly different functions but they're also structured quite differently from state to state. Some authority boards are elected, while others are appointed by governors or mayors. A few cross political boundaries, such as the Delaware River Port Authority, whose board is appointed by the governors of Pennsylvania and New Jersey. Some receive appropriations from legislatures, but most authorities can raise money on their own, from tolls, fares or user fees, and some can levy taxes on the public at large.

One thing that is clear about authorities is that their number is growing faster than that of any other slice of American government. It's difficult to pin down an exact figure for the whole country, precisely because they are so loosely defined from one state to the next. Nevertheless, the U.S. Census Bureau makes an effort. In 2002, it counted some 35,000 "special district governments"—a label that does not include school districts. By contrast, there were only 26,000 of these quasi-governmental institutions in 1977.

Much of this growth is in booming suburbs and exurbs, where development means that there are new water systems to manage, new parks to build, new bus systems to run. More often than not, a public authority is given these responsibilities. But some of the authorities' growth also reflects the changing needs of states and older cities. In Moses' day, many authorities literally paved the way to a new automobile era by building the first highways and bridges. These days, in urban areas, newly minted authorities are more likely to be building arenas and convention centers, or playing the role of lead developer in publicly financed real estate deals.

A new authority's strongest selling point is often its ability to stay focused on a single goal. For example, Washington, D.C., just created a new corporation to finance an $8 billion redevelopment plan along the Anacostia River. The job could have gone to the D.C. economic development department, or to an existing authority that does redevelopment work citywide. But planners didn't want to risk seeing the Anacostia program get lost in an overstuffed portfolio. They preferred to create a separate institution whose managers have one job—redeveloping the waterfront—rather than many.

Another reason why the number of authorities keeps growing is that old ones rarely seem to go away. Look at the Pittsburgh Stadium Authority, created in the 1960s to build and manage Three Rivers Stadium. Pittsburgh demolished that facility four years ago, replacing it with twin football and baseball stadiums—built by yet another authority. Still, the old Stadium Authority lives on, an oddity that nobody paid much attention to until charges hit this summer that an authority accountant had embezzled $193,000. The authority's ostensible *raison d'etre* is to pay off the bonds on Three Rivers, but Pennsylvania state Representative Jack Wagner thinks that's a bogus excuse. "There's no reason why that authority and the debt can't be merged into another authority," Wagner says. "This is nothing more than a duplication of government services."

CLOSED DOORS

A swell of complaints about alleged impropriety at authorities is what put reform on the agenda in New York. The MTA's budget scam and the canal land giveaway were only the beginning:

- The New York Racing Association, the quasi-governmental agency that runs three horse-racing tracks, was indicted as a body and many tellers were convicted of tax fraud and money laundering.
- The head of the New York State Bridge Authority, who was also the father-in-law of a close Pataki adviser, resigned when it was revealed that he had spent $25,000 of the authority's money on personal trips and rung up $80,000 worth of questionable credit card bills.
- Former U.S. Senator Alphonse D'Amato, now a lobbyist, received a $500,000 fee for a placing a phone call to the MTA and persuading the authority to help his client get a loan. (An investigation cleared D'Amato of any wrongdoing.)

"Here's the reality," says Hevesi, whose audits have turned up a few of the latest transgressions. "Some authorities are very effective and well run. But a lot are mismanaged and some are corrupt."

Pataki thinks that assessment is too negative. Like New York governors before him, Pataki, a Republican, influences many of the state authorities through his appointment power. His aides say he wants reform, but that much of the recent controversy is little more than political grandstanding. They insist that Spitzer, a Democrat, mostly wants Pataki's job, and another authorities critic, Democratic Assemblyman Richard Brodsky, wants Spitzer's job. Hevesi, too, is an elected Democrat. "We're proud of the work of our authorities," says Joe Conway, a Pataki spokesman.

But it is not just partisans who are calling for reform. Good-government groups have come to see the authorities as a subset of Albany's legendary governance problems (the state budget is typically decided in secret by three men, universally known as the "triumvirate": currently Pataki, Democratic Assembly Speaker Sheldon Silver, and the Senate's GOP Majority Leader Joseph Bruno). "Getting a

What Special Governments Do

Function	Percent
Natural resources	19.9%
Fire protection	16.2
Water supply	9.7
Housing and Community Development	9.7
Sewerage	5.7
Cemeteries	4.7
Libraries	4.4
Parks and recreation	3.7
Highways	2.2
Health	2.1
Hospitals	2.1
Education	1.5
Airports	1.4
Utilities (excluding water supply)	1.4
Other single functions	6.2
Multiple functions	9.0

Source: U.S. Census Bureau, 2002

handle on what the public authorities spend and how much money they raise is very difficult," says Diana Fortuna, president of the nonpartisan Citizens Budget Commission.

Authorities haven't had to report their finances in any consistent way, and their budgets don't show up on the state government's books. Authorities aren't subject to the same contracting or lobbying rules that state agencies are, even though they spend billions of dollars every year. If you want to know why an authority picked one vendor over another for a important contract, it is nearly impossible to find out. Nor is it easy to track how much lobbying contractors do, or how successful they are at it.

Top jobs at authorities are considered plum positions in New York, with salaries that often exceed six figures. Patronage is the prerogative of any governor, of course, but Albany insiders say that Pataki, more than his predecessors, has used the authorities to enrich his friends and campaign contributors. For example, a former mayor of the town of Peekskill, who is also a childhood friend of Pataki's, found his way to an executive vice president job at the New York Power Authority. Another friend, who had headed Pataki's security detail, also got a top job with the power authority. Blair Horner, a lobbyist with the New York Public Interest Research Group, argues that the conversion of authorities into patronage mills defeats their original purpose. "The idea that these authorities are semi-autonomous entities staffed by career civil service types who are divorced from politics has changed. They're now agents of the executive branch who are not subject to the same oversight."

BIG-TIME DEBT

Who are the authorities accountable to? That answer isn't always clear. Pataki is prone to issuing press releases anytime an authority generates good news, such as when the Lower Manhattan Development Corp. (LMDC) opened four reconstructed ball fields in a park on the East River. When events get politically dodgy, however, Pataki tends to emphasize the authorities' independence, keeping his own hands clean.

The messy debate over rebuilding the World Trade Center—detailed in Paul Goldberger's new book *Up from Zero*—is a good example of this. Pataki, more than any other public official, held great sway over Ground Zero: His appointees led the Port Authority, which owned the land, as well as the LMDC, which ran the planning process. As early as the beginning of 2002, Pataki could have settled key questions regarding the lease on the Trade Center. But he was in the midst of a re-election campaign that year and might have offended voters who preferred one rebuilding plan over another. Rather than set clear terms for the planning process, he let the governmental, quasi-governmental and private parties involved squabble with each other. "Pataki talked about bringing consensus and public input to the process," Goldberger writes. "But he seemed often to be working to assure that the process would be slow, convoluted and more than a little bit opaque."

Finally, there is the huge amount of debt that New York's authorities have run up. The state is not allowed to borrow money without voter approval, but that rule doesn't apply when it's authorities that are doing the borrowing. Consequently, these entities are used like credit cards. State authorities are currently carrying approximately $114 billion in debt—28 times more than the $4 billion issued by New York State. Much of the authorities' debt is backed by highway tolls, subway fares or other fees. But a staggering amount of it—$43 billion—is supported by state government, meaning that if the authority that issued those bonds defaulted, taxpayers would be on the hook.

It is the job of an institution called the Public Authorities Control Board to ensure that that doesn't happen. But the operations of this board are even harder to decipher than those of the authorities. The PACB was created in 1976, when one of the largest state authorities, the Urban Development Corp., nearly collapsed. The control board must approve any debt issued by the 11 largest state authorities. There are three voting members—each a representative of the Pataki-Silver-Bruno triumvirate—and decisions must be made by consensus. What that means in practice is that the PACB makes its decisions the Albany way: behind closed doors.

Not that the PACB doesn't meet in public. It does, every month, in a vaulted pink room on the first floor of the Capitol. But by the time this happens, all the decisions have been worked out in advance. At its public hearing in September, the PACB zipped quickly through a lengthy agenda, approving $384 million worth of authority financing in exactly 20 minutes. All that remained for public consumption was a pro-forma flurry of motions, seconds and ayes.

Barbara Bartoletti, a lobbyist for the League of Women Voters, attends these meetings regularly, "just so that they know the public is watching." After five years of observing from the back of the room, Bartoletti says the PACB remains a mystery to her. "We're talking about billions of taxpayer dollars," Bartoletti says. "We can't crack why decisions are made the way they are. We don't have a clue about where the money is going and whom it's going to."

GROPING FOR SUNLIGHT

Exactly what can be done about the problems with authorities is open to argument. Pataki favors an approach that aims to do for authorities what the federal Sarbanes-Oxley law did for corporate governance. In February, Pataki's chief of staff issued a memo to the 31 state authorities most tightly under the governor's control. The memo called upon them to implement so-called "model governance principles," developed by corporate governance expert Ira Millstein. Pataki also asked Millstein to head a commission, whose June draft report fleshed these principles out further.

Millstein's suggestions include standardizing financial reporting among the authorities, and making more of it publicly available. He also would have each authority appoint an independent audit committee. The bulk of Millstein's recommendations, however, have to do with the authorities' boards. Many boards have developed reputations for rubber-stamping management decisions. Millstein thinks boards should be structured to have more independence. He also thinks that if board members went through extensive training, they might take the oversight part of their job more seriously. "Sunlight and active boards will be as much of a cure as we can get at this point," Millstein says.

Hevesi and Spitzer agree with most of Millstein's proposals, but don't think he goes far enough. They have joined together on more sweeping legislation that would, for the first time in 50 years, prune back the number of authorities in New York. The plan is to have a commission sort out those authorities that have outlived their usefulness, or whose duties can easily be handled elsewhere in government.

Hevesi and Spitzer would make other changes. Their proposal would rewrite lobbying and procurement rules so that authorities and state agencies are treated the same. That means the controller would get a veto over large authority contracts. It also means that anyone who lobbies an authority would have to register with the state lobbying commission. In September, Hevesi added another reform he would like to see: He wants authority spending to be considered "on budget" in the state's books.

Assemblyman Brodsky proposes a different approach, one that was passed by the Democratic Assembly in February, but died in the Senate. Brodsky would create new layers of oversight, including an inspector general's office for public authorities, as well as an independent budget officer. In September, Brodsky upped the ante, calling for a constitutional amendment that would abolish all public authorities, wrapping their functions back into state agencies. That was more a statement of principle than a realistic policy proposal. Still, Brodsky says, "anything authorities can do can be done directly by government on-budget, instead of hidden off-budget."

All the reform rhetoric makes officials at some authorities cringe, especially those that are widely acknowledged to be well run. In over-reacting to a few scandals, they warn, reformers might take away the independence that has allowed some authorities to thrive. Take the state Dormitory Authority, which started in the 1940s building dorms at teachers colleges, and has since become a well-regarded all-purpose builder of school and hospital facilities. Claudia Hutton, the authority's spokeswoman, cautions that a cookie-cutter reform package could cause more problems than it solves. "The New York Power Authority is a power company," Hutton says. "That's awfully different from what we do."

It's unlikely that she has much to fear. Talking about reform in Albany is easy. Doing it is another thing. Individual authorities such as the MTA and Canal Corp. have tweaked the practices that landed them in the headlines. But more sweeping reform of authorities isn't likely, if only because the desire to create more of them remains such a powerful force. Steve Malanga says the situation with authorities is a lot like New York's budget process in general. "It's broken, but it doesn't suit the people in power to fix it."

5

The Great GASB

Michele Mariani

States and localities now have to account for the real value of everything from city halls to drainage systems.

William Raftery remembers the darkest times. Those would be the waning weeks of winter 1999, when it became clear to Wisconsin's controller that GASB 34 was not going to go away, that he, like hundreds of other state and local financial officers, would have to deal with the new accounting rule that asked governments to put an up-to-date value on infrastructure—bridges, jails, libraries, city halls and the like—built since 1980.

Implementation of the rule seemed formidable, even frightening, given the lack of additional resources available to fathom the complex guidelines and figure out the worth—the depreciated value, to be exact—of, say, a highway interchange built in 1984. Although dictates of the Governmental Accounting Standards Board—known informally by the way its acronym is pronounced, Gasby—don't carry the legal weight of a legislative mandate or gubernatorial edict, it was clear to Raftery that he and his office would have to comply with the first stages of GASB's Statement 34 by the time their fiscal year 2002 came to an end. Without compliance, the state couldn't earn clean audits of its Comprehensive Annual Financial Report. And a muddied CAFR could bring about a host of fiscal horrors.

But a funny thing has been happening on the way to the 2002 deadlines. Many states and localities are finding the valuation challenge not nearly as daunting as it first appeared.

There is, of course, more to Statement 34 than price tags. The rule calls for several accounting changes, including non-number statements that explain what the numbers mean. GASB's objective was to make state and local financial reports more valuable to readers. For many outside government in particular, the dozens of pages

From Governing, April 2002.

of seemingly endless numbers make it difficult to understand what their state, city or county is trying to convey through traditional financial reports. Looking at all the changes GASB 34 will bring to financial reporting, Roberta Reese, a GASB project manager sees Statement 34 as bringing governments closer to GASB's objective. "Someone who looks at financial statements is going to have a more complete picture of what government does," she says.

Not that it's been easy to get the valuation piece in place or that everyone will get there together. The 50 states, along with municipal governments with $100 million or more in annual revenues, go first. They must implement the reporting changes, including infrastructure values, at the end of their 2002 fiscal year. Localities with lower revenue levels have another year or two leeway.

In general, what they will have to do is put a price tag on both fixed assets and infrastructure. (In GASB-speak, infrastructure refers only to bridges, roads, parks and drainage systems.) While governments have long reported depreciated values for fixed assets that are part of self-replenishing proprietary funds, such as water and sewer systems, they now need to report depreciated values for assets that fall under the primary government. That includes reporting on buildings, bridges and roads. To do this, governments have to compile comprehensive inventories, backtrack to find original costs and find a way to depreciate those assets over time—and get it done within a few years.

Given the complexity and enormity of the effort, it shouldn't be surprising that when GASB first came out with the rule, fear and trembling ran through the ranks of financial officers. GASB 34 sessions at national conferences overflowed with angry and confused participants. Government officials from large states to small cities protested that they didn't have enough time, staff or money to complete the task. Controllers feared what is, to them, the worst outcome: a qualified opinion on the annual financial audit.

> "[Under GASB 34], someone who looks at financial statements is going to have a more complete picture of what government does."
>
> Roberta Reese,
> GASB project manager

Now that the jurisdictions that have to meet the 2002 deadline are into the process, there's a more sanguine air. "Two years ago, people were asking, 'When are you going to repeal this thing?'" GASB's Reese says. "Now they're a lot more practical, and there's less resistance."

It may be that finance officers changed their tune when they found some of the infrastructure reporting to be much simpler than they expected. That's due in part to the comprehensive records most transportation departments keep to fulfill reporting requirements linked to federal transportation funds. "Everybody has been pleasantly surprised that the records are as good as they are," says Relmond Van Daniker, executive director of the National Association of State Auditors, Comptrollers and Treasurers. "Fears haven't been borne out, and infrastructure has not become nearly the problem people thought it would be."

GASB also helped by offering an alternative for road and bridge reporting. Rather than insist that governments use the same straight-line depreciation method for infrastructure as they use for other fixed assets, Statement 34 allows for a "modified approach," an approach that calls for maintenance of infrastructure to be reported as an expense. Governments must meet three criteria to use this method: They must commit to maintaining the assets at a predetermined level, estimate the amount necessary to fund that maintenance level and conduct condition assessments at least every three years. More than half of the states are opting for the modified approach.

Wisconsin is among them. Bridges and roads were already on an assessment cycle, and to William Raftery and his staff, it seemed to be the most sensible format. "That's the way most DOTs manage highways," Raftery says. "That information is much more valuable than depreciation."

Some governments took the depreciation route because, for them, it was an easier-than-expected task. Portland, Oregon, for instance, already had depreciation costs built into its fixed-asset computer system. Once a useful life span is entered into the computer's system—15 years for a road, or 40 years for a building, for example—the computer automatically depreciates the asset's value. "I don't understand why people are up in arms," says Lena Ellis, the city's accounting manager, of the initial furor over the GASB depreciation rule. "That's our least concern. If that's all we had to do, we'd be elated."

For governments without built-in depreciation data, the experience has been more trying. Florida's computer system didn't include depreciation costs—it was 20 years old and hadn't been improved in about 15. So it took state workers months to enter the data to generate depreciated values. "Property was our number one headache, without a doubt," says Molly Merry, the state's financial administrator for financial reporting.

Oklahoma, which managed to beat the deadline and implement GASB 34 with its fiscal year 2001 CAFR, also chose to report its infrastructure using depreciation. For Oklahoma, the modified approach was too big a hurdle. "We didn't have the detail," says Steve Funck, a financial reporting supervisor. "We couldn't do it if we wanted to."

But there is another factor for states to consider when making a decision about which approach to use. Condition assessment data from the modified approach can be used for political advantage, such as convincing a legislature of the need for repair dollars. And that may, in fact, be one of the more positive fallouts from GASB 34. Departments in charge of, say, highways and bridges can, says Jay Fountain, assistant director of research for GASB, "get their story out there. They can get more funding for an adequate level of maintenance."

It is possible to switch to the modified approach after beginning with straight-line depreciation, and big-picture watchers expect to see more governments sign on as years pass. Coincidentally, just as GASB released Statement 34, the Federal Highway Administration opened its Office of Asset Management, which helps states develop systematic management methods for their highways. That dovetails nicely with the changes in infrastructure reporting, particularly with amassing the information to explain the data associated with GASB 34.

Luckily, GASB has built breathing room into compliance deadlines: In stage one, governments must report the value of all assets under construction or completed by the beginning of their implementation year. They then have an additional four years to report on assets built as far back as 1980. Assets constructed before 1980 won't have to be reported at all, although GASB has encouraged governments to stretch their reporting back as far as their records will allow. So, as interesting as it would be to find out the value of the Brooklyn Bridge, New York City won't be required to troll back to 1883 to come up with the number.

There are some numbers that localities have to come up with that may be difficult to determine, however. Some jurisdictions, especially those experiencing fast growth, are stymied by how to book the value of donated assets, such as streets built by developers. Orange County, Florida, which grew 32 percent in the 1990s, hasn't systematically tracked the value of donated streets and drainage systems.

The city of Alexandria, Virginia, faced a similar issue but had a built-in solution. Most of the 223-year-old city was built well before 1980—the heart of the city is called "Old Town." But the streets running beyond Old Town are under great growth pressure. Fortunately, developers are required to post bonds with the city before building, even for assets they donate. The city simply looked up those records, and there were its values.

New York City managed to become the largest government yet to implement GASB 34 with its fiscal year 2001 CAFR, despite the hardship of having to continue doing the work immediately after the trauma of September 11. The city was set on 2001 implementation, however, knowing that in 2002 it would have to deal with a new mayor, new comptroller and new outside auditors. The city's process moved relatively smoothly, even as it booked more than $5 billion in assets. The final CAFR is "more complex, if anything," according to Warren Ruppel, assistant comptroller for accounting.

Complexity wasn't what GASB had in mind with Statement 34. Its hope was that the new reporting guidelines—particularly the inclusion of capital costs—would provide the general public with a clearer idea of the full costs of providing services.

Will GASB 34 achieve that? Some finance officers remain unsure that GASB's vision will be recognized. "This is change, and change is difficult. Whether people understand better, they'll have to tell us," says Linda Steele, city comptroller in Mobile, Alabama. "From our perspective, it's just change." Looking forward to her own city's September 30 implementation date, she says that "so far it's not been too bad, but when we get down to the wire, it may get a little painful."

6

Insufficient Funds

Dennis Farney

Half of the states are embroiled in lawsuits charging that school spending is inadequate. How much money is enough—and where will it come from?

Kansas state legislators, whose job is to somehow square state needs with state political realities, can perhaps be forgiven for regarding their 1992 education funding formula as a pretty good piece of work.

The formula was derived in response to a court ruling that had found the previous formula unfair and unconstitutional. It began by mandating the same base or "foundation" amount of educational spending for every "full-time equivalent" pupil in the state and also required every district to levy a minimum property tax of 20 mills. If this levy didn't raise enough money to enable a district to meet the foundation level, the state would make up the difference. If it raised more money than necessary, the state would reallocate the excess to needy districts.

Then, responding to political pressures from multiple directions, legislators went on to tweak their basic formula. They cranked in extra weighting—and money—for small rural districts. To placate large urban districts, they added extra weighting for them, too. They also added extra weighting for districts with "at risk"—poor—pupils, districts that built new facilities, districts with high transportation costs and districts offering bilingual or vocational education. They allowed districts to tax themselves beyond the 20-mill minimum (and keep the extra money) if they wished. Finally, there was "ancillary weighting," a rather mysterious factor that seemed to apply only to a few of the wealthiest districts in the state.

Although this may have been a good-faith response to concerns about fairness, 11 years later state district Judge Terry L. Bullock swept the whole thing into the dustbin. The formula was the flawed

From *Governing*, December 2004.

result of a "political auction" and "in blatant violation" of both the Kansas and U.S. Constitutions, he ruled in *Montoy v. State of Kansas*. Bullock then ordered the cash-strapped state to add $1 billion a year to its education budget, a big jump from the $3.6 billion it spent in 2002-03.

Kansas had collided with an "adequacy" suit— and lost. It has a lot of company. Two dozen states are now embroiled in these lawsuits, all of which maintain that a state's total education spending is too low. The tide is running strongly in favor of the plaintiffs. State after state is being told that it has no choice but to spend more— usually a lot more—on its constitutional obligation to educate its children, even if this means cutting back on other programs and/or raising taxes.

Advocates of poor and minority children hail these cases as the latest wave in the decades-old battle for civil rights, with the courts once again leading the way. "These suits are the progeny of *Brown v. Board of Education*," says Molly A. Hunter, director of legal research for the Campaign for Fiscal Equity Inc., the group spearheading the suits in many states. "Brown wasn't just about desegregation for desegregation's sake. It was also about access to educational opportunity."

Others see the suits as an end-run around state legislatures and governors. "This is a fairly brazen attempt to extort more money," says Kansas House Speaker Doug Mays, a Republican. The state promptly appealed the Bullock ruling to the Kansas Supreme Court, with a decision expected before year's end.

A BIGGER PIE

These adequacy suits are quite different from the "equity" suits that compelled some states—including Kansas—to re-write their school finance formulas in the 1970s, '80s and '90s. The equity suits were "Robin Hood" suits, explains Julie Underwood, general counsel for the National School Boards Association. That is, they challenged the unfairness of wealthy school districts spending far more per pupil than poorer districts. Equity suits were about dividing up the education pie in a fairer way.

Adequacy suits are about getting a bigger pie—considerably bigger. They assert that total state funding isn't high enough to ensure that all pupils have a reasonable opportunity to meet state educational goals. Adequacy suits put plaintiffs in a stronger position than was the case in equity suits, where the state could sometimes pit district against district in court. As the NSBA notes, "school boards [now] can present a united front."

Often, the facts speak for themselves. *Hoke County Board of Education v. State of North Carolina* spotlighted deplorable conditions in one of the state's poorest counties. Testimony revealed that in the mid-1990s, only 41 percent of high school freshmen went on to graduate—the worst retention rate in the state. Those who did graduate sometimes lacked the skills to perform "even basic tasks."

Clearly exasperated, the North Carolina Supreme Court ruled in July 2004 that the state had failed in its constitutional duty. The court also noted that the case had already dragged on for a decade, costing North Carolina taxpayers "an incalculable sum of money. . . . One can only wonder how many additional teachers, books, classrooms and programs could have been provided by that money. . . ."

States are the underdogs in adequacy suits because 49 states have education clauses in their constitutions. (The lone exception, South Carolina, repealed its clause in response to the Supreme Court decision in *Brown v. Board of Education*. These clauses, however perfunctory, make these cases constitutional cases. And courts, of course, are the arbiters of constitutional questions.

Because the cases hinge on constitutional issues, it doesn't do a state much good to argue that it simply can't afford a major increase in education expenditures. When Kansas tried that argument, among

> "State after state is being told that it has no choice but to spend more—usually a lot more—on its constitutional obligation to educate its children, even if it means cutting back on other programs and/or raising taxes."

Key Cases Around The Country

New York In August 2004, after legislators failed to meet a July 30 deadline, a Manhattan court appointed three special masters to resolve the state's long educational funding battle. The action came 13 months after the state's highest court had set that deadline and 11 years after the Campaign for Fiscal Equity filed the original suit seeking more money for New York City schools. The special masters were directed to come up with a formula by year's end. *Campaign for Fiscal Equity v. State of New York*

Missouri In 1993, a judge concluded that Missouri schools ranged from "the golden to the god-awful." That ruling led to passage of Missouri's Outstanding Schools Act of 1993, which established higher educational goals and a new funding formula. But in January 2004, the Committee for Educational Equality sued on grounds that the funding system distributes money unequally among districts even as it holds all districts to the same level of performance and accountability. The plaintiffs argue that $900 million more is needed annually. *Committee for Education Equality v. State of Missouri*

Arkansas The state Supreme Court voted 4 to 3 in June 2004 to approve a new state funding formula hammered out by the legislature. It increases state education spending by $370 million annually. But part of the package was the closing through consolidation of 57 small districts—including the one that originally brought the suit. *Lake View School District, No. 25 v. Huckabee*

Massachusetts A state superior court has ruled that despite a 1993 school reform measure and an average increase in state funding since then of 12 percent a year, Massachusetts is still failing to meet its constitutional obligation to adequately educate pupils in poor school districts. Oral arguments before the Massachusetts Supreme Judicial Court began in early October 2004. *Hancock v. Driscoll*

Montana In April 2004, a district court ruled that Montana's school financing system is unconstitutional on adequacy grounds and ordered the state to come up with a formula based on "educationally relevant factors." The court stayed its order until October 1, 2005. The state appealed to the Montana Supreme Court, which issued a preliminary order in November (for the benefit of the 2005 legislature) unanimously upholding the lower court's decision. *Columbia Falls Public Schools v. State of Montana*

New Jersey The state Supreme Court ruled in 2003 that cash-short New Jersey could freeze spending in so-called "Abbott districts." A 1994 ruling in *Abbott v. Burke* had concluded that these poor urban districts were denied "a thorough and efficient education" and ordered spending increases. The 2003 ruling was a setback for advocacy advocates. However, they could take some solace from a separate appellate court ruling in January 2004 that found the state Department of Education had erred in cutting $124 million from these districts.

Texas A state district judge ruled in September 2004 that the Texas education finance system is unconstitutional because it is inadequate and also fails to give districts meaningful discretion in setting local property tax rates. The judge set no dollar figure and delayed the effect of his ruling until late 2005 to give the Texas legislature time to act. But the state appealed to the Texas Supreme Court, and concerns are growing that the high court may not rule before the regular 2005 legislative session is over. *West Orange-Cove Consolidated ISD v. Neeley*

Ohio In perhaps the most convoluted struggle of all, the Ohio Supreme Court initially ruled in favor of the plaintiffs. But then the composition of the court changed and it effectively reversed itself. "We have a legislature that won't obey court orders and a Supreme Court that won't enforce court decisions," says William Phillis, executive director of the Ohio Coalition for Equity and Adequacy of School Funding.

---

others, it got a sharp rebuff in district court. " 'Money doesn't matter?' That dog won't hunt in Dodge City," retorted Judge Bullock.

Ironically, states are even more vulnerable now because many of them have crafted more rigorous and more specific educational standards. Plaintiffs can now argue that the states haven't matched their money to the new mandates.

Al Lindseth, an Atlanta attorney who has represented states in several suits, points out an additional irony. "The legislature isn't even a party to the lawsuit in most of these cases. But guess who gets handed the bill when it's all over?" He notes that typically the formal defendant is the state education department, "and half the time they are sympathizing with the plaintiffs. They want more money and, frankly, more state control."

Even states that are already spending heavily on education, such as New York and New Jersey, are not immune to adequacy suits. If anything, Lindseth adds, they seem to be more vulnerable. He says it's a matter of political climate: Higher-spending states tend to be more liberal, with liberal courts that, in turn, are more receptive to such suits.

Wherever they occur, school finance battles are intensely emotional. Few things are as potent as schools in shaping a state's, or a community's, image of itself. And few factors loom larger in efforts to attract business and industry. Indeed, for smaller, rural communities anxious about possible consolidation, the loss of their schools is seen as tantamount to losing their towns.

FIGHTING TO A DRAW

All these forces came together in Kansas after Judge Bullock declared the state's 1992 funding formula unconstitutional last year. He emphatically concluded: "Whether any Kansas child is of a minority race, or is a slow learner, or suffers a learning disability, or is rich or poor, or lives east or west, or any other consideration, that child is 'our child' and our Constitution guarantees that child an equal educational opportunity consistent with his or her natural abilities."

In 2004, the battle moved from the courtroom to the political arena. Ideologically, Kansas—to an even greater extent than many other states in recent years—is divided into three "parties": conservative Republicans, moderate Republicans and Democrats. Likewise, the geopolitical landscape also has three identifiable parts: rural, small-town Kansas, where the population is drying up and schools are having to consolidate; the wealthy suburbs of Johnson County (bordering Kansas City, Missouri), which take pride in their fine schools and lament taxes that subsidize poorer school districts across the state; and finally, small to mid-sized cities, such as Dodge City (25,568), Salina (45,833) and Wichita (354,617), which are trying to educate substantial numbers of immigrant children. The Dodge City and Salina districts, in fact, brought the Kansas suit.

Against this political backdrop, the first move went to Governor Kathleen Sebelius. A first-term Democrat, she is the daughter of former Ohio Governor John J. Gilligan (who served in the early 1970s) and married to the son (Gary) of a popular former Kansas Republican congressman, Keith Sebelius.

Sebelius seems to be very much aware of her father's fate: defeated for reelection because he was perceived as too liberal for Ohio. Thus, although the court was demanding $1 billion, she responded cautiously with a $300 million plan, to be phased in over three years. It was to be financed by increasing sales and income taxes. "If we wait, the courts, not legislators representing local school districts, could determine how much we must spend on our schools," she warned.

Her plan was quickly dismissed by the legislature. But lawmakers then stalemated over what to put in its place. The House approved $155 million. The Senate countered with $72 million—for one year only. The House rejected the Senate's plan. As the session ground on, figures filled the air like confetti: $108 million, $128 million, $95 million, $82 million, $92 million. With the state's rainy day fund already depleted, one plan would have tapped the state highway fund, another the state pension fund.

Finally, having fought itself to a draw, the legislature adjourned. "To paraphrase Aesop: The mountain labored and brought forth nothing at all," an irritated Judge Bullock would later write.

FEAR FACTOR

In the legislative melee, some moderate Republicans had stuck their necks out—only to pay a political price. One was first-termer Bill Kassebaum. The son of former Kansas Republican Senator Nancy Kassebaum Baker and grandson of legendary GOP Governor Alf Landon, Bill Kassebaum is a rancher and assistant county prosecutor. His hometown of Burdick, population 60, is so small that its high school has been boarded up since 1957.

"I was so upset with the representation we had, ducking the issues," he says. So in 2002, Kassebaum challenged the incumbent Republican state representative, Shari Weber. He ran a Mr. Smith Goes to Washington kind of campaign, saying up front that he would be open to tax increases in order to resolve the state's school finance problem. Against the odds, he won the primary—by 145 votes—and went to the Kansas House.

Kassebaum was as good as his word. He put together a bipartisan coalition to pass the $155 million House plan. The money was to come from increased state sales and income taxes. All 45 House Democrats and 36 of its moderate Republicans voted for it. Forty-three conservative Republicans voted against it.

But Kassebaum's bill died in the Senate. And when he ran for reelection in the 2004 primary, he again faced Weber, who ran as an anti-tax, anti-abortion social conservative. She had financial support from the Kansas Club for Growth, an offshoot of the anti-tax, Washington-based Club for Growth, and beat Kassebaum by 288 votes. "It's easy to influence people on fear," he says. "It's difficult to counter that."

Where does Kansas go from here? If its legislature couldn't pass even 15 percent of the $1 billion ordered by the court, can it come up with a full billion? It seems doubtful, although Judge Bullock pointedly noted that the money could be raised simply by rescinding tax cuts passed in recent years.

House Speaker Doug Mays says flatly that the $1 billion "isn't going to happen, or anywhere close to it." He does venture that it is "possible to go up to $200 million or so," given an improving Kansas economy and saving on other social programs.

Bullock's order does offer some leeway. It says, "there must be literally hundreds of ways" the legislature could structure an acceptable formula. Moreover, the judge took pains to say that he isn't demanding that every student receive exactly the same amount of support. He just insists that any deviation be justified by a "rational explanation premised on the varying actual costs incurred in providing essentially equal educational opportunities for each of those children."

It's possible that the adequacy suits could ultimately be the catalyst for broader educational reforms. But attorney Al Lindseth thinks that whatever Kansas and other states decide to do, they would be well advised to have lawyers sitting at their elbows. He adds: "There are more ways than [just] money to skin this cat."

Kansas—and states around the country—may have to look at every one of them.

> "If we wait, the courts, not legislators representing local school districts could determine how much we must spend on our schools."
>
> Governor Kathleen Sebelius

7 The Well That Dried Up

Anya Sostek

Pittsburgh has weathered some tough economic times and there are encouraging signs. If only the government weren't broke.

In the heat of an August afternoon in Pittsburgh, construction workers laid shingles and power-washed bricks in a new housing development called Summerset. They were building homes that will sell for as much as half a million dollars, rising up on land reclaimed from Nine Mile Run, a polluted slag heap overlooking the Monongahela River.

It is an impressive project. But as the residents of Summerset move into their new homes, they are discovering that the city won't be controlling rodents or funding community recreation centers. Their property and income taxes—already among the highest in the state—may be increased again. And when the Summerset homeowners drive downtown, they'll have to pay as much as $22 a day to park in a garage.

These are confusing, troubling times in Pittsburgh. In overall terms, the city is doing fairly well. Rebounding from the rapid decline of the steel industry in the 1980s, it has nurtured and created high-paying jobs in the hospital, university and financial sectors. But while Pittsburgh as an economic entity is in reasonably healthy shape, its government is critically ill. Throughout the last decade of relative prosperity, the city's budget ran structural deficits every single year. In the past two years, the budget has collapsed.

In August 2003, Mayor Tom Murphy closed nearly all city swimming pools and recreation centers, cut basic services, increased the parking tax to 50 percent and laid off about 600 municipal workers, including nearly 100 police officers. "This is Pittsburgh's Waterloo," says city controller Tom Flaherty. "It's an abysmal scene here." Two state oversight boards have taken control of the finances and operations, leaving local elected officials nearly powerless.

From *Governing,* October, 2004.

In June, the city council voted 5-4, amidst great emotional anguish, in favor of a plan drafted by one of the two boards. The plan called for deep cuts in the city budget and a $40 million package of new tax increases. The scene surrounding the council meeting was nothing short of ugly, with protesters taking their fight to the homes and neighborhoods of council members. "It's hard medicine and it is hard to swallow," says Sala Udin, a council member who voted for the plan. "But I think that most of what they recommend and require is a better way of doing business." The tax plan still has to be approved by state legislators, who may or may not be willing to allow the city to raise new revenues.

THE PITTSBURGH PARADOX

It all amounts to a problem that might be described as the Pittsburgh Paradox. And it raises new questions about the whole relationship between economic vitality and fiscal solvency. How does a city with ongoing new construction and ubiquitous help-wanted signs go bankrupt? Is it possible for a government that can't pay its bills even in the best of economic times to turn its budget around in much less favorable circumstances?

In fact, the reasons for Pittsburgh's plight are relatively simple to explain. They lie primarily in the tax structure. More than anything else, it is Pittsburgh's tax system that created the mismatch between its economy and its fiscal health. "The government is starving while the economy is robust," says Udin. "We have made an amazing recovery from the collapse of the steel industry, but city government revenues have not grown as the economy has."

In the 1950s, the city had 600,000 residents. Two out of every three people who worked in Pittsburgh lived there, and 60 percent worked in heavy manufacturing. Today, 600,000 people still come into the city every day. But nearly 300,000 of them live outside its borders, and do not pay its income or property taxes. Pittsburgh's ratio of city jobs to city population is the second-highest in the country (sprawling Atlanta is first). "It's not as if when the people moved out, the jobs moved out," says Harold Miller, president of the Allegheny Conference on Community Development. "The city has the challenge of providing services to people who do not live in the city."

Not only does the tax system fail to reach half of Pittsburgh's daytime population, but the taxes themselves are based on the heavy-industry economy of a half-century ago. There is, for example, a business privilege tax whose collection is crucial to keeping the city solvent. But the state of Pennsylvania has exempted many broad categories of businesses from paying it, including utilities and financial services companies. The result is that 45 percent of Pittsburgh companies pay no business taxes at all. That group includes 44 of the city's top 50 corporations, such as Mellon Bank, Heinz and Alcoa. The city is reluctant to raise tax rates for the remaining small businesses that bear a disproportionate share.

Businesses such as Mellon and Heinz do pay a property tax, but it is based on land use, and today's businesses take up much less land than steel companies did. Even more significant is the fact that the non-profit sector, whose hospitals and universities spurred much of the city's economic renaissance, are exempt from property taxes. If foundations and religious institutions are added into the mix, nearly 40 percent of city land is tax-exempt. When Duquesne University recently turned a private high-rise apartment building into a dorm, for example, the city instantly lost more than $350,000 a year in property taxes. The small commercial revenue base leaves city residents paying the bulk of the property tax bill—at a rate of nearly $3,000 per $100,000 of assessed value.

Pittsburgh citizens also pay a 3 percent income tax to the city and their local school district—the highest in the region. "It doesn't work as a solution to load more taxes on residents," says Jim Roberts, a lawyer who is heading up one of the oversight boards. "It's not fair and it's counterproductive because people will

> *It's hard medicine,' says Councilman Sala Udin. Mayor Murphy agrees. But, he says, 'it's not enough to simply nickel and dime the government.*

leave." State law has prohibited the city from levying a commuter income tax on its workers and has held an occupational privilege tax paid by all workers to $10 per year since the 1950s.

Pittsburgh's structurally inadequate revenue base has led it to some desperate taxing solutions to capture a part of the cost imposed by its commuting workers. Last year, it had the highest parking tax of any city in the country: 31 percent. Now it has raised that to 50 percent. The parking lot at the city's largest office tower, the U.S. Steel Building, charges $22 per day. The early-bird "special," for those who arrive before 9 a.m., is $15.

OUT OF GIMMICKS

The way Pittsburgh has dealt with its underlying fiscal problem is to balance its budget every year based on one-time tricks and financial manipulations—such as selling its water company to itself. "It's been 25 years of robbing Peter to pay Paul and putting off tough decisions," says Bill Lieberman, chairman of the Intergovernmental Cooperation Authority (ICA), one of the two oversight boards. But last year, after the layoffs and service cutbacks still didn't yield a balanced budget, the city had run out of one-time fixes. "We have no more tricks," says Udin. "We have nothing left to sell. We are honestly broke and we are honestly on the brink of disaster."

The existence of a structural revenue problem is not a revelation to city officials. No less than five independent reports on the city have recommended changes. But state legislators have repeatedly refused to grant new taxing powers until Pittsburgh reduced its expenses. Of those expenses, a sizable portion goes simply to service the city's debt. Pittsburgh currently has more than $935 million in debt, with payments making up nearly 25 percent of its operating budget for 2004. Credit rating companies consider debt at 12 percent of a city's budget to be high; Pittsburgh's debt of $2,800 per capita is the highest in the country.

Some of the debt was unavoidable. For example, the city of 330,000 today is still paying the pension benefits for the city of 600,000 in the 1950s and '60s. In 1998, Pittsburgh borrowed $250 million to shore up its pension fund, which is still only about 50 percent funded. What could have been avoided was making those bonds non-callable, meaning that they cannot be refinanced. In recent months, with interest rates at their lowest point in modern history, Pittsburgh has been legally required to pay its creditors at or above 6.5 percent. The preliminary report of the Intergovernmental Cooperation Authority called the bond financing structure "ill-advised and a tragic error."

Then there are public safety costs, which make up about half of the budget. Here, too, Pittsburgh has incurred expenses beyond those of most other cities, due in part to the political influence of its public employee unions and the state-mandated binding arbitration process. In particular, critics say that spending on the fire department, which comprises more than 40 percent of public safety costs, is overly generous. "We have somewhere in the range of 300 more fire fighters than we need," says Jim Roddey, the former Allegheny County executive. "We have 32 fire stations and we could easily cover with 20. Organized labor is very powerful in Pittsburgh." Fire union president Joe King vigorously disagrees with that assessment, saying that Pittsburgh's geography of numerous rivers and steep mountains makes fire service comparisons with other cities difficult.

Put aside debt service and public safety, and three-quarters of the entire budget is spoken for. Public works, parks and general services all have to be incorporated into the remaining 25 percent. What critics of Mayor Murphy tend to seize on, however, is spending on economic development. In the mid-1990s, Murphy, an unabashed supporter of development incentives, reserved a portion of 1 percent of county sales tax revenues for an economic development fund.

Over the years, that fund has had some visible successes, such as the Summerset residential project, a Home Depot in a depressed neighborhood and a Cheesecake Factory on reclaimed brownfields. But the fund has had equally visible setbacks—most notably the failure of Lazarus-Macy's and Lord & Taylor stores downtown after more than $50 million in combined incentives. The fund began with a $60 million bond issue and receives $6 million per year.

Some legislators and councilmen argue that the fund should be redirected to cover deficits in city operations, but Murphy has been adamant on continuing economic development. "Some people will give me credit for being tenacious and some will criticize me for stubbornness," he says. "We need to have a vision. It's not enough to simply nickel and dime the government."

JUNK STATUS

By November of last year, the city's finances were practically down to nickels and dimes. An audit report from the consulting firm KPMG questioned whether the local government would be able to make it through the year, and publicly raised the possibility of bankruptcy. In response, the three major credit rating agencies lowered Pittsburgh's bond rating to junk status—making Pittsburgh the only major U.S. city in that category.

At that point, after another losing battle with the state legislature over new taxes, Murphy asked that the city be declared distressed under a state law known as Act 47, originally designed to help small cities cope with the loss of the steel industry. The law authorizes new revenue sources for cities, such as commuter taxes, but requires the cities to accept whatever remedies are prescribed by the Act 47 administrators.

The threat of a commuter tax sent suburban legislators scrambling for an oversight board of their own. Hence, the creation of the Intergovernmental Cooperation Authority, under Act 11 of state law. While the Act 47 team is made up of the Pittsburgh law firm of Eckert Seamans and a Philadelphia-based consulting firm, Public Financial Management, the ICA members were directly appointed by legislative leaders.

No other city has ever been under two oversight boards at the same time, and city officials were unsure which group would take precedence if the recommendations differed. In the end, those concerns never materialized. The oversight boards were able to agree on the same set of recommendations—with the Act 47 team releasing theirs in June and the ICA coming out with a similar plan in September. The Act 47 team has focused on the nuts and bolts of reorganizing city services while the ICA has worked primarily on the legislative tax package. When the Act 47 recommendations were unveiled in June, they were greeted by the *Pittsburgh Post-Gazette* with a headline that said, "Recovery Plan Has Pain for Everyone."

On the spending side, the Act 47 plan is harshest on the fire fighters, who face a 17 percent salary cut, as well as staffing reductions and station closures. With Act 47 status, cities are no longer subject to binding arbitration and can make changes to future labor contracts. For King, the fire president, the Act 47 process has been devastating. "Act 47 is nothing other than a back-door approach to establish a right-to-work state," he says. "What managers weren't successful at in negotiation and arbitration, they are going through the back door to circumvent the rights and privileges of workers."

In addition to the firefighters, all city employees face a two-year wage freeze, the implementation of a 15 percent health premium contribution (employees currently contribute nothing) and the elimination of retiree health benefits. "I think it's an abomination," says Flaherty, the city controller, who believes that more money should have been required of the state and nonprofits. "The city employees took the hit," he says.

Spending cuts in the plan will make up more than half of the city's $70 million deficit for 2004. The Act 47 board has recommended filling the remaining gap with a $40 million tax package that would require approval by the legislature. This would replace the current business taxes with a payroll tax, under which all businesses in the city would pay a specified amount per employee. The plan also would raise the occupational privilege tax from $10 per year to $120 per year, effectively getting some contribution from workers who live outside the city. If the legislature does not go along with some or all of the tax increases, the Act 47 team has a Plan B: Use its power to levy a commuter tax to keep the city afloat. Under that scenario, Pittsburgh residents might also face increased income and property taxes.

The long-term fate of the city is now in the hands of the legislature, which is expected to take up the issue of Pittsburgh's tax package in November. What the tax-averse legislators will do is up in the air. "We're asking for fairness in our tax structure," says Mayor Murphy. "I have always believed that at the end of the day, logic will prevail."

8

Risky Ventures

Christopher Swope

Private investors are pushing a complex venture-capital scheme that involves big risks and uncertain rewards for states.

There is a phrase that venture capitalists, the investors who bet on small start-up companies, use to describe business locations that aren't worth their time: "flyover states." For any place in America that is watching jobs move to China or India, to be labeled a flyover state is an ominous sign. Information technology, biotechnology and nanotechnology are the future, and growing these industries without venture capital is like growing a rose without water.

The distressing truth, however, is that venture investors and the money they manage are concentrated in frustratingly few places. Silicon Valley accounts for one-third of all venture capital in the country, followed by a handful of smaller hubs such as Boston, Austin, San Diego, New York and Seattle. The lack of venture capital almost everywhere else makes it likely that any inventor with an idea, any professor with a patent or any entrepreneur with a business plan who aspires to launch a start-up company will move to where the money is. States are understandably desperate to hold on to their entrepreneurs. So it is easy to see why governors and legislators are increasingly willing to use public funds to jump-start a local venture-capital industry.

What is harder to understand is why so many of them have latched onto one controversial strategy, lobbied for by a small cadre of private investors, that critics call a rip-off for taxpayers and a sweetheart deal for both its promoters and insurance companies. Nine states have earmarked nearly $2 billion to "certified capital companies" or CAPCOs. Yet many state economic development officials contend that CAPCOs don't much resemble typical venture-capital deals in which investors pouring large sums of money

From *Governing*, April, 2004.

into risky start-up companies expect to be highly rewarded. With CAPCOs, the state is taking on nearly all of the risk in exchange for little, if any, of the financial rewards. In fact, states are not really "investing" their money at all. They are essentially handing it over to the CAPCOs, which, after fulfilling their obligations, are free to keep the remainder.

Ever since a Louisiana law gave birth to the CAPCO program in the 1980s, three CAPCOs in particular have been quietly but aggressively pushing this venture-capital model around the country. They make big campaign contributions and use well-paid lobbyists to win over lawmakers. And in states where they have secured funding once, they have nearly always come back and pressed for more.

The CAPCO trend hasn't attracted much public interest, however, because the funding structure is so complex. Last year in Alabama, while voters were souring on new taxes for education, state officials were quietly implementing a 2002 law that gave CAPCOs $100 million in tax credits. In November, Washington, D.C.'s city council passed a $50 million CAPCO bill without triggering a single mention in the *Washington Post*. Texas and Georgia are preparing to fund CAPCO programs worth $200 million and $75 million, respectively. "These CAPCO guys are good at lobbying," says George Lipper, who tracks CAPCOs for the National Association of Seed and Venture Funds, a group that monitors economic development efforts in the states. "They show up at the table with a solution to the state's lack of venture capital. Most state legislators don't have any knowledge of venture capital at all, and what they have in front of them is a promise to answer that problem. So they're very vulnerable to it."

The beginnings of a backlash are visible, however. The Wisconsin Assembly last month beat back the CAPCOs' push for a second round of funding. Florida is refusing to

> "The former [Colorado] House speaker, who originally sponsored the CAPCO measure is having second thoughts. 'As a legislator, I passed 80 good bills,' says Doug Dean, who is now Colorado's insurance commissioner. 'And one bad one.'"

fund a 2002 law giving the CAPCOs a second $150 million. The situation is even more heated in Colorado. When the legislature passed a CAPCO law in 2001, funding was split into two $100 million installments, the first of which was disbursed two years ago. Policy makers in Colorado are so angry with how the first $100 million is being used that they raced to divert the second $100 million before the CAPCOs got it this April. Even the former House speaker who originally sponsored the CAPCO measure is having second thoughts. "As a legislator, I passed 80 good bills," says Doug Dean, who is now Colorado's insurance commissioner. "And one bad one."

BUY NOW, PAY LATER

To understand the CAPCO controversy, it is helpful to look at how venture capital traditionally works. After pooling together money from pension funds, foundations and wealthy individuals who become limited partners in a fund, venture capitalists invest in start-up companies in exchange for an equity stake in the business. This kind of early-stage investing carries big risks—more than half of those start-ups typically won't survive. But occasionally one hits it big, earning limited partners large returns on their investments. If all goes well, an investor who gives $100 million to a venture capitalist would expect to get his $100 million back, and in addition a share of 80 percent of the fund's profits. The venture capitalist takes 20 percent of the profits, plus an annual management fee of about 2.5 percent, or roughly $2.5 million a year.

CAPCOs work quite differently. In order to raise a $100 million venture pool, states turn to insurance companies. Insurers give $100 million upfront to the CAPCOs, in exchange for the same amount in tax credits to be taken over 10 years. The CAPCOs then begin investing the money in local start-up companies. It is a buy-now, pay-later formula that elected officials find

The CAPCO Flow

1. State allocates tax credits (State → CAPCOs)
2. Insurance companies make loan (Insurance Companies → CAPCOs)
3. CAPCOs give tax credits, plus guaranteed rate of return (CAPCOs → Insurance Companies)
4. CAPCOs invest in start-ups (CAPCOs → Start-up Companies)
5. Start-ups grow and pay taxes (Start-up Companies → State)

Source: Colorado State Auditor's report, October 2003

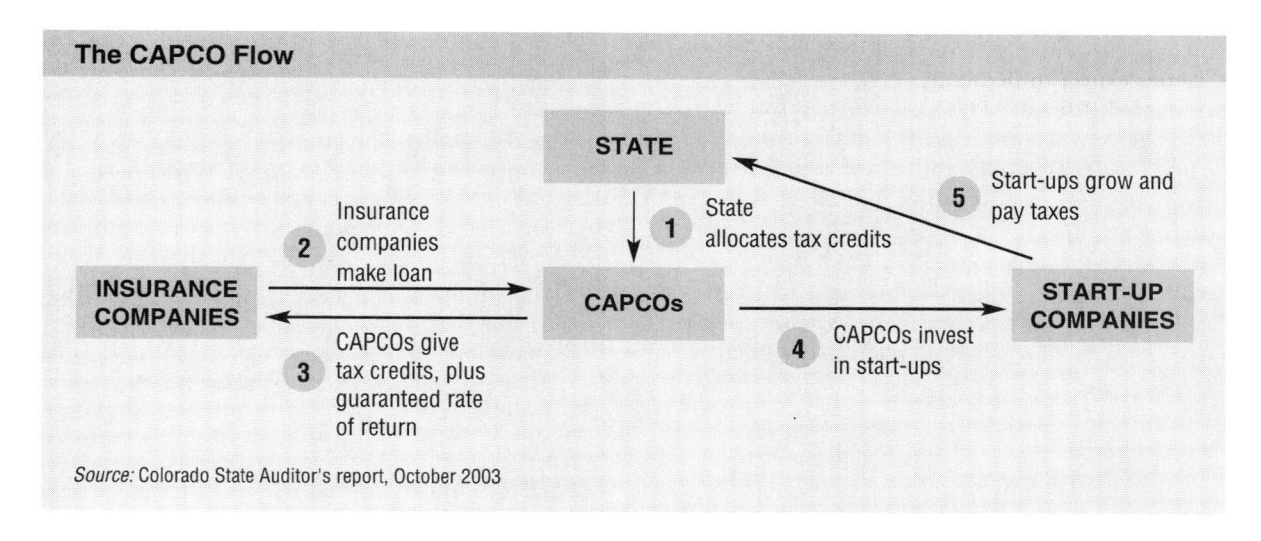

hard to resist. The state, however, is the only party in the deal who bears much risk. The CAPCOs have none of the fiduciary responsibilities to the state that a venture capitalist owes to his limited partners. In fact, much of the "investment" here—the state's $100 million in forgone tax revenues—actually lands on the CAPCOs' books as income.

Almost any group of investors may form a CAPCO, as long as they have a couple of years of venture-capital experience, $500,000 in the bank and agree to set up an in-state office. But the states' boilerplate laws, crafted by CAPCO lobbyists, subtly favor a few established national players who have been around since the early days in Louisiana. Not coincidentally, they are the same players who are lobbying legislatures the hardest. Of the $1.5 billion that seven states have so far funneled to CAPCOs via the insurance tax-credit mechanism, only $1 billion is traceable through public records. Those records clearly show who the Big Three nationally are:

- Advantage Capital Partners in St. Louis has received at least $261 million.
- The Wilshire Group, a subsidiary of Newtek Business Services in New York City, has received at least $140 million.
- Stonehenge Capital Corp., based in Columbus, Ohio, and affiliated with Bank One, has received at least $226 million.

The insurance companies, in addition to receiving the tax credits, negotiate with the CAPCOs for a guaranteed rate of return. Exactly how much insurance companies make off the deal is not public record, although Colorado regulators believe the insurers' overall return is as high as 10 percent a year. According to state records in Florida, New York and Colorado, insurers Metropolitan Life, Travelers, John Hancock and Northwestern Mutual, among others, have taken CAPCO tax credits in each of those states.

To be sure, states do attach a few strings to CAPCO money. The CAPCOs must invest in start-ups located in the state. Start-ups typically must begin with a small number of employees, and firms practicing law, accounting, medicine or real estate often don't qualify. Otherwise, state laws are generally silent about how to measure outcomes. It is hoped that the CAPCOs will create jobs and taxable income, but they are not required to show any economic benefits. Instead, the laws gauge success by how quickly the CAPCOs pump out dollars. They typically must have 30 percent of their funds invested within three years and 50 percent invested within five years.

These laws leave much open to the CAPCOs' interpretation. The Wilshire Group, for example, uses the states' CAPCO programs primarily as an income stream for Newtek, its parent company. Newtek is a publicly traded company that performs credit card processing and financial services for small businesses. Its corporate strategy, laid out in filings with the Securities and Exchange Commission, is to channel the states' money into Newtek's own subsidiaries. In 2002, state CAPCO programs accounted for 88 percent of Newtek's gross revenue.

Newtek calls its tactic a "hands-on approach" to investing and says in its latest annual report that "the states' objectives of job creation and economic development are unquestionably met." Indeed, all of Newtek's "partner companies" are based in CAPCO states. But Alice Kotrlik, who oversees the CAPCOs for Colorado's economic development office, says, "Legislators never intended this to be free capital for a company to expand its own product line. That's not anybody's perception of venture capital."

SAFE BETS

When the CAPCOs came calling in Colorado three years ago, the state was already in an enviable position—ranking among the top 10 for venture-capital investment. Nevertheless, high-tech industries were complaining that early-stage seed funding was still hard to come by, particularly in biotechnology. The CAPCOs finally won over lawmakers by agreeing to spread the venture-capital wealth beyond Denver and Boulder and make one-quarter of their investments in rural counties.

It didn't take long for policy makers to realize that the CAPCO approach wasn't quite what they expected. Their first shock was learning that $100 million worth of tax credits yielded a pool of only about $40 million for the CAPCOs to invest. That's because the CAPCOs placed nearly half of the $100 million in safe havens such as treasury bonds in order to pay the insurance companies back. This would not have come as a surprise to anyone who had looked at other states' CAPCO programs. Still, even legislators who originally supported the CAPCOs didn't understand how this so-called "defeasance" worked. Nor did they seem to grasp the fees CAPCOs were allowed to charge: $11 million to set up their offices, plus an additional $4 million in management fees the first year.

This is not to say that the CAPCOs won't make $100 million worth of investments. In fact, the law encourages them to do so—and quickly. The CAPCOs are deregulated once they have put 100 percent of the insurance companies' money to work. What that means though, is that in order to turn a $40 million pool into $100 million worth of investments, the CAPCOs must roll over some of the money a few times. That prompts them to make safe bets, which is at odds with the very goals of a venture-capital program. Indeed, more than half of the CAPCOs' investments to date have been in the form of loans, some of them short-term.

The last straw for Colorado officials, however, was the revelations in a state auditor's report last October: Not only had the CAPCOs spent $472,000 on lobbying in four years, but $85,000 of that was financed with state-backed money from the venture-capital program. And the CAPCOs were meeting only the letter, not the spirit, of the rural investment requirement. Three portfolio companies landed in an office park in "rural" Clear Creek County, 600 yards from the border of Denver's western suburbs.

AN INNOVATIVE MODEL?

Although CAPCO critics harp on these anecdotes, if you look at the 23 Colorado companies in the CAPCOs' portfolios many are high-tech start-ups of the nature that lawmakers had in mind. Ischemia Technologies, for instance, is a biotech company based in the Denver suburbs. Ischemia sells a blood test that helps doctors determine quickly whether a patient reporting chest pains is having a heart attack or just heartburn. The market for Ischemia's product is huge: 6 million Americans show up at hospitals with chest pains annually.

A year and a half ago, Ischemia was burning through cash while waiting for the U.S. Food and Drug Administration to approve its product. To get through the crunch, it sought its fourth round of venture capital, but the dot-com meltdown had made such funding hard to find. Two CAPCOs, Advantage and a smaller one called Murphree Colorado Capital, came through with $700,000. Ischemia also raised $7.6 million from other venture investors, but Chief Financial Officer Steven Joanis says, "The CAPCOs were instrumental to closing the round. In an era when not many others are doing deals, the CAPCOs are."

The FDA approved Ischemia's device in February 2003. Now that the company is selling a product, cash flow is improving and the focus of its 25 employees is shifting from research toward marketing and manufacturing. According to Peter Crosby, Ischemia's president and CEO, the company likely would have downsized some had the CACPO funds not come through when they did. "Our payroll is $3.5 million. We pay lots of state taxes. Who can tell me this isn't making money for the state?"

The CAPCOs point to other small-business success stories. Federation Inc., another company in Advantage's portfolio, is a software integrator in the defense aerospace market that moved to Colorado from Israel. The company's staff has grown from two to nine since it landed $7 million in venture capital a little over a year ago (Advantage's stake was $300,000). Another start-up, called StorePerform Technologies, sells software to retailers. It has grown from 18 employees to 30 since one of the CAPCOs, Enhanced Colorado Issuer, invested $750,000 in it. The new positions came about during Colorado's toughest job market in years.

As the CAPCOs see it, they've created an innovative model for financing venture capital—persuading insurance companies, who are safe investors by nature, to put money into high-risk investing. This approach is particularly effective in flyover states, they say, where CAPCOs pull in co-investors from other states. That is beginning to break down venture capital's geographic barriers, according to John Neis, a Wisconsin-based venture capitalist who manages Advantage Capital's CAPCO there. "You need a local lead investor who has a meaningful amount of capital to be credible to attract folks from the coasts," he says.

But since this isn't traditional venture capital, the CAPCOs say, the costs and benefits should be evaluated differently. The CAPCOs are fusing together two worlds—profit-driven venture capital with jobs-driven economic development—and those goals sometimes contradict each other. Normally, venture capitalists seek the best deals, period. But CAPCOs are restricted to in-state deals and limited by other political considerations, such as Colorado's rural requirement. Which is why, they argue, states should reward them more handsomely than a typical limited partner would reward a venture capitalist. "There's a lot of great deals I have to pass on in the CAPCO model," Neis says. "The objective is economic development more so than return on investment. We're trying to get a return, but the expectations are vastly lower for the CAPCO model."

According to the CAPCOs, success can be measured only in the long run. And the main test is whether the benefits outweigh the admittedly expensive costs. A January study of Missouri's seven-year-old CAPCO program, funded by the CAPCOs' own trade association, found that $52 million worth of CAPCO funding had leveraged $1.3 billion in co-investment (this assumes that CAPCO money always pulls in other investors, not the other way around). Using liberal assumptions on job creation, the study concluded that state and local governments were receiving $3.30 in tax revenues for every $1 the state had invested in the program. "Without our actions through the CAPCOs, these ventures would not happen," says Joe Maxwell, Missouri's lieutenant governor. "Missouri wins when we create new jobs that would not otherwise have been created."

BANG FOR THE BUCK

The question, however, is not whether the CAPCOs might produce some positive results. Nobody doubts that aiding high-tech, high-paying companies such as Ischemia Technologies are good for Colorado. The issue is cost-efficiency. Are there ways to accomplish the same goals that give states more bang for the buck?

A report by the National Governors Association in 2000 outlined at least a half-dozen approaches to state venture-capital programs. A few states, such as Connecticut, Maryland and Massachusetts, directly invest public funds in local companies. Others, such as Pennsylvania and more recently Oregon, have asked public pension funds to place a small percentage of their investments with local venture-capital firms. States such as Maine, Ohio and Virginia offer tax credits to wealthy individuals, known as "angel investors," for investing seed money in local start-ups. Another model from Oklahoma, copied by Arkansas and Iowa, uses tax credits a bit like the CAPCO programs, except that the credits act only as a backstop. After 11 years in Oklahoma, investors have poured $30 million into local start-ups and the state has yet to give up any tax credits. "The best programs treat the state as a valued financial partner, not as a chump," says the NGA report, which was co-authored by Robert Heard, who runs the Oklahoma program.

SPLITTING THE DIFFERENCE

The CAPCOs counter that the alternatives have flaws as well. The closer the state is to investment decisions, they say, the more likely it is that those choices will become politicized. A worst-case example of that is Mississippi, whose Magnolia Venture fund folded in 1998 and wound up with its director in prison on fraud charges. Pension fund managers, for their part, hate it when lawmakers tell them how and where to invest retirees' money. And the CAPCOs are right when they say that no other venture-capital program pumps as much money into a state's economy as quickly as they do. Clearly, to many election-minded state legislators and governors, that is all that matters.

Colorado officials weighed all of this in February when they debated what to do with the second $100 million worth of CAPCO tax credits. They were convinced that CAPCO could not be reformed, that its underlying structure was defective. But a state law prevented them from simply wiping those tax credits away. Bob Lee, then the state's economic development director and now chief of staff to Governor Bill Owens, wanted to try a new venture-capital model. Mike Coffman, the state treasurer and the CAPCOs' leading critic, wanted Colorado out of the venture-capital business altogether. "It's an inappropriate role for state government to be picking winners and losers," Coffman says.

In the end, the legislature split the difference. It diverted $50 million of the tax credits to a state health insurance fund. The other $50 million will go toward a new venture-capital program. Insurance companies will still fund it, in exchange for the tax credits. But a quasi-public authority will manage it, rather than the CAPCOs. The authority won't pick the investments itself. It will invest the money with private venture funds (the CAPCOs may participate if they wish). And if there are profits, the authority expects to be rewarded the way normal investors are in the real venture-capital world.

According to Chris Christoffersen, a Boulder venture capitalist who helped craft Colorado's new program, the real highlight is that it's an "evergreen" fund. Where the CAPCOs' record is to seek successive infusions of tax credits, Colorado's program, if it works, will build on itself and grow in perpetuity. "CAPCO was almost the antithesis of a real venture-capital program," Christoffersen says. "To call it venture capital was a misnomer."

9

Worth the Money?

Jonathan Walters

The competition for top talent is producing a cadre of highly paid public executives.

Like a baseball coach working his way up the organizational ladder, Rhoda Mae Kerr recently had to abandon her hometown team and make the move to a new city in order to take the top spot. Last January, Kerr took over as chief of the Little Rock fire department after a career in Fort Lauderdale that was capped by three years as deputy chief. Whereas the pattern in the old days was to stay in one place for an entire career, Kerr says, today it's typical to see executives in the fire service move around in order to move up. And for a handful of recognized achievers in her field, such moves bring with them something besides greater challenges and prestige: They bring increased salaries and perks along with a burgeoning reputation that, if nurtured, can put a public-sector career onto an all-star track.

While insisting that she has no plans to leave Little Rock, Kerr admits that some of her employees already have expressed concern that this might be just a short stop for her on the road to somewhere even bigger. That's because Kerr has now entered an elite corps of hired public-sector executives whose expertise makes them hot properties across the country. "There's been a confluence of forces," says Bob O'Neill, executive director of the International City/County Management Association. "There's this incredible pressure that's brought to bear between scarce resources, the demand for and focus on performance, and the political environment in which these people have to operate. People who are effective in that environment are worth their weight in gold."

Indeed, in this new world, hired-gun attorneys negotiate six-figure salaries on their behalf, headhunters make regular contact, and some even speculate that the day will come when the hottest

From *Governing*, July 2004.

public officials will have agents to shop around for the most lucrative deal.

Some members of the "gold" club, such as Los Angeles Police Chief Bill Bratton and former New York City School Superintendent Rudy Crew, have managed to become household names. Robert Kiley, who is credited with rebuilding both the Boston and New York City subway systems, was recently the subject of a full-blown feature story in *The New Yorker* magazine, which chronicled his elevation to savior of the London Underground. Kiley was lured overseas by a compensation package estimated to be worth well over half a million dollars.

Because of the aggressive recruitment of top talent, members of the gold club can command heftier salaries and beefier benefits, whether it's big-ticket sweeteners such as generous contributions to pension funds, performance bonuses or help with housing costs, or littler treats, such as cars, cell phones and take-home computers. Meanwhile, the elite are increasingly opting out of traditional, at-will employment and insisting on multi-year contracts with clauses that ensure any falling out with their elected or appointed handlers will end up in a very soft landing.

Add to the dynamic a shortage of top people willing to take on what in many cases are considered impossible jobs and it makes for a lively, lucrative mix. "You have a lot of school districts chasing a few superintendents and that makes for a lot of churning and also for a significant increase in salaries and perks," says Paul Houston, a former school superintendent who is now executive director of the American Association of School Administrators. "In the past decade, it has really shifted from a buyer's market to a seller's market."

Eric Smith, the school superintendent in Anne Arundel County, Maryland, who reportedly was on the short list of candidates for the superintendent's job in Miami-Dade County (a position ultimately accepted by the aforementioned Rudy Crew), says it's the high profile and the high stakes, in particular, that require the combat pay. "It's an area that's covered intensely by the press and that is much analyzed and debated. And if you're trying to drive change, you'll draw a fair amount of fire."

Smith, who makes $200,000 a year, says that while these forces make for an improved salary picture, the downside is that peripatetic school officials can't draw upon the generous pension layouts afforded most state and local employees, who put in their 25 or 30 years in one place and then reap the benefits. Anne Arundel is contributing a decent sum to a 401(k)-style pension plan as part of his compensation package, says Smith, but he still lives in a world of defined contributions and not guaranteed benefits upon retirement. And Smith arguably is now on the modest end of the high-profile superintendent salary structure. Crew's compensation package in Miami-Dade is estimated to be around $550,000, including salary, bonuses and a housing allowance.

For public-sector superstars, goodbyes sometimes can be as lucrative as hellos. Interim District of Columbia School Superintendent Elfreda Massie, who was paid $75,000 to fill in for about six months last winter, was handed a bonus check for nearly $34,000 on her last day of work in April. Members of the city council and the mayor harshly criticized the bonus, but D.C. school board members saw it as much-deserved pay for a job well done. In recent months, D.C. Mayor Anthony Williams seems to have come around to a new way of thinking about compensating the city's chief education officer. A *Washington Post* article in May had the mayor's office speculating that the city might have to come up with as much as $600,000 to attract a top-flight candidate to fill the job. In mid-June, the city was attempting to lure Carl A. Cohn, former Long Beach, California, superintendent.

PERSONNEL PILFERING

While such remuneration indicates just how much of a seller's market it has become for some top executives, the lucrative talent trade can also be gauged by the amount of public-sector personnel larceny going on as governments jockey to secure the best and the brightest. "It's not unusual for any high-profile administrator to be contacted once a month and offered a job," says Professor George Frederickson, who has spent decades helping train future public managers at the University of Kansas. Rod Gould, city manager for San Rafael, California, say he is frequently on the receiving end of such queries. "I'm amazed at all the calls from recruiters." The 47-year-old Gould adds that part of what's driving demand is a rapidly aging and retiring cadre of experienced managers.

And it's not just high-profile players in traditionally high-profile jobs such as city manager, police chief or school superintendent who are being approached. Planning directors, public works directors, chief information officers—those in the more utilitarian trenches of government—are also routinely recruited by other jurisdictions intent on a little personnel pilfering. "I get called every so often," says Bob Hunter, the long-serving executive director of the Regional Planning Commission in Hillsborough County, Florida. Hunter says he's happy to stay put for now, but as one of the most respected planners in the country, he could probably write his ticket on any given day.

And while few lay people have probably ever heard of Peter Park, the city of Denver knows him as one of the top urban planners in the field. "The reason that I just about killed myself to get Peter Park is that planning is as important as anything else when it comes to what a city does," says Denver Mayor John Hickenlooper, who spent weeks wooing Park. "Park is not just a New Urbanist, he's one of the national and international leaders in urban planning." And probably a significant bargain to Denver at $115,000 a year.

Michael Armstrong has been the assistant city manager for information technology in Des Moines for the past six years. He knows that there aren't very many people with his level of technical skill and knowledge who can also work cooperatively on large projects that span departments citywide. If he wanted to, Armstrong could no doubt move to a bigger municipality on either coast. According to the International City/County Management Association's 2004 salary survey, Prince William County, Virginia, pays its IT director around $130,000 a year; San Diego County pays $160,000; Phoenix pays almost $145,000. But Armstrong says his salary of $125,000 goes a nice distance in the Midwest, which is one of the reasons he has stayed put; salaries may be higher elsewhere, he says, but so is the cost of living. As for being contacted by headhunters, Armstrong says, "It's nothing like two or three times a week, but every once in a while."

Who Makes What

■ Kerr	$102,000
■ Park	$115,008
■ Pataki	$179,000
■ Neff	$190,000
■ Wood	$250,000
■ Bratton	$256,155
■ Crew	$305,000
■ Bush	$400,000
■ Saban	$400,000

Jerry Newfarmer, who finished his city manager's career in Cincinnati after stints in Fresno and San Jose, says that the job has always paid pretty well. But clearly things have gotten better in the past couple of decades as competition for top talent has warmed up. For example, when Newfarmer took over as San Jose's city manager in 1983, the salary was $90,000; the job now pays $209,000. And whereas the big perk for Newfarmer was having the city contribute to a 401(k)-style retirement plan, employment packages in numerous California jurisdictions now include the ability to tap into the state pension system, CalPERS, as well as housing allowances and generous severance packages.

Rod Wood, who at $250,000 a year may be the highest-paid city or county manager in the country, worked out an arrangement with his new employer—the city of Beverly Hills—whereby the city subsidizes his annual housing costs to the tune of $70,000. Wood, who made his name in other cities by thinking up creative ways to finance sewage expansion and affordable housing projects, is also a pioneer in fashioning creative financial packages to attract top talent to public service in a high housing-cost environment. He believes he was the first to work out an equity-sharing deal with a city when he became manager of Indian Wells, California, back in 1989. "I think Indian Wells may have the second-highest per capita income of any city in the country and it costs a ton of money to live there." So he proposed an arrangement whereby the city helped subsidize his mortgage but also profited from the sale of his house when he moved on.

LOCAL LARGESSE

In analyzing who pays how much, it's clear that high pressure and high stakes are only part of what drives salaries. ICMA's salary survey shows that big cities and wealthy suburbs are where the money is. Bratton makes upwards of $250,000 in L.A.; the chief financial officer for Washington, D.C., rakes in more than $170,000. Meanwhile, the fire chief in the well-heeled Boston suburb of Needham earns more than $110,000. Rod Wood's old haunt, Indian Wells (population 3,816), pays its public works director $114,000. Greenwich, Connecticut, pays its police chief more than $110,000. The economic development director in Lake Forest, Illinois, makes around $112,000.

If it sounds like the big-salary and generous perks action is all at the local government level, that's because with a few exceptions—notably state university presidents, athletic directors and football or basketball coaches—it is. "Our experience is that there are fewer restrictions on pay for local officials," says Bob Lavigna, the former head of recruitment and selection for the state of Wisconsin who now works for CPS Human Resources Services, a Sacramento-based human resources consulting firm. "In many cases, by law or by tradition, state officials can't make more than the governor." (New York's George Pataki is the highest-paid governor, at $179,000.) It's a quirky restriction that in some places even extends to municipalities. For example, when CPS was asked to help Minneapolis find a public works director, Lavigna says, the task was made much trickier by the fact that state law caps municipal salaries at 90 percent of the governor's annual $120,000 salary. Minneapolis recently sought and got a waiver from the state legislature in order to hire a police chief at $128,000.

There may be other reasons that local governments offer salaries more commensurate with the market—not to mention actual job responsibilities. "It's a riddle that always perplexed me," says Alisoun Moore, who left her $101,000 job as chief information officer for the state of Maryland to take the $155,000 CIO job in Montgomery County, Maryland. "But I think that county legislators and executives know that their primary job is to deliver very direct services, so they're willing to pay competitive wages to attract good folks, whether it's firefighters or executives."

Despite all the talk about big bucks and generous perquisites, one point needs to be made clear, say those who follow issues of pay and benefits for public officials: Given the incredible responsibilities heaped on upper-level

> *Given the incredible responsibilities heaped on upper-level public executives, they are still arguably underpaid.*

public-sector executives and the frequently volatile political environments in which they're asked to operate, they are still arguably underpaid. Whether it's taming the streets of Los Angeles, raising student test scores in Miami-Dade, or trying to pull Denver's disparate districts and neighborhoods together into a cohesive, economically dynamic metropolitan whole, lots of upper-level public executives are atop gigantic, sprawling organizations that are charged with accomplishing nearly impossible tasks. Kevin Baum, assistant fire chief in Austin, Texas, and a rising star in his field, says that he is probably paid one-third of what one of his organizational counterparts at Austin-based Dell Computer makes, "minus the stock options," he adds wryly. And it hardly needs stating that the Dell executive's job is sandbox play compared to what Baum faces every day.

Baum says he could move up a salary notch if he listened to any of the headhunters who he says call every so often trying to woo him out of Texas hill country. Baum's next logical move, he says, would be to chief in a mid-size city, which would set him up for the jump to the big league—a Chicago, Boston or Seattle. And certainly there are plenty of six-figure jobs in smaller cities around the country, from Birmingham, Alabama, to Downers Grove, Illinois, to Costa Mesa, California, which pay $115,000, $102,000 and $140,000, respectively, according to the ICMA salary survey. But the politics of fire chief have become more volatile and the job strains more pronounced since 9/11, he says. In fact, he's seeing a lot of longtime chiefs getting out altogether, with fewer and fewer experienced candidates willing to step up. That, along with the fact that average tenure of larger city fire chiefs is getting ever shorter, says Baum, has him thinking twice about the whole idea of pulling up stakes. "I have to ask myself if I really want to move to another city and be chief."

It's a sentiment that's expressed by others who find themselves at the edge of superstar status, not sure if it's worth the extra money to step into the frequently unforgiving limelight that is populated by the public sector's executive movers and shakers. Kevin Duggan, city manager for Mountain View, California, says he could certainly be making more money working somewhere else. But he adds that many of those jobs are in "meat grinder" cities, and he's just not sure he's ready for the blades to swirl his way, regardless of pay.

LURE OF THE LIMELIGHT

But for others, the prospect of taking on seemingly impossible high-level jobs is an enormous part of the appeal. "It's an interesting combination between a really true and altruistic sense of public service, on the one hand, and enormous ego, on the other," says the school administrators' Paul Houston. "It's the adrenaline buzz. There's a lot of pressure, but a lot of people thrive on that and become addicted to it."

When Oakland City Manager Robert Bobb, who had co-existed for five years with the famously egotistical Mayor Jerry Brown, was finally ousted last summer, he received a $275,000 severance package. But rather than riding off into the sunset or choosing some easy assignment, Bobb soon headed for Washington, D.C.—a city with comparable problems and egos. As the District of Columbia's top administrator, Bobb now earns $185,000. That's a step down from the $224,400 and generous benefits he had negotiated with Oakland but $50,000 more than D.C. paid his predecessor.

But even given the potential for high-visibility failure or feuding, the money and the personal satisfaction of doing a hard job that matters make it all worthwhile, says San Rafael's Rod Gould. "If you've got the chops for it, there are few things better than taking on the variety and challenge of being a city manager."

And of course it's not always a jungle out there. Just ask Rod Wood, who was actually contemplating a switch to the private sector before a headhunter talked him into giving Beverly Hills a try. Shortly after taking the job, he was at one of the many after-hour events that city managers view as obligatory. "There was a band," says Wood, "but nobody was dancing. Well, they started playing a particular song, and I just couldn't resist and so I started to sort of move my feet a little." As he got into his groove, an attractive young woman who just happened to be wandering by joined him.

For any public officials out there looking for signs that they have hit the big time: It has arrived when a city gets down on bended knee to offer a compensation package worth a quarter-million dollars. Or, as in the case of Rod Wood, when the job includes taking a quick twirl on the dance floor with Britney Spears.

10

Going Outside

Jonathan Walters

The push to privatize is expanding beyond service delivery into the areas of policy making and program design.

While governors and legislators scramble to deal with American jobs moving offshore, many of these same policy makers are creating anxiety about outsourcing within their own state's borders—among their own public employees.

Texas, for example, is poised to make a radical change in the way it administers welfare benefits. Anyone seeking public assistance will no longer visit a local government office but instead dial up a call center staffed by private-sector operators. Those corporate employees will be linked to a computer system that allows them fingertip access to a vast array of financial data. Using such information, the new-style eligibility workers will then tell callers whether or not they qualify to receive a variety of benefits—from food stamps and Temporary Assistance to Needy Families to child health insurance and Medicaid.

The "call center" approach to qualifying citizens for public benefits is the front edge of a wedge aimed at opening up a huge new area of traditional government work to the private sector. If it receives federal approval, the Texas privatization strategy could trigger a wave of state and local outsourcing nationwide worth billions of dollars, affecting millions of citizens and tens of thousands of state and local employees, while at the same time opening up whole new business lines for eager vendors. Frank Ambramcheck, who heads up public sector consulting for Unisys Corp., calls it the "the bow wave" of a private-sector push into government work, an expansion that is beginning to go beyond what has typically been privatized—service delivery to citizens—and into program design and decision making.

From *Governing*, May, 2004.

"If Texas gets its toe in the water," says Celia Hagert, an analyst with Progressive Policy Institute who has been tracking the issue, "then a whole lot of states will be diving in right behind it." Hagert, along with many health and social services advocates nationwide, is concerned about private companies deciding who ought to get government benefits, arguing that it has always been too sensitive a job to sell off.

The drive to privatize in Texas is part of a massive consolidation that will distill 12 health and human services agencies into four. The job of administering the four new departments falls to the Health and Human Services Commission, which formerly had more casual oversight over the sprawling bureaucracies. The law that engineered the consolidation also directs HHSC to turn as much other work as is practicable over to the private sector.

The commission already has sent out a request for proposals to run the human resource management function—not just payroll administration but a broad range of HR work, from recruitment of new employees to initial screening of job candidates. Other administrative basics such as procurement and information technology will also be on the table.

But that's not all. In keeping with the outsourcing theme of the overhaul, the reorganization itself is being quarterbacked by the private sector. Deloitte Consulting, Maximus and Accenture are doing everything from reengineering how work gets done, to ensuring that whatever system Texas ends up with squares with federal cost-accounting requirements.

As of this spring, the commission's "contracting opportunities" Web site had more than a dozen RFPs listed, ranging from such specific work as studying the closure or consolidation of certain facilities, to doing feasibility studies on community-based treatment for emotionally disturbed kids. What's more, vendors also are helping HSSC to do the analyses that will become part of the "business case" that the agency uses to evaluate the efficacy of contracting out.

> "I am a very strong proponent of free enterprise and private-sector solutions to meet the needs of government."
>
> State Representative Arlene Wohlgemuth

The math and the mindset driving the privatization effort are straightforward: Texas is facing a $10 billion budget deficit and in the view of many influential Republicans there is only one way to deal with that number: Let the private sector in on state work to lower state costs. "I am a very strong proponent of free enterprise and private-sector solutions to meet the needs of government," says state Representative Arlene Wohlgemuth, who sponsored the consolidation bill. Through reorganization and consolidation, she says, the state is slated to save billions of dollars, in part through programmatic changes to such big-ticket items as Medicaid but also by turning work over to contractors. Under the Wohlgemuth plan, more than 2,500 state health and social services jobs are scheduled to be handed off to vendors in the next two years. Ultimately, the plan could directly impact the lives of thousands more state workers across Texas.

But if Texas is shaping up as a privatizer's dream come true, some who have been watching the process closely view it as an exercise in outsourcing gone amok. Patrick Bresette, executive director of the Austin-based Center for Public Policy Priorities, calls it the "the big-bang theory" applied to scaling back government service. There is scant evidence, according to the center's analysis of the consolidation plan and early outsourcing efforts, that it will actually result in improved services at lower costs.

Texas employees, meanwhile, express their own brand of skepticism. The state is "stepping over dollars to save dimes," says Gary Anderson, executive director of the Texas Public Employees Association. While he understands the cost-saving imperative, he believes the state isn't thinking much beyond a single budget cycle in assessing the actual value of outsourcing so much work. "In the short term, you may see some savings," he acknowledges. But in the long run, Anderson contends, the state loses valuable institutional knowledge along with the capacity to easily take work back if vendors don't pan out. That could saddle the state with huge down-the-road costs, for both rebuilding internal capacity and compensating for non-performance of basic work.

Anderson sees one other potential and ironic cost to the plan: If vendors are really going to save the state money, then they will probably have to do that by using low-wage, low-benefit workers, which means the very people taking over pieces of food stamps, TANF and Medicaid administration could end up qualifying for all those benefits themselves.

BRANCHING OUT

The issues of cost, performance and capacity have long been at the heart of what drives outsourcing—and the heated debates about it. "More (and better) for less" has been the longstanding rationale for using private contractors to do everything from mowing grass to placing kids in foster care. But recently privatization has been taking on a more ideological edge. A new generation of elected officials—top-level executives, in particular—is making no secret of its conviction that government should not only "be run like a business" but also, in many cases, be run *by* business. And that has led to a new aggressiveness in what states such as Texas are looking to contract out.

Adding heat to the simmering outsourcing debate is the current controversy over where, exactly, the privatized work is going. Offshore outsourcing began to capture the attention of lawmakers at the beginning of this year, fueled by a string of stories about private contractors sending state work—especially call-center work—to foreign countries. The image of employees in India handling Virginians' and Vermonters' queries about food-stamp benefits had governors and legislatures nationwide arguing all spring about whether they ought to limit state contracts to vendors who agree not to send jobs abroad.

But the issue of offshore outsourcing is clearly a sideshow to the main event: the increased interest in domestic outsourcing fueled by new, more market-friendly political leadership in combination with tough budget times. Faced with a $350 million budget deficit, South Carolina Governor Mark Sanford is among those identifying areas where the private sector might do the job better for less.

One of the items on Sanford's list—outsourcing inmate health care—has fallen to John Davis, the acting health services director for the Corrections Department. A veteran of past privatization efforts, Davis well understands that coming up with a list of areas to consider for outsourcing is one thing, and actually doing the contracting in a way that delivers quality service at reasonable cost is quite another. In fact, the state had been contracting out part of its inmate health care prior to Sanford's election, and that experience wasn't altogether satisfactory. The state dropped its contract with a private health services provider working at 10 state facilities for a very simple reason: The company wanted more money, and the state didn't want to pay more.

Now health care for the *entire* corrections system is on the table, and Davis is wrestling with the RFP process. It is a daunting task. First, the state doesn't have a good handle on costs, so it's hard to judge if outsourcing will really be a better deal. "We break things down in large categories. What it costs for hospitalization, pharmaceuticals and personnel. But we don't know how much it costs to treat diabetics or cardiac patients," he says. Although the state is currently working on a cost-coding system that will help it to capture such data, for now it is negotiating RFPs absent such detailed breakouts. Cost, of course, is what makes the outsourcing world go around, and as part of the back-and-forth with potential vendors over the RFP, private-sector companies also are asking that liability for cost overruns be shared by the state. That has made for dicier negotiations.

Also complicating the contracting effort is the fact that the state operates on an annual budget, so it's hard to lock any company into a long-term contract. That raises the specter of a low-ball bid just to get the work, with ever-escalating contract requests to follow. The state may be particularly susceptible to such a syndrome in this case, Davis notes, because this contract involves outsourcing health care services at all 29 of its facilities, which would mean the state would lose the capacity to do the work itself. "Once you've dismantled the system, it's tough to put it back together," he says, "and vendors know that."

Still, the RFP process proceeds apace. Davis thinks that given the state's past experience, things are going a little smoother this time, and that the state is doing a better job of bargaining.

In all cases, though, whether it's outsourcing human resource management or inmate health care, the basic question is the same: Does it really add up to cheaper and better government? Organized labor challenges that notion, arguing that it frequently adds up to more expensive government and worse performance. Free marketeers, meanwhile, argue that privatization is the only way to break expensive government—and government employee—monopolies. Such a break wrings greater performance and productivity from government bureaucracies, argue proponents, while applying fresh ideas and strategies to government administration and programs.

With states and localities spending upwards of $400 billion a year on contracts, and with the recent incursions into new outsourcing territory, it's not an argument that's likely to ease up anytime soon. But even Adrian Moore, executive director of the pro-privatization Reason Foundation, admits contracting out is not a panacea. "Like all policy tools, it is neither good nor bad," he says, "It depends on whether or not you do it right."

THE CALCULUS

Stories and data abound illustrating how and where government does it wrong, say outsourcing critics. Joe Fox, vice president of the New York State Public Employees Federation, says he understands there are times when outsourcing makes sense—when a temporary spike in demand calls for some outside help or for certain kinds of seasonal work. But Fox argues that because of outsourcing, New York state government is currently paying more for a wide range of traditional government work and is getting lower quality service for the money.

According to PEF calculations, the state could save at least $160 million a year if it brought nursing, pharmaceutical, psychiatric, computer and engineering work back in-house. The federation's stand is bolstered by a March 2001 letter to the New York State Department of Transportation, in which the state comptroller declared, "It is generally less expensive for the department to design and inspect projects in-house rather than use consultants." For Fox, the game being played by New York and other states is obvious. "Politically, it looks good to say, 'I don't have this huge workforce.' But it's smoke and mirrors."

Outsourcing critics also say some politicians pursue privatization in order to offload difficult policy areas. In looking at the highly volatile area of child protective services and foster care, Richard Wexler, executive director of the National Coalition for Child Protection Reform, says Florida is a national model of how outsourcing the administration of child protection is an effort to dump responsibility and accountability. "The only motivation for privatization of child welfare in Florida is that it is a political liability, and Governor Jeb Bush doesn't want that liability," says Wexler.

The governor's administration rejects that criticism out of hand. "If you look at that area, it's one where states have been outsourcing for 100 years," says Bill Simon, secretary of the Florida Department of Management Services. The whole concept of sending kids to foster homes instead of orphanages, Simon notes, is one where outsourcing has proved "wildly successful." And he adds, "It's not much of a step to then look at outsourcing its administration."

But Florida is a state that has come in for heavy criticism for its aggressive, big-ticket and low-accountability outsourcing efforts. In particular, the governor has been pounded over the state's high-profile and so far unhappy effort to outsource a significant portion of its human resources management function. A $280 million contract with Cincinnati-based Convergys Corp. to take over the job has bogged down badly, which means the state is spending millions of dollars keeping its old system up and running while Convergys tries to work out kinks in the new system.

Still, DMS secretary Simon believes that much of the criticism aimed at Bush is simply on account of the "blistering pace" with which the governor has pursued privatization. So far, state action on the outsourcing front has included everything from collecting tolls to investigating allegations of child abuse.

Not all of Florida's privatizing has gone badly. In several multi-million-dollar deals, the contractors have performed as advertised. But both the governor's own Inspector General and the legislature's Office of Program Policy Analysis and Government Accountability have released papers taking the state to task for its less-than-businesslike approach to contracting out. The legislative oversight office, for instance, said agencies need to make a better business case for privatization and look more at performance-based contracting. It also suggested the need for central oversight of contracting.

Florida has received enough official criticism about its privatization efforts that Governor Bush in March created a Center for Efficient Government in the state's Department of Management Services to oversee the state's outsourcing efforts. One of the center's main jobs will be to provide technical assistance to agencies not used to negotiating large contracts with experienced, savvy vendors. "We have state agencies that might do a $100 million contract every one or two years, whereas IBM does one a week," Simon says. The center will also be the central repository for information on cost and performance.

NEGOTIATING WITH THE FEDS

While Florida has received much attention for its outsourcing efforts, most eyes right now are on Texas and its decision to privatize eligibility determination—and whatever else it can—as part of its health and human services overhaul.

Texas is still negotiating with the feds for permission to outsource all the eligibility determination work that it would like to—particularly in the areas of food stamps and Medicaid. Gregg Phillips, a former consultant with Deloitte who is now HHSC's point man on reorganization and contracting out, is confident the state will be allowed to hand the work off to contractors. Other states are watching the action carefully.

Phillips is well aware of concerns about contracting out. But he says that Texas won't repeat the mistakes of other aggressive privatizers that have gone before it. Furthermore, he argues that the state already has been using the call-center approach in such areas as the child health insurance program and workers' compensation with no problems. "Right now with our CHIP program," he says, "every eligibility determination is being made by a private-sector company. Texans seeking service don't care who they're talking to as long as who they are talking to is courteous, accurate and performs well."

Furthermore, says Phillips, every outsourcing effort that HHSC undertakes has to be justified by a business case, and where contracting out is deemed cost effective—and he's confident there will be lots more cases—contractors will always be held to high standards of performance with clear penalties for failure to meet those standards. He also believes there are enough vendors around that are interested in picking up state work that HHSC will never be held hostage by any private-sector monopolizer.

Still, even the staunchest advocates of outsourcing, including Representative Wohlgemuth, understand that building that kind of contract-writing, administration and oversight capacity in state government is in and of itself a daunting task. But she has a ready answer for how to deal with any shortfall in state contracting capacity: "You can contract that out, too."

11 Payout Planning

Christopher Swope

As older workers retire, state pension funds are finding they've made more promises than they can keep.

When Oregon lawmakers looked into the state's beleaguered public pension system this spring, they couldn't escape one conclusion: Retirees simply weren't dying early enough. Actually, the blame lay not with the retirees, who like all Americans are living longer these days, but with the outmoded life-expectancy tables Oregon was using. The pension fund's assumption dated to a time when people lived to an average age of 73. Now that people are living to about 77, however, Oregon retirees are collecting more monthly checks than the state has money to pay them.

Old mortality tables were just one of several things that were draining Oregon's retirement fund and slowly bankrupting both the state and local governments. Add in the three-year stock market slump, and Oregon had an actuarial disaster in the making. By early this year, the system's unfunded liability hit a whopping $16 billion. In contrast, the state's entire annual budget is only about $6 billion. "We couldn't ride out this storm," says state Senator Tony Corcoran. "The system was going to implode."

Oregon responded with a sweeping pension overhaul that updated those life-expectancy tables and made other key structural reforms. Yet there is a good chance that many of the changes will get struck down in court. Public employee unions have already filed suit against the plan, arguing that Oregon is illegally cutting their benefits. The new mortality rates, for instance, mean that monthly checks will shrink because they'll have to last longer.

From *Governing*, September 2003.

The Fix the Funds Are In

State pension assets as a percentage of liabilities

- 100% or more
- 90% to 99%
- 80% to 89%
- 70% to 79%
- Less than 70%

Source: Wilshire Associates, 2003

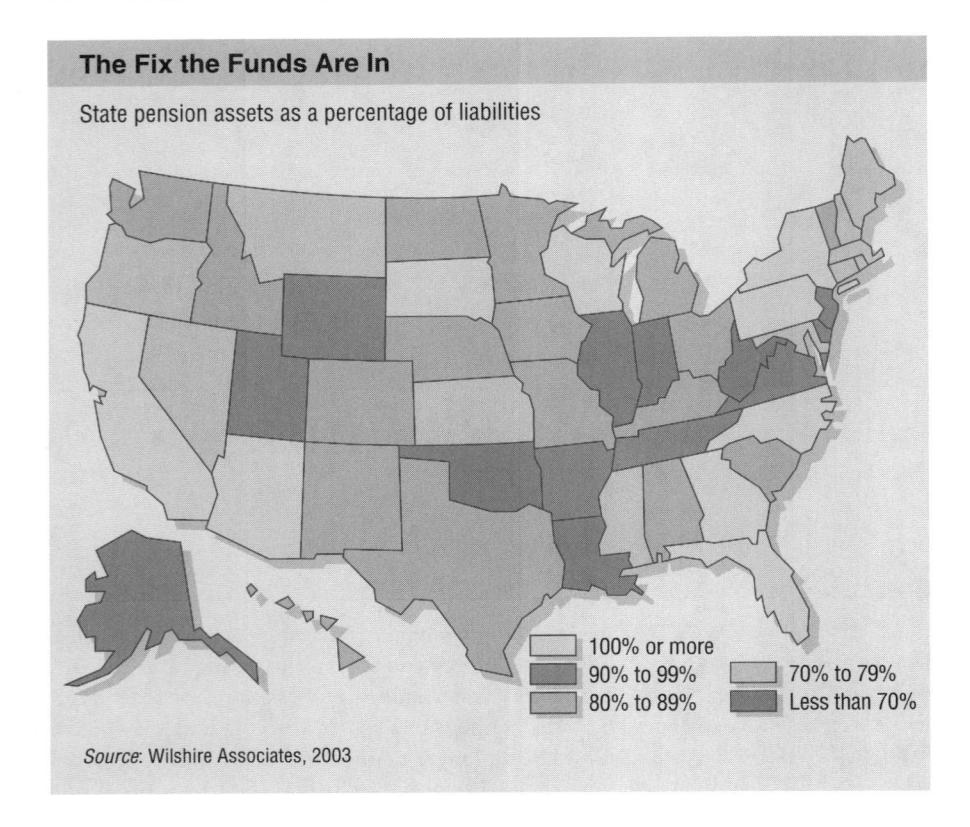

HARD TIMES

These are the cold calculations dozens of state and local pension funds are faced with today. According to a controversial March report by Wilshire Associates, an investment advisory firm, 79 percent of those systems are underfunded. That figure alone isn't so troubling; pension funds are long-term investors, and it's not unusual for them to owe more money than they have in the bank. What's disconcerting is how deep the holes are. Some 27 states face pension shortfalls that run more than half as large as their entire state budgets. In nine states, the gap actually exceeds the size of their budgets. These states, topped by Nevada, Oregon and Oklahoma, look like dejected gamblers playing their last chips at the blackjack table: It's difficult to see how they'll get out of this mess.

How did things get so bad? The easy answer is the stock market's three-year slide, but that's only part of the problem. The fact is that many state and local governments brought this quandary on themselves. During the go-go 1990s, when funds were pulling in sky-high returns, they failed to save up for harder times. Some, such as Contra Costa County, California, looked at their billowing pension funds as a cash register from which they could take money to fund other programs. Others, such as the New York Retirement System, used the wind-fall to hike up benefits for retirees. These choices only compounded the crisis when stocks crashed: Pension funds now have more obligations to pay but less cash on hand to pay them. As Fred Nesbitt, the head of the National Conference on Public Employee Retirement Systems, puts it: "The hens have come home to roost, and at a very bad time."

To be sure, not all public pension funds are suffering. More than two dozen major plans are better than 100 percent funded. And this spring's stock market rally lifted the fortunes of nearly all pension funds. In July, North Carolina's fund for teachers and state employees reported that its investments finished fiscal 2003 in the black by 7.6 percent. That was enough to wipe out all of the fund's losses from the previous years and to help make up for the legislature's decision to nearly zero-out contributions to the fund during the budget crisis.

For the worst-off pension funds, however, logic suggests that there are only four ways out of this jam, and none of them look good. Governments can pay more into the funds, which isn't easy with the big budget deficits most of them already face. They can try cutting benefits to retirees, which is nearly impossible in most states because benefits given usually can't be taken away. They can ask retirees to pay more into the system, which is unpopular with unions. Or they can just wait it out, in hopes that the bulls will run wild again on Wall Street—living in a very reasonable fear that they won't.

Actually, there's a fifth option, but it is perhaps the riskiest of all: borrowing money. Illinois is floating a hefty $10 billion in bonds in order to pay down some of its fund's $36 billion unfunded liability. This is by far the largest offering of pension-obligation bonds ever. Essentially, Illinois is making a bet: The state's money managers will invest the cash, and if they make a 7 percent return or more, Illinois wins.

Illinois Governor Rod Blagojevich, who pushed the bond plan, is confident that the pension fund will come out ahead. On the other hand, if Illinois loses its bet, the fund will fall even deeper into trouble. This is what has happened in New Jersey. In 1997, under then-Governor Christie Whitman, New Jersey floated $2.8 billion in pension-obligation bonds. At first, the high-flying stock market made this look like a smart move, but after stocks crashed, New Jersey had to dig deep into its pockets in order to pay those bonds back. "It's a long-term play," says Parry Young, an analyst with Standard & Poor's Corp. in New York. "Lord knows what the market will return for the next 15 to 20 years."

PROMISES, PROMISES

Even if more Oregon retirees were dying "on time," the state's pension fund would still have begun 2003 in deep trouble. There wasn't one structural problem. There were many. They grew quietly out of decisions made as long ago as the 1950s and as recently the late '90s.

In Oregon's pension system, each employee, whether he works for the state or a local government, has an account. For most employees, the state guarantees those accounts an 8 percent annual return, which is about equal to the fund's historical performance. During the most recent bull market, however, Oregon's system, like most pension funds, earned astronomical returns: an average of 18.5 percent from 1996 to 1999. Pension board officials decided not to sock the extra money away. Instead, they funneled it into individuals' accounts, which ballooned in value. What's more, when the stock market began to slide and the fund's returns went negative, the state remained on the hook for that 8 percent guarantee.

As workers retired after the boom, they took advantage of another feature of Oregon's system: the money match. This dated back to just after World War II, when Oregon agreed to double the amount in an employee's account upon retirement. At the time, it was intended to bring retirement checks up to subsistence levels. Now, it meant that state and local governments were sometimes shelling out enormous sums to match bubble-inflated accounts. Many people wound up collecting retirement checks that exceeded their biggest paychecks. Governor Ted Kulongoski calls this the result of a series of unintended consequences. "The system was never designed to return 100 percent to 105 percent of pre-retirement income," he says.

Kulongoski, a freshman governor who years ago litigated a major pension case when he was attorney general, pushed the legislature to overhaul the system. Lawmakers had little choice but to accept the challenge; the pension gap loomed so heavily over state finances that they couldn't begin working on a budget until they dealt with the pension issue. The result was a series of reforms, passed in May. One change converted the 8 percent guarantee from something the state had to meet each year into something the state could calculate over an employee's entire career. Another change temporarily did away with some retirees' cost-of-living adjustments. And of course, the mortality tables were brought up to date. In all, the fixes were expected to take a $16 billion unfunded liability and cut it down to about $8 billion.

Taking the state to court, Oregon's public employee unions are arguing that the changes amount to a cut in benefits. In June, Attorney General Hardy Myers said that he, too, thought the courts would declare the reforms unconstitutional. AFSCME lobbyist Mary Botkin counsels patience. "We continue to believe that at some level the stock market will recover and dig us out of some of these problems," she says.

State Senator Corcoran, himself a former labor organizer, disagrees with his old labor allies. He doesn't see much hope in waiting out the stock market. "Nobody expected the crash in 1929, and it took us 11 years to get out of that," Corcoran says. "We're in uncharted territory here."

High Five

Five state systems with high-return,

	Expected Return
Colorado State & School	8.3%
Minnesota PERA	8.2
Pennsylvania PERS	8.2
Louisiana Teachers	8.2
Michigan SERS	8.2

Source: Wilshire Associates Inc., 2003

12

Civil Service Tsunami

Jonathan Walters

Florida's radical overhaul of its personnel system is making big political waves.

As Florida's commerce secretary, John Ellis Bush had a notion for how to streamline personnel management in the Sunshine State: make every state employee "at will"—subject to being hired and fired as easily as a waitress in a Tallahassee waffle shop.

That was in 1987, and the state wasn't ready for such a radical plan. But in 1999, Jeb Bush was back—and not as a single, voice-in-the-wilderness cabinet member. He was governor. And when Bush took aim at civil service this time, it was with conviction and clout. On May 14, 2001, Bush signed into law a sweeping civil service overhaul package dubbed "Service First," a set of changes he hailed as a significant modernization of personnel administration in Florida.

Service First is a revolution in the wake of evolution: In the early 1980s, Florida began chipping away at civil service, decentralizing authority for personnel management to departments, experimenting with broadbanding of job titles and pay, and reducing the emphasis on formal exams and tightly ranked lists of eligible candidates as an avenue into and up the ladder of state service.

But compared with the waves of personnel administration reform that had been washing over Florida, Service First is a tsunami. In particular, Service First makes three major changes: Most significant, it eliminates seniority for all state workers. The long-standing idea that more-senior employees ought to be protected during downsizings and accorded the right to "bump" newer staff out of jobs during layoffs is gone. At the same time, Service First moves a huge cohort of employees—anyone with even a remotely managerial or supervisory title—into a "selected exempt

From *Governing*, May 2003.

service," all of whom do serve at will. Third, the law lays the groundwork for a major overhaul of job titles and pay, reducing thousands of job classes to dozens of occupational groups, and assigning to each group a pay band that allows management wide discretion in how to compensate individual employees.

In adopting Service First, Florida became one of only three states to substantially eliminate civil service protection for executive-branch employees. Texas has never had much in the way of a centralized merit system, and what it did have it abolished back in 1985. But Florida's reforms most closely track those of Georgia, which passed legislation in 1996 that eliminates civil service for state workers over time: State employees hired after July 1, 1996, serve at will, completely outside an ever-shrinking civil service system. They can be hired, promoted, disciplined and fired quickly and with relative impunity; they accrue no seniority and therefore have no bumping rights whatsoever.

FIERCE FIGHT

But whereas there wasn't much of a fight in Georgia over the merit system's overhaul, the battle in Florida over Service First was—and continues to be—fierce. Mark Neimeiser, political director for the American Federation of State, County and Municipal Employees Council 79, which represents most of the state's rank-and-file employees, calls the law "Service Worst." He and his colleagues in Council 79 see the law not as a rational attempt to fix what might be wrong with civil service but as a frontal assault on organized labor and on state government employees. With a governor who seems determined to shrink government employment and privatize everything from the state library to child protective services to personnel administration itself, Service First, critics say, is a thinly disguised mechanism for simplifying the removal of public employees for whatever reason: political, practical or ideological. "This is about management control of the most radical kind," says Neimeiser. "This is a governor who just wants to be able to do whatever he wants with state employees."

Two concerns in particular are raised by those who view Service First as a wholly cynical effort on the part of the Bush administration to seize control of state hiring and firing. First, it exposes state workers who enforce regulations and license businesses and professionals to the risk of retribution for pursuing cases against politically well-connected Floridians. Second, it leaves higher-salaried senior staff exposed to the whims of departmental budget cutters who, like a sports-team owner trying to meet a salary cap, might be tempted to off-load more senior, high-paid staff just to save money, regardless of what it means by way of institutional brain drain or employee morale.

With regard to the first concern, it is certainly not hard to find Florida whistleblowers who claim to have been fired for political reasons—either because they took regulatory action against an ally of the governor, or simply because they were registered in the wrong party and were picked off for political reasons. A Florida Web site—www.whoseflorida.com (a twist on the Bush administration's official home page myflorida.com)—is packed with allegations of politically driven personnel shenanigans. Depending on one's view of the spoils system and what it ought to deliver to whom, such stories are either shocking or just par for the political course and no different than stories that filter out of Albany, Springfield or Sacramento whenever there's a change of party, regardless of the civil service rules.

As for dumping senior staff, there is evidence of the widespread removal of long-time employees. In the wake of Service First, releasing a couple hundred senior employees has become very simple—there is no imperative to find them other jobs in their department or anywhere else in government. A number of agencies have experienced significant downsizings, including, health, transportation and juvenile justice. The Bush administration says that most laid-off employees were given the option of taking other jobs in government. Critics of Service First say the jobs offered typically represented demotions in both rank and pay. For example, a group of employees in the Department of Business and Professional Regulation were terminated, then allowed to reapply for jobs paying 25 percent less.

FLEXIBLE MANAGEMENT

While it's not hard to find critics of Service First in every corner of state government, there is one notable group of long-time Tallahassee denizens who couldn't be more pleased with the new law: department personnel directors who for years have been laboring under the strictures of what they view as an onerous set of rules that have far outlived their usefulness.

David Ferguson, head of personnel for the Department of Transportation for the past 30 years, says unequivocally that Service First is the best thing that's ever happened in Florida with regard to personnel administration. The ability to freely and quickly hire, promote, transfer or offer raises to employees has allowed his department to manage personnel in a rational, business-like way, competing for the best and brightest and retaining top-performing staff, he notes. "It gives us the flexibility to operate like we need to operate to get the job done for the citizens of Florida."

Personnel directors in Florida acknowledge that all state employees are now more vulnerable. When it comes to potential political pressure on state regulators, Alyce Parmer, head of human resources management for the Department of Environmental Protection says, "I can see where that potential is there. But I don't know that it's had a chilling effect at DEP and our ability to vigorously address [enforcement] issues. We haven't seen that."

To the extent that political pressure might be brought to bear, personnel managers say, state whistle-blower laws offer ample protection for wronged employees. Florida whistle-blowers vehemently disagree. One former Florida regulator, who says he was fired for taking action against a well-connected businessman, notes that whistle-blowing is a lonely, difficult and ultimately career-threatening activity. "It takes a special kind of person with the right kind of support," he says.

As for potential brain drain that might come with off-loading senior staff for fiscal reasons, David Ferguson says that the budget and staffing squeeze in his department has actually led his organization to do the opposite. His department is trying to hang on to veterans because of their depth of knowledge and ability to handle a variety of different jobs.

The specifics of Service First and its day-to-day impacts aside, HR managers in Florida make a more global argument about new personnel policies in an era of a new kind of employee. Tightly wound civil service laws are simply no longer relevant in today's employment world, they say, where it's understood that individuals will be job-hopping for their entire work lives. In the view of personnel directors like Ferguson and Parmer, the approach represented by Service First is simply part of a natural evolution in an emerging new view of state service: No longer should states be looking for people who will make working for the state a lifelong career. Rather, government should, like the private sector, accept the fact that workers in modern times are inclined to do three and four-year stints here and there and then move on. The state needs to adapt to the wishes and habits of these new-style employees. In fact, to accommodate a more peripatetic work force, Florida now allows employees to opt into a 401(k)-style defined-contribution plan that workers can take with them when they leave state service, as opposed to the traditional defined-benefit plan that requires a minimum length of service for vesting and that gets sweeter with time.

If state personnel directors have any criticism of Service First, it is that it still contains too much micro-managing language, instances where departments must go to the Department of Management Services—which oversees state personnel policies—or the governor's budget office to ask "mother may I," Parmer says. "I view agency heads as CEOs. If you have confidence in them, then give them the authority and the flexibility to manage and then hold them accountable."

DETAILS, DETAILS

For a law that supporters say is all about management flexibility, it does contain some oddly meddlesome provisions, ranging from major to minuscule. For example,

> *Government should, like the private sector, accept the fact that workers in modern times are inclined to do three and four-year stints here and there and move on. The state needs to adapt to the wishes and habits of these new style employees.*

it requires that agencies get gubernatorial approval to work temporary employees longer than 1,040 hours in a year. At the same time the law takes on the weighty matter of how much can be spent on congratulatory plaques for state service: "Each department head is authorized to incur expenditures not to exceed $100 each plus applicable taxes for suitable framed certificates, plaques or other tokens of recognition."

Service First actually gets into quite a bit of detail on a wide variety of issues. It caps the ratio of upper-level managers to rank-and-file employees. It makes all of the personal secretaries of key executive branch officials at-will employees. And it calls for the establishment of a professional development program to help employees understand strategic planning and performance measurement. Yet the law also contains at least one notable omission: There is no language at all about how the effects of Service First itself will be assessed.

One effect to date is very clear, though: It has organized labor in Florida riled up, especially Council 79. Because of organized labor's opposition, the fight over Service First from the outset was much tougher, acrimonious and ideologically divisive than was Georgia's push to eliminate civil service. While hardly a political powerhouse—Florida is an "open shop" state, which means that unions can organize but employees can't be compelled to pay dues—AFSCME 79 is at least a presence in Florida politics, with enough resources to lobby and sue.

Also nettling to labor is that key support for the measure comes from the Florida Council of 100, an influential corps of top businesspeople statewide who haven't exactly evinced great affection for unions. Where Georgia Governor Zell Miller invoked an arguably disinterested Philip K. Howard, author of *The Death of Common Sense*, in declaring that civil service in Georgia had outlived its purpose, Governor Bush invoked *Modernizing Florida's Civil Service System: Moving From Protection to Performance*, a report released at the end of 2000 by the arguably very interested Council of 100.

At the beginning of the report, the Council's chairman, Charles E. Cobb Jr., states "one of the primary reasons for the public's mistrust [in government] lies in the antiquated and cumbersome personnel system for most of Florida state employees called Career Service." However, no survey is cited in the report to demonstrate broad Floridian disgust with step and grade, bumping or cumbersome appeals processes for coddled state staffers.

In fact, the whole report is extremely thin on data about the negative impacts of civil service on state government. But the report's tone and message are unmistakable: In the mind of business, Florida's civil service system was public enemy number one and needed to be rubbed out. The report called for at-will status for all state employees, a move that would eliminate what the report described as a "complicated web of restrictions" for removing employees "called 'due process.'"

AFSCME 79 fought the law hard, and it won at least a partial victory. In its original form, Service First took both the governor's and the Council of 100's cue and made all state employees at will, in effect doing instantly what will take a few decades to do in Georgia. The Florida House passed a version of the law embracing immediate, universal at-will status for all state employees, but the Senate pulled back, which is when Bush administration strategists decided to carve out as many employees as possible for the selected exempt service. The 120,000 or so employees left in the "career service" category, however, didn't escape unscathed.

The new law makes it considerably easier to discipline employees, and it curbs the Public Employee Relations Commission's authority and discretion in deciding such appeals. Meanwhile, it overturns the long-standing practice of reimbursing employees for their legal fees in cases where they appeal adverse personnel actions to PERC and prevail. And in a major shift in how the state goes about collective bargaining, the law short-circuits the traditional process for working through contract impasses, allowing the governor to bypass mediation and kick deadlocked negotiations directly to the legislature for final resolution. In Neimeiser's opinion, the new language reflects an overall attitude of the Bush administration: They don't want to negotiate anything. "It's catch me if you can; sue me if you can," he says.

COPS ESCAPE UNSCATHED

Key pieces of Service First aren't about reform at all, Neimeiser and other labor activists argue. Rather, they are aimed at weakening organized labor. But Service First does not treat organized labor monolithically. Specific language in Service First excludes certain professions from coverage under the new, flexible personnel regime, including police, fire fighters and dietitians. It is a curious combination, and certainly begs the question of what the three occupational groups might have in common when it comes to what state personnel rules ought to apply.

In fact, what the three groups have in common has nothing to do with their job responsibilities, says Democratic Senator Al Lawson Jr., who was on both the Senate and conference committees that worked on Service First. He says the police and fire unions endorsed Bush in 1998, as did the union that represents the state's dietitians, nurses, psychologists, physical and speech therapists, dentists and pharmacists. Furthermore, Lawson says, language removing the three groups from coverage under Service First was inserted at some point between when the joint committee finished its work—or thought it had—and when the law was printed. "That was a secret deal," he says. "I went to bed that night and woke up the next day and there they were. It was nothing that ever came before our committee."

If it had the feel of a midnight hit-and-run political payoff to it, supporters of Service First didn't care. Even though such freelance tinkering violates legislative rules, Governor Bush and Republican lawmakers forged forward. "We tried to hold them up and they said, 'We're going to roll you,' and they did," Lawson says.

Certainly the Bush administration would have an easier time defending Service First as management reform without such exceptions. If Georgia's radical overhaul of civil service treats state employees roughly, as some believe, it at least treats them all equally—no job title is spared from evaporating protection. In considering the exceptions crafted in Florida, even some supporters of Service First have questions. Florida TaxWatch, a business-financed, nonpartisan, nonprofit group that advocates for fiscally responsible state policies, backed Service First on the grounds that management flexibility in personnel administration is a good thing. But TaxWatch head Dominic Calabro says the exceptions weren't anything his group endorsed. When it comes to who is covered under Service First, says Calabro, "what's good for the goose is good for the gander."

Asked about the special exceptions, Simone Marstiller, interim secretary at the Department of Management Services, says they were extended to job titles that "are demanding, both physically and intellectually." As for the charge that politics had more of a role to play in the exceptions than anything else, Marstiller says, "That doesn't sound like anything that makes a whole lot of sense. I've not heard that from anybody."

ONGOING CONTROVERSY

Whether such exceptions serve a legitimate purpose or whether they were just a routine political payoff, they certainly have added to the controversy surrounding the whole Service First effort, and they are just one of the many reasons why the fight surrounding the law shows little sign of abating at the moment.

Also keeping the issue very much alive is the fact that AFSCME 79 is in the middle of a three-count lawsuit against the state and Governor Bush, claiming, among other things, that Service First has "unconstitutionally waived and impaired collective bargaining rights protected by the Florida Constitution." A decision on the suit is expected later this year; other legal skirmishes around Service First have not ended happily for organized labor.

Regardless of the motivation for Service First, or how the controversy surrounding it plays out, the law gives management a powerful new hand in all matters related to personnel administration, including the freedom to pursue the kind of aggressive downsizing the state has seen in the past few years. Already lean, Florida went from ranking 47th on the national list of state employees per capita in July 2000, to 49th in July 2002, with 24,000 positions lopped off the payroll during that time period.

A recent Florida State University survey of employees who were shifted into the at-will, selected exempt class by Service First found that nearly two-thirds of them believed that "a goal of Service First is to downsize government." Indeed, in considering the most significant effects of Service First to date, Florida state employees probably can't be blamed if they're feeling more and more like they've joined the manatee and black panther on an expanding list of the state's endangered species.

13

The Dot-Bomb's Silver Lining

Ellen Perlman

In the wake of the tech sector's tumble, governments are finding it easier to fill IT positions.

When Kevin Tanner was laid off by 2ndwave, a dot-com company in Austin, Texas, he first considered applying for other jobs in the private sector. But it quickly became clear that few, if any, of the available opportunities would allow him to go to an Austin office each day and be home in time for dinner. He either would have to relocate or do some heavy traveling. "I had been a road warrior with IBM for six years and that was enough for me," says Tanner.

Instead, two months ago, he signed on as a systems analyst with the Texas Department of Information Resources—even though his new job pays one-third less than what he had been earning. Of the 35 or so former colleagues who were laid off along with him, Tanner hears that many are moving to California or Wyoming or Washington. But others—like him—don't want to pull up stakes. About 10 of them are actively pursuing state government IT positions. "The governor's job bank is a very popular site among networking groups," Tanner says.

Texas officials are hardly happy about the collapse of local dot-coms or the belt-tightening by formerly high-flying technology companies in the Austin area. Yet they are realizing benefits from all the problems related to the ailing economy and private-sector layoffs. More than at any time in the past several years, skilled technology workers are knocking on their doors looking for state government jobs. "The quality of our applicant pool has skyrocketed," says Carolyn Purcell, chief information officer. So has the number of people applying for each open position.

State and local governments have always offered security, stability and good benefits, if not great salaries or cutting-edge technolo-

From *Governing*, March 2002.

gies. And employment security seems to have moved higher on the list of priorities for many people who were burned by the implosion in the technology sector. That shift has enabled some state and local governments to hire and keep IT workers more easily than in the past.

Where there used to be a flood of talent exiting or avoiding government in search of high-paying dot-com jobs, many governments are finding they are looking pretty good to people turned out into the street by companies that went under or downsized. "We are having a very different experience this year than last year," says David Lewis, chief information officer of Massachusetts. "We have no problem at all attracting people."

Interestingly, a survey done in late 2001 by Gartner, an IT research and consulting firm, found that most of the governments surveyed still had IT vacancies. Nearly 90 percent of state governments and 80 percent of the local governments surveyed said they suffer from a critical shortage of qualified IT staff. But many governments are startled by those findings. "I was very surprised at the Gartner survey," says Lewis. "It's not our experience." Nor is it the experience in many other state and local governments, where applications for government jobs are pouring in.

Interest by IT workers in government jobs has been particularly pronounced in places that are home to a dense high-tech sector, such as regions in California, Massachusetts, Texas and Virginia. In addition to the increasingly likely risk of being laid off, much of the luster of start-ups and stock options has been tarnished by the reality of pressure-cooker jobs that entail long days or frequent travel.

Massachusetts sought to take advantage of the bleary-eyed fatigue some IT workers were experiencing. "Two years ago we hired a recruiter and came up with a strategy of who we can appeal to," says Lewis. "It was people in their 40s, who may have made some serious money already and now would like a job that is more than 10-hour days, Cheetos and 'Did you make the monthly number?'"

The state ran ads asking potential recruits if they were sick of traveling and interested in having more of a family life. In person, recruiters appealed to those who wanted to make a difference in other people's lives. "Would you rather work for Fidelity on some Byzantine mutual-fund system or here, at a social service application?" Lewis might inquire. He finds that a lot of applicants agree they would gain more satisfaction from placing children in foster homes. A lot of those recruits happen to be women.

Lewis was surprised at the highly experienced, top-notch people the state was able to attract, including a woman hired three months ago to work on a project for the courts. She had done several large projects in the private sector, including one involving a court system.

Still, for some of the high-end project managers and the 30 or so CIOs of various Massachusetts agencies, the search usually takes longer. For instance, if the state wants to hire a CIO for Medicaid, someone who has knowledge of the complicated payment systems, it must compete with local health maintenance organizations, hospitals and insurance companies in the region. "It's a hot, hot area," Lewis says. "We do not compete on salary with the world."

In positions that pay up to about $60,000, the state is quite competitive. Higher than that, though, there's an ever-widening gap between what the state can pay and what a private company can offer. For the majority of mid- to upper-range technicians, the state is probably 25 percent below market. "When you get to a position like mine, there's a dramatic difference," Lewis points out.

But governments are trying to address the difference between government and private-sector compensation as best they can. In the past several years, Texas has taken steps to lure people by raising state IT salaries. In the most recent session, the legislature granted all state workers with a year's tenure an automatic 4 percent pay raise, effective September 1, 2001.

And over the past four to six years, the legislature passed various laws to pull in IT workers, including raising the maximum salaries and offering recruitment and retention bonuses for systems analysts, programmers and other IT workers willing to commit to at least a year with the state. Texas also has tried to encourage its agencies to develop flexible work schedules and telecommuting policies that might appeal to workers who want to work from home sometimes or come into the office later or earlier than is typical.

Tanner was willing take a one-third pay cut to work for the state, but he says he couldn't have taken a 50 percent cut, which would have been the case if Texas hadn't increased salaries last session. "It put state jobs on the radar screen, made them at least possible," he says.

Human resources officials are heartened by the way the hiring picture has improved. "If we compare this year to last year, we have about twice as many applicants for our IT jobs," says Bob Eason, deputy executive director of the HR division of the Department of Transportation. When economic times were better for IT people, human resources had to extend job postings or re-post job openings to get a decent pool of qualified applicants. "Of course we can't accommodate them all, but it's refreshing to have them come to us rather than us dig, dig, dig to find them."

California, too, is buoyed by an influx of highly skilled job applicants from the private sector. It's the high point of a rollercoaster ride over the past three years. Leading up to Y2K, the state had a hard time getting skilled IT people. "The whole world was taking those resources," says Eli Cortez, the state's CIO. Then California launched its e-government initiatives and continued to face challenging times trying to recruit and retain IT people. Lately, however, the state has started to be more proactive about hiring and has found the shrinking technology sector aided its efforts.

Although California has not specifically raised the salaries for IT workers, it revised the classification system and changed minimum qualification requirements so that employees could be brought in at higher levels and therefore earn higher salaries to start. The state now takes into account work experience and competence. A college degree is no longer a prerequisite for an IT job. "High school students have been playing with computers all their lives," notes Sandra Sales, statewide information technology recruitment and retention manager. "The classification systems and qualifications established many years ago are not reflective of the needs of industry today."

The state also holds job fairs, uses employment Web sites and has made it easier to apply by putting applications and exams online. When Cisco and Intel were laying people off, the state worked directly with the companies to provide opportunities to those losing jobs, explaining to people how they could match their personal interests with state technology jobs in water or air quality or the parks system. Outplacement firms have contacted the state for other private companies reducing their workforce. State recruiters also work with local colleges on job fairs.

It's not that surprising that governments in high-tech corridors would reap the benefits of local technology company downsizing. But the effect is showing up in some unexpected places as well. For instance, IT hiring has become noticeably easier in Kansas City, Missouri. "I'm not ready to attribute it all to the crash of the dot-coms," says Gail Roper, the city's IT director. "But I can say without over-analyzing that we're able to find people."

An additional factor may be that the nature of IT jobs is changing. People are getting hired at top levels for project management and business analysis, rather than for purely technical expertise. "We've gone from being, historically, primarily a programming shop to being an organization that is finding technical business solutions," Roper says. Kansas City recently hired a young woman from Phoenix who had worked for American Express, which had a major layoff. She was "project oriented" and when her job dissolved, Kansas City was able to snap her up and put her private-sector talents to work. "Strong project management is what we were looking for," Roper says.

Along with the good news on hiring comes a more disheartening reason why some states are finding it easier to fill IT positions: The current recession has led governments to reduce the number of positions or impose hiring freezes. "We're not pounding the pavement to the degree we were a couple of years ago," says Massachusetts' Lewis.

In California, Governor Gray Davis issued an executive order, effective October 23, 2001, that froze all state hiring until mid-year 2003, because of fiscal constraints. The Department of Information Technology still has some flexibility to hire if it makes its case to the Department of Finance, but it's clear that with budget problems affecting just about every agency, it's not likely there will be scads of new money for technology projects.

In any event, a much more worrisome IT-staffing issue is looming on the horizon: Between 11 percent and 20 percent of state government IT workers are eligible to retire within five years, according to a Gartner survey of 28 states and 40 of the largest counties and cities.

Massachusetts is getting an early taste of what that could mean. The state recently offered an early-retirement package to employees, who had to decide by mid-February whether to take it. Those who did will be gone by March 15. Of 300 state technology employees, about 75 were eligible. Lewis was expecting to lose as many as 15 to 20. The fact that a quarter of the staff was eligible for early retirement speaks volumes about what the vacancy situation might be like in just a few years.

So even though times are good for IT hiring right now, Purcell in Texas has no illusions about hiring and retention problems being solved for good. "I worry some that it's easy to become complacent. I want to continue to have good recruiting and not let the opportunity slip away."

14

Legislators Who Get IT

Ellen Perlman

Politicians hold the purse strings for big technology projects. But few are interested in or informed about IT issues.

As recently as last year, the Arizona Senate was using a 1980s-era roll-call system that showed lawmakers' names and a bar that turned green or red, depending on whether their vote was yea or nay. When it worked, the system was adequate, if antiquated. The problem was, it often didn't work—forcing senators back to voice votes tabulated on pieces of paper. Repairing the system meant flying people out from Washington, D.C., since there was only one company left in the country that knew how to maintain it. Since the upkeep was more expensive than the purchase of a new system, a decision was made to rip out all the old equipment and start fresh.

With the installation of a fully computerized video system that has a large screen that drops down from the ceiling, senators got a personal look at the benefits of upgraded technology. The state-of-the-art system not only turns voting legislators' names green or red—or yellow if they haven't voted yet—it also provides a screen where they can show presentations to enhance their remarks in debate.

Since most lawmakers are not well versed in information technology issues, any firsthand experience with and lessons on the benefits of technology are sorely needed in legislatures. "Sometimes it's difficult for legislators to see the potential of technology," says Arizona state Senator Dean Martin, who is the founder of a digital media development company and one of the few lawmakers there with a technology background. "They balk over a million-dollar expenditure when it would result in a $10 million savings over 10 years in man hours or overhead."

From *Governing*, May 2002.

Martin figures that if technology is integrated into legislators' way of life and their job duties, they will be more likely to understand what executive-branch agencies are asking for when they seek funding for technology projects. Right now, the level of understanding of even basic technology varies widely among legislators. "There are people who don't know how to turn on a computer and are afraid of e-mail," Martin says. "They have assistants who print out e-mails for them and respond to them. If you have a legislature that's been doing things the same way for 100 years, they may not be as willing to have other agencies upgrade."

Getting legislatures to understand the technology needs of executive-branch agencies has been a tough assignment for chief information officers and department heads. Legislators often have great interest in technology from an economic development point of view; that is, the business of attracting technology companies to a region or laying fiber for more sophisticated use of technology around the state. And there's been no shortage of ideological stands taken on technology issues, such as stopping Internet pornography and using filtering software in schools.

But when it comes to understanding and overseeing the complex technology projects that run state governments and their agencies, legislators often are at a loss or just not interested. "Legislators don't get it," Ohio CIO Gregory Jackson told vendors who sell hardware and software to state and local governments, at a recent technology conference. He called on the private sector to help educate local legislators on technology issues.

Few legislators would argue with the assessment that although they hold the purse strings for millions of dollars in technology spending, most of them don't stay on top of technology issues very well. In some cases, legislatures are getting better at it. They've had to. Embarrassing, expensive and highly public failures of large IT projects have forced the issue into the spotlight. "There have been some bad stories of cost overruns," says Minnesota state Senator Steve Kelley. "Projects have been either poorly conceived or poorly executed. Legislators have had to pay attention to those issues."

Yet getting legislatures to routinely focus on state IT projects is an ongoing process, one that gets interrupted with every election cycle. Some states have done better than others at making room for legislators at the IT table, and keeping them there. Washington State formalized a structure that brings the legislative branch into the loop with the executive and judicial branches early on, as IT projects are being discussed. A little more than half of the states have created technology boards or councils with legislators as members, and some develop policy and formulate spending guidelines for statewide IT projects. Thirty-one states have set up House, Senate or joint IT committees to focus on technology.

Some states benefit from a convergence of factors that leads to effective technology policies and practices. In Utah, the stars have aligned with a savvy and technology-oriented governor, Mike Leavitt, and a number of individual legislators who happen to have technology know-how and interest. State legislators sit on an IT commission with executive branch and private-sector members. And legislators all have laptops that they use for constituent e-mail and to read and review amendments and bills, so they have a basic comfort level with technology.

If legislators aren't at ease with technology or aren't interested enough to spend time on it, they can't just pick up and start talking about it. "It takes awhile to understand what's going on," says Mary Winkley, who worked as a legislative analyst in California, after a stint as a technology staffer to state Senator Debra Bowen, who chairs the Energy, Utilities and Communication-New Technology Subcommittee.

That's why the role of the executive branch is so crucial. "It has really been up to the administration to get

> "The legislature is missing how important technology is for making executive branch programs successful," says Mary Winkley, [who worked as a legislative analyst in California, after a stint as a technology staffer].

folks in position to understand the cost savings, and go to legislators with proposals," says Arizona's Martin. CIOs and department heads who do the legislative handholding, educating lawmakers and building relationships with them, have a leg up when it comes time to request funding for a big project. "You have to constantly give the big picture," says Susan Patrick, strategic communications manager of the Government Information Technology Agency in Arizona, an executive-branch agency that does oversight, planning and coordination of IT projects and is headed by the state's CIO, a member of the governor's Cabinet.

Patrick and others from GITA not only present information formally at the beginning of a session, but also during the summer when study committees are meeting and at informal meetings throughout the year. Patrick recalls speaking with a rural economic development committee made up mostly of rural legislators who felt they had little interest in technology. Once she talked to them about steps the state was taking to bring broadband capacity to rural areas for telemedicine and distance learning, "they had much more interest in technology—versus rural issues—than they realized they did."

When Iowa legislators have questions about the value of IT projects being proposed, they can refer to the state's return-on-investment program, a methodology for evaluating the benefits of IT projects. The program summarizes, analyzes, prioritizes and explains the specifics and the worth of all the technology projects being done across government in any year. Technology projects are ranked and get points based on whether the project will improve customer service, whether there are requirements mandating it, whether it will have a direct impact on Iowa's citizens, whether the project will be for one agency, multiple agencies or the entire state government enterprise.

As to the request for vendors to help educate legislators, Richard Varn, Iowa's CIO, believes there is a useful way and a not-so-useful way for them to do so. When it comes to their own economic well being, technology companies don't need to be persuaded to approach and educate legislators. They do what it takes to get IT contracts signed. But when it comes to promoting the technology industry in general, Varn notes, vendors are conspicuously absent.

Everyone would benefit from legislators becoming more informed about issues such as telemedicine, distance education, e-government services, digital signatures and identity theft. But vendors do not typically engage in those discussions, Varn says.

Legislators agree that few technology companies seek them out. "A lot of people in the IT industry stick to their knitting," says Minnesota's Kelley. "They're not comfortable breaking out and working with politicians." They do make their way to the executive branch to lobby for contract awards and promote their wares. But in his state, Kelley says, they have not figured out how to make themselves effective at the capital nearly as well as, say, the chamber of commerce. "I partly attribute that to the fitful motivation of folks in the technology industry. Most of them would rather government go away. They'd rather not deal with us at all." Nor have there been many IT-types who run for office, producing instant legislative experts.

How can legislators do their homework and learn what they need to know about technology? California's Bowen says she learned from experts. When she observed agencies in state government that were good at delivering projects on time and on budget, she focused on what they had to say in hearings. Over time, her staff has developed a list of questions to ask others based on that knowledge, such as "How do you know when to pull the plug on a project" and "How can you divide that project into segments so you build on success, rather than take on big projects without knowing how well they'll do?"

The California legislature is certainly more sophisticated than it was in 1994 when it approved a welfare IT project that quickly fell to pieces. The welfare system was supposed to automate the calculation of benefits for welfare recipients

Arizona Tech Snapshot

Hardware	$56 million
Software	$23 million
Telecom	$51 million
External services	$20 million
Employee-related expenses	$88 million
Repair & maintenance	$8 million
Other	$3 million

Source: Arizona Goverment Information Technology Agency

and was piloted in a few counties. But an audit determined it wasn't robust enough to handle the entire state's caseload and the project was stopped.

Back then, the budget committee was presented with no deliverables, no benchmarks and no evidence of strategic planning, Bowen says. Very few legislators were thinking about how to achieve service-delivery goals or efficiencies, or eliminate errors. They thought more in terms of how to automate an existing paper trail. Bowen didn't claim to know the ins and outs of IT but was able to turn to the auditor's office and the legislative analyst's office for their expertise. Both have the authority to retain IT consultants.

California now has House and Senate committees and subcommittees on technology. Some officials consider the existence of such committees in state legislatures as vital for overseeing technology matters. Others say technology shouldn't be channeled so narrowly. All agencies should be focusing on technology, even within program areas such as health and social services. Legislators who get a judiciary committee assignment may think they have to deal only with judicial issues but may find themselves voting on whether to modernize data tracking systems in the judiciary.

In any case, technology committees are not generally considered plum assignments. "A lot of legislators like to get into committees that can make major changes or major splashes in the media," says Arizona's Martin. "Technology committees are more oversight of upgrading government. Most people don't give you an award for making the DMV line move 10 percent faster," he says. "But for most people, if a three-hour wait becomes a two-hour wait, it's still an accomplishment."

Minnesota does not have formal technology committees. Instead, the legislature created an ad hoc IT committee as a forum for technology discussions, education and information. "We tried to get everybody together to look at issues that cross functional boundaries," Kelley says. But for the most part, busy legislators failed to show up. "Until a particular committee forces you to make a decision, time-budgeted legislators aren't going to get background on an issue." As a result, there's less of a build-up of IT expertise in the legislature and more reliance on the executive branch or staff.

As term limits sweep out the old guard in some states, opportunities open up for younger legislators to step in. In theory, at least, the thirty-somethings that come into office would seem likely to push legislatures up to speed on technology issues. "To the extent there are term limits and younger members of the legislature, the use of technology will become matter of fact," says state Representative Ed Jennings, a member of the Florida House Committee on Information Technology.

But even though these young professionals have been using technology most of their adult lives, that doesn't guarantee they have the know-how to oversee complex, enterprise-wide technology projects that change the way government does its business. "People come in who know technology better, but they don't stay long enough to know the business processes of government," says Iowa's Varn.

When legislatures are not knowledgeable in technology, it leaves a lop-sided arrangement in government. "In the absence of participation by the legislature, the executive branch has no checks or balances," says Winkley. "The legislature is missing how important technology is for making executive branch programs successful."

15

Dealing in Data

Ellen Perlman

Forget about building a big all-purpose database. There are other ways to integrate state and local information.

In the days leading up to Smarty Jones' run at the Kentucky Derby, state and local officials had more to think about than who would win a horse race. Thunder Over Louisville, an air show with skydiving teams and hundreds of planes, would be drawing a crowd of half a million people, and the dazzling pyrotechnics after dark would keep them there for hours. The extravaganza, which stretches over both sides of the Ohio River between Louisville and southern Indiana, would call on police, firefighters, emergency personnel and others from several jurisdictions to work together to monitor the scene and respond to emergencies. And two days later, the Derby would require similar vigilance.

The job of covering two weeks' worth of high-profile events is a big one, and officials wanted to have a lot of useful information fingertip-ready for watching and controlling crowds and responding to emergencies. That's why Louisville-area governments brought on board "special events situation awareness" software to bring together pockets of disparate information from multiple databases located at several levels of government. The program gave them quick-click access to Web pages and GIS maps of the area. Officials could simulate an aerial flyover of the region, get weather reports in case Derby crowds had to be moved inside and monitor real-time traffic cameras on the highway. Moreover, the Internet-based information was available to Centers for Disease Control and Prevention officials in Atlanta and FBI officials in Washington, if needed.

Governments have been trying to break down the silos of data that have been built up agency by agency, government by government. It's a never-ending quest to make information available government-wide, and technology vendors and officials have talked for

From *Governing*, September 2004.

years about finding a way to integrate underlying systems so that information is merged. Of course, before that can happen, all levels of government have to go electronic and get onto the Internet. "The bottom line is to get digital," says Steve Kolodney, the former CIO of Washington state who is now with CGI-AMS, a government technology consulting company. "If not, you don't have a prayer."

Full integration is not likely to happen anytime soon—if ever. But with a boost from ever-evolving technologies, the silos themselves have become porous and many agencies are looking at translating and connecting data from different places and assembling it on the fly. That is, rather than trying to force all data into one big compatible base, the idea is to tap into existing databases for the bits and pieces of information—and integrate them for a specific use.

In Louisville, law enforcement and emergency management agencies took the lead on sharing data. But officials in areas such as health care, social services and the environment, in Louisville as well as other jurisdictions, see the value and efficiencies not only in automating and sharing data but also in figuring out ways to make it happen. In addition, enterprise resource planning systems that connect all the financials or payroll information in a jurisdiction and 311 systems that tap into data from many departments to help resolve constituent complaints or problems have given officials and employees a taste of looking beyond their own departments—and an idea about the value of doing so.

ENVIRONMENTAL INTEGRATION

There is one basic prerequisite that has to be met before any data merging can take place. Government agencies have to take the information that lives on paper and convert it into digitized form. That's still a work in progress in many places. Once it's taken care of, however, advances in technology are available to make the most of that information.

The Michigan Department of Environmental Quality was paperbound and chose to go from 0 to 60 to reach a digitized state. The department's aim was not just to move environmental data from paper to an electronic form. It was also to share that data electronically with the federal government and others, including the private sector. Michigan undertook the move as one of more than a dozen states participating in the Exchange Network, a Web-based state-U.S. Environmental Protection Agency cooperative venture that will make it possible for federal, state and local environmental officials to get their hands on important environmental data in real time and make good use of it. District engineers, for instance, can tap into up-to-the-minute data to generate a report or a graph that shows a trend in a particular region or of a particular chemical so that officials can respond quickly.

Getting participating states up to speed on the network hasn't been easy—nor is it a mission that's been fully accomplished—but Michigan has helped blaze the trail and has already saved time and money from having done so. The starting point was meeting a long-standing federal requirement: The state's environmental quality department has to submit to the U.S. EPA monthly reports on the amount and concentrations of chemicals in the effluent discharged by the 1,200 automobile, manufacturing and other permitted facilities in the state. The same data are used by engineers in the field who would, says Mike Beaulac, state assistant administrator for the department, "take handfuls of paper copies, put it into a temporary database, crunch the numbers and throw the database away." And they did that every time they needed to examine what was going on with wastewater facilities—something that was sometimes necessary on a weekly or even daily basis.

The facility data were also submitted to the state in a similarly inefficient manner. "Chemical companies had all this chemical effluent information in their computers they would handwrite, throw in the mail and we would put it in state computers," says Beaulac. Then they would enter the data a second time into a federal Web-based system to send to the federal government. The repeated replication of the data at different levels resulted in many errors, lowering the quality of the information.

In May 2003, Michigan launched a process to allow permitted facilities to send their computer data directly to the state database. In January of this year, that same electronic process was extended so that the information from the state database could be sent electronically to the feds. Michigan estimated that within a year, 10 percent of the permitted facilities would participate. It was wrong. The participation rate reached three times that number and is growing. The state expects to save up to half a million dollars a year in administrative costs—staff no longer have to type in so much data and district engineers no longer have to keep creating temporary databases.

What has made the connections possible between pools of data residing at the local, state and federal levels and with the private sector is a universal computer language called XML that lets one database communicate with another no matter what kind of operating systems or platforms are being used. Part of the conversion process also requires human beings to sit down and come up with data standards so the information can be exchanged smoothly. Previously, every time EPA made a change to a database, states would have to figure out how to change their programs for extracting data to match up to EPA's changed format. The Exchange Network's job is to make that unnecessary by defining the way in which information will be shared. "The language has to be standardized enough so all different users across the nation can use it," Beaulac says. Eventually, all 50 states will be able tap into the network. They don't have to but, Beaulac says, "once they do a cost-benefit analysis, it's a no-brainer."

CONNECTING THE HEALTH DOTS

In Wisconsin, the silo-busting project is in the area of health care. Linking up isolated data in public health labs, the clinical community and state and local health departments is essential for early detection and analysis of disease, and alerting the community. Wisconsin is putting together a Public Health Information Network (PHIN), a program funded by the CDC. All states eventually will have one.

The Wisconsin PHIN is collecting and analyzing related sets of health information electronically so health and emergency workers can be alerted to and prepare for a crisis. For instance, if a railroad car hauling a chemical crashes and spills its contents, the first responders need to know what they're dealing with and what sort of skilled responders to call for help in treating casualties. Appropriately trained people might not be in the area,

> *Linking up isolated data in public health labs, the clinical community and state and local health departments is essential for early detection and analysis of disease, and alerting the community.*

and the system would help emergency workers on the scene locate the personnel they might need. "You have to reach into some system to find out who is trained and how quickly they can get there," says Michael Enstrom, project manager for Wisconsin's Division of Public Health. "This transcends county lines, sometimes state lines."

Once they're fully developed, PHINs will be composed of five pieces that range from detection and monitoring to response. Wisconsin is up and running with the health-alert piece that marries 2,500 trained users at health departments in counties and states to emergency management personnel and local police. The state's health department has the ability to reach across agencies to find personnel and use various forms of communication to reach them.

The state also is pilot-testing an electronic lab reporting system that can relay lab data back to counties that send in information about problems they're seeing. If a clinic somewhere has a hepatitis case, for instance, it will be tracked internally in its own reporting system but it can also be linked to Wisconsin's PHIN. Through a secure network, information about further developments would be sent back to the jurisdiction, as well as to the CDC and the local health department.

What Enstrom likes about the health information network is that the data remain in the silos from which they came. "The real focus is on interconnectivity," he says. A chief medical officer has a specific set of things he needs to look at, while law enforcement has a different set. "It doesn't make sense to shovel it all into a big database."

Governments have to look at organizational rules for connecting each department's or division's data by entering into agreements between agencies and setting the tone for how integration is to be set up, Enstrom says. Departments can define where it makes sense to share and where it doesn't, taking into consideration the need for privacy and security.

Public health departments, for instance, should be looking at linking up with the courts, human services and corrections, three different realms with the same set of participants, so that each set of data on a case can be useful to all. How these insulated groups work together has a bearing on how the state gets funding and accounts for funding. "The guts of this integration is to make the business case for integrating wholly different data sets and why it is appropriate to do that," Enstrom says.

ELIGIBILITY DETAILS

Social services agencies have long needed the means and the will to share information on cases. Multnomah County, Oregon, took a highly fragmented eligibility system serving the neediest of its residents and smoothed it out for simplicity. The result is Oregon Helps!, a Web site that provides low- and moderate-income people with a one-stop shop for information on their eligibility for 27 local, state and federal social service programs.

The databases for each of the 27 programs are scattered throughout agencies and offices. So are the application forms. People in need often were sent to several places while trying to figure out what they were eligible for and where they should go for applications. Many times, people in one program, such as food stamps, didn't realize they were also eligible for other programs that could help them. The county also discovered that a lot of the questions on the forms were too complicated.

Multnomah started its sharing process by launching a pre-screening Web site in 1999. There was enough interest and support from other agencies and foundations to take the county program statewide. The county also took the publicly available questions, applications and eligibility rules for 27 social services programs, combined them and made them multilingual. A sixth-grade reading consultant was asked to rewrite questions that were unclear or so complicated that they drove away deserving people. The county also programmed into the system an algorithm that can determine whether someone is likely to be eligible for various benefits.

The Web site sticks with basic technologies so that people living in rural areas can use it even if they have access only via a slow modem. Needy residents in rural areas, for instance, can sign on and check to see if they'd be eligible for programs, or if, say, their benefits have changed after a job loss. That way, says project manager Van Le, they can decide whether it's worth driving what could be a long distance to apply for a program. If the system tells them they don't qualify, they can save themselves an office visit that will only disappoint.

Those who are eligible are told what types of forms they should have in hand so that they can arrive at a government office with the appropriate paperwork. The Web site lets them know, for instance, that they can provide proof of income and resources using bank records or life insurance policies. "It's a self-service one-stop before people get into navigating the system," Le says.

EDUCATION'S CONGLOMERATES

Data sharing in education may end up changing how teachers are paid or trained. At the Texas Education Agency, agency employees are looking at a variety of sources of data to figure out how to distribute appropriate programs, staffing and funding throughout the state. The agency first tried using activity-based costing—a way of pulling together into a mathematical formula every detail of cost—to track costs for the efficient purchase of textbooks, computers and other learning tools. It didn't turn out as successfully as hoped, mainly because the publisher's costs were private and could not be obtained to plug into the formula. "Sometimes you go down the road and find that road's under construction, and you need to take an alternate route," says Bill Monroe, former chief of operations at the agency who is now with PeopleSoft.

But there is plenty of useful information in public records that can be taken out of silos and when conglomerated, provide insights that can be used strategically. Texas is pondering the possibilities.

It's been a long-held belief, for instance, that all teachers should be paid the same no matter where they are, but an idea that's emerging is to differentiate pay to attract teachers to poorer neighborhoods. With data pulled out of stovepipes, there is a way—at least technically—to make this possible, and officials are wrestling with the issue.

Shared information could also make connections between teachers, the quality of teaching and teacher training. "Policy people have to deal with these things," says Monroe. "But the devil's in the details. Until people start sharing data in silos, they don't have good concrete information to work with."

16

Computer games offer citizens the chance to see how government works and the trade-offs involved in policy making.

From *Governing,* December 2003.

Honey, I Shrunk the Deficit!

Christopher Conte

Step aside, and let me show you how it's done: I'm going to balance the budget.

My tool in this exercise will be the Utah Budget Simulator, a game devised by Utah's Office of Planning and Budget. After downloading the game software from the state's Web site, I click through a series of ledger sheets briefing me on the myriad issues I must resolve. Before I type in each of my decisions, I can click a button that brings up a picture of the governor offering his recommendations, or another that shows what the fictitious *Standard Deseret Tribune* is saying about my performance.

I'm still trying to get my mind around the $78 million deficit when a "news flash" pops up telling me that the U.S. Congress has reduced social services block grants to states. The projected deficit swells to $81 million. Ignoring a sign that reads "No Pork," I reject the governor's advice and increase the state's revenue forecast by 5 percent. That shrinks the projected deficit to $31 million. I know how the game is played.

Then a second news flash tells me that state colleges need $45 million to fix computer problems, and a corpulent character in dark glasses pops up to remind me to take care of his special project. I plow ahead, but while taking a break from boning up on Utah's "weighted pupil unit" formula for funding education, I make the mistake of reading the "newspaper." Under the headline "Utah Out of Balance—Conte Budget Preposterous," it cites "economic experts" saying my revenue assumptions are overly optimistic. Lambasting me for breaking the law by trying to slash the state legislature's budget, it quotes an unnamed legislative leader saying that "forces are mounting" to remove me from office. I retreat from the revenue ploy and the legislative cut. The deficit balloons to $111 million.

Hmm. This may not be as easy as I thought. But that, of course, is exactly the point. "We wanted to show that this is hard," says Lynne Ward, director of Utah's budget office and one of the game's creators. "It is complex, and there are many decisions you have to make."

The Utah budget simulation (www.governor.state.ut.us/budget/fy2000/) is one of a small but growing number of experiments that seek to use computer games to teach people how government works. Budget games have proven popular not only in Utah but in California, Maine, Massachusetts, Minnesota, New Hampshire and Texas as well. Government agencies and news organizations in Savannah, Georgia, and Seattle offer games that focus on water conservation (www.savannahnow.com/features/water/calcBryan.shtml and www.savingwater.org/waterbusters/). In Pennsylvania, legislative Republicans and Democratic Governor Edward Rendell this year prepared competing online tools to let taxpayers assess the impact of proposed tax-law changes (www.pasenategop.com/calculator.htm). And in New York, a grassroots group has created online games letting citizens register their ideas for redeveloping the World Trade Center site (www.gothamgazette.com/rebuilding_nyc/groundzeroplanner/) and highlighting corruption in the Brooklyn Supreme Court (www.gothamgazette.com/judgesgame/).

If this keeps up, the word "gaming" soon could come to mean something more to state and local officials than lotteries, slot machines and Indian-run casinos. The Woodrow Wilson International Center for Scholars in Washington, D.C., has launched a "Serious Games Initiative," which seeks to encourage development of games simulating policy making and management. In a workshop it convened earlier this year, game designers and policy makers brainstormed about games involving management of parks, high schools and hospitals, and

> "The goal of electronic-based gaming is not just to raise a generation of digitally ambidextrous kids but to create intellectually ambidextrous decision-makers as well."
>
> David Rejeski, director, Foresight and Governance Project

David Rejeski, director of the center's Foresight and Governance Project, says he hopes to see other games that would help citizens and government officials learn how to orchestrate disaster relief, make better health care choices and grapple with urban sprawl. "The goal of electronic-based gaming," he explains, "is not just to raise a generation of digitally ambidextrous kids but to create intellectually ambidextrous decision-makers as well."

WEIGHING IN

Games are effective communication tools because they are fun and engaging. Moreover, advocates believe they may leave a deeper and more lasting impression than brochures, public service advertisements and traditional news stories because they turn viewers into active participants in gathering information, rather than passive recipients of it. A game designed by Boston's WBUR-radio in Boston during the 2002 gubernatorial campaign demonstrates their allure. Rather than spoon-feed canned position statements to its Web users, the public-radio station invited them to scroll through statements by five unnamed candidates on 10 issues, each time selecting the statement closest to their own views. At the end, the station showed them which candidates agreed with them on each issue.

The game may not have made deciding how to vote any easier; when I took the quiz, I was surprised to find that I agreed with an independent candidate on one issue, the Green Party candidate on three, the Republican on three, the Democrat on one and the Libertarian on two. But the game sparked my curiosity, forced me to think more carefully about my own views and plumb the candidates' statements for subtle distinctions.

Games also can give players an opportunity to weigh in on issues. In 2001, the *Topeka Capital-Journal* created the "Topeka City Council Survivor" game (www.cjonline.com/webindepth/survivor/). Modeled after the "reality-TV" program of that name, the game called on Web users to symbolically vote one member off the city council each week. Designed to hold a spotlight on a council that had become rife with bickering, the game sparked a lively online discussion about how council members should behave. And while it lacked the finality of a recall election, it was a big hit in some circles. Players included a virtual "Who's Who" of Topeka government and business leaders, according to the newspaper.

Not surprisingly, the game wasn't popular with council members. "The job of a newspaper, you would think, is to report the news and not create it," fumed Topeka city council member Jim Gardner, who was the third of 10 officials to be figuratively drummed out of the council. But proponents say that misses an important point: Citizens increasingly want to participate in decision making rather than be treated as mere spectators, and technology makes that possible, they contend. "Now, with the Internet, [journalists] have the power to not only start stories but then capture how the world interacts with it, reacts to it and changes it," argue Shayne Bowman and Chris Willis of the Atlanta-based consulting firm Hypergene. Bowman and Willis presented their views at a 2001 workshop sponsored by the Institute for New Media Studies at the University of Minnesota. The gathering, which explored how news organizations could create games to convey information, was entitled, "Playing the News."

While the *Topeka Capital-Journal* designed its game with satire in mind, the Everett *Herald*, just north of Seattle, offers its games in earnest. Its "Waterfront Renaissance" game (http://waterfront.heraldnet.com/develop2.cfm) let Web users weigh in on urban renewal projects by placing icons representing their preferred land uses on city maps. The project was crude; players were not forced to consider the cost or feasibility of their proposals, and the game's graphics didn't allow them to do any actual designing. But sponsors were convinced it made a difference, since many of the players' preferences later showed up the city's actual redevelopment plans. That led the *Herald* to join two media partners in offering a more elaborate game called "Fix Your Commute" (http://fyc.heraldnet.com/). In that game, players peruse maps and identify which transportation problems they think are most in need of corrective action. Then, they decide how to pay for the road improvements they want. Only plans that are fully financed are accepted, and players get a bonus if they address regional needs rather than their own parochial concerns.

All this suggests games could become a new channel of communication between government and citizens. "Games like this can serve almost as a surrogate public hearing process," notes Jan Schaffer, the former executive director of the Pew Center for Civic Journalism, which underwrote the Waterfront project. The Pew Center, which encouraged journalists to become more actively involved in seeking solutions to public issues, closed its doors in May after 10 years in operation. Schaffer now runs an organization called J-Lab at the University of Maryland, which seeks to encourage games and other forms of interactive journalism.

J-Lab (www.j-lab.org) exists in part because Americans take games—whether football or fiscal policy—very seriously. When Minnesota Public Radio put a budget game on its Web site (http://news.mpr.org/features/2003/03/10_newsroom_budgetsim/), some 7,000 people played. But they created 11,000 budgets, suggesting that many put in more than a casual effort. The hard work appeared to change more than a few minds. In a survey, many players said they went into the game opposed to tax increases but came out convinced that the state needed new revenues. "When people have to make choices, they don't stick with their ideological positions," notes Michael Skoler, the station's managing director of news.

HEALTHY CONTROVERSY

Such games may really make people think more clearly about the ramifications of different policies. But what if games subtly manipulate players to reach predetermined conclusions? You only have to listen to complaints from parents whose teenagers steal cars, drive recklessly and even visit prostitutes in the popular video game "Grand Theft Auto" to know that there are concerns about the influence games might have over people. Some analysts see the potential for subtle coercion in policy games, too. "Only a few can penetrate the black box and understand what is inside," warned Paul Starr, a Princeton University social scientist and co-editor of the *American Prospect,* in a 1994 review of popular games such as SimCity. "As a result, those who have technical authority over the black boxes acquire an extraordinary degree of influence in the political process."

I decide to test Starr's theory on MassBalance (www.playmassbalance.com/), a budget game created under the guidance of Richard Moore, a state senator in Massachusetts. Moore, a Democrat, describes himself as "relatively conservative." When I try to balance the budget by raising state taxes, the results are troublesome: I'm told my budget worsens a recession, hurts retailers near the New Hampshire border and exacerbates a loss in economic productivity. When I revise the budget by making steep spending cuts and eschewing tax increases, the results are less harmful. (Yes, lack of funding for the corrections system helps set off a prison riot, but I'm told the system survives.)

I infer from these results that Senator Moore leans against tax increases. But the lawmaker says the only complaints he has received about the game have come from anti-tax groups. They have a point: The game gives players only the option of raising taxes or holding them at their current level. In response to complaints, Moore has promised to add options to his next version of the game that will enable players to reduce taxes or even eliminate the state income tax entirely. "I think it will be disastrous," he says, "but we'll put in what the libertarians want."

Far from reflecting badly on a game, controversy over its parameters is actually a healthy development, according to educational researchers. Some experts suggest that most learning comes not from games themselves but from the thinking, discussion and further study they inspire. "Any game is, at best, a simulation," notes Kurt Squire, an assistant professor at the University of Wisconsin. "You have to play it, discuss whether it is realistic or not, and consult other data to confirm its validity." Squire formerly worked on the Massachusetts Institute of Technology Games-to-Teach project, which develops educational video games. "The bottom line," he says, "is that the game alone is much less important than the game plus social interaction plus additional research."

For the moment, few policy games are as technically sophisticated as those produced by the entertainment industry. But that may change. The Woodrow Wilson Center's "Serious Games Initiative" envisions a time in the not-too-distant future when policy games will be just as sophisticated as top-of-the-line entertainment games, and universities and government agencies will use them to train a new generation of government decision makers. The model for what they hope will be any number of new games is Virtual U (www.virtual-u.org/), which puts players in the shoes of an imaginary university president.

THE NEXT LEVEL

Virtual U goes far beyond the typical budget simulation game. Consisting of several hundred thousand lines of computer code, it allows players in a few hours to explore secondary and tertiary effects of a couple of years' worth of actions they might take as academic administrators. What's more, they can customize it by adjusting everything from the size of the faculty and student body to the cost of maintaining campus roads and buildings. If you don't believe it's a serious game, consider this: It took four people two years to build it, at a cost of more than $1 million. But the investment has paid off. Virtual U has been used in some 25 master's and Ph.D. programs to train more than 3,000 aspiring university administrators, and some 50,000 copies have been downloaded from the Internet.

The game gives administrators something that has been sorely lacking in the public sector—"an understanding of the big picture," argues the Woodrow Wilson Center's David Rejeski. "That understanding, coupled with the ability to rapidly test hypotheses, run multiple experiments and fail softly—without a loss of life or loss of face—would go a long way in improving public policy and management," he says.

State and local officials soon will have an opportunity similar to what Virtual U has given college administrators. BreakAway Games Ltd., a Baltimore software developer, recently started designing a game that will enable local officials to practice dealing with crises such as terrorist attacks or environmental disasters. "Incident Commander" will use technology that BreakAway has developed for the military to create games depicting real geographic locations. (The next time American soldiers are deployed abroad, they'll be able to use this game to familiarize themselves with the place they will be landing—down to the layout of city streets.)

BreakAway's federal funding will enable it to distribute the homeland security software, free of charge, to 18,000 municipalities. But any city that is interested will be able to purchase a customized version that will show its actual streets and buildings. "As long as we have satellite data, we will be able to recreate a 10-square block area in 48 hours," says BreakAway President Deborah Tillett.

But who will pay for high-level policy games? The most likely candidates so far appear to be private foundations and the federal government. The Alfred P. Sloan Foundation, for instance, financed Virtual U and the U.S. Department of Justice is paying for the homeland security game. But advocates say that state and local governments could get into the act, too. "I'd look for seed money from the federal government, and I'd look for ways to collaborate across boundaries," says Colonel Casey Wardynski, director of the U.S. Army's Office of Economic and Manpower Analysis and Army Game Project. He oversees "America's Army" (www.americasarmy.com/), a game that leads players through realistic simulations of Army life, including basic training. After the game first came out, on July 4, 2002, the U.S. Department of Health and Human Services approached the Army to add a component that would teach players basic first aid information. The Army, eager to defray its costs while enriching the game and performing a public service, jumped at the idea. As a result, players now receive basic instruction in first aid.

To those who are dubious about the value of the project, Wardynski has some interesting figures. More than 2 million Americans have played "America's Army" in its first year and a half of operation, and more than 1 million have completed its basic training components. In all, Americans have logged 24 million hours playing the game. To get that kind of exposure using public service advertisements and other traditional forms of publicity would have cost the Army $120 million, compared to the $10 million it spent creating and distributing the game, Wardynski notes. And the exposure has been high in quality. In a recent survey, the Army found that 19 percent of young Americans have a favorable impression of the Army thanks to the game, making it the single most effective public-relations tool in the military's arsenal.

Of course, the Army has one thing that few state and local governments have today: plenty of resources. It may be a stretch to imagine a governor or mayor willing to risk the public criticism that might come from using precious taxpayer dollars to finance a game. Then again, maybe they should try some games themselves, and see what lessons they bring away from them.

After despairing of finding any solution to Utah's budget dilemmas, I finally knuckle down to making some hard decisions. It takes me almost an hour, and the cuts I make are deep and painful. And, when I feel I can cut no more, I swallow hard and impose modest increases in both the sales and income taxes. With trepidation, I brace myself to be excoriated by the *Standard Deseret Tribune*. Sure enough, the headline blares: "Tax Freedom Day Gets Further Away." But buried in the imaginary newspaper story are some surprisingly kind words. My tax decisions, my erstwhile critics concede, were "a gutsy move."

17 Trading for Clean Water

Tom Arrandale

States and localities are intrigued by proposals to create market mechanisms for solving intractable water-pollution problems.

For thousands of years, the shady forests that grew along the banks of Oregon's Tualatin River kept the water chilly enough for salmon, steelhead and cutthroat trout. The temperature began to rise, however, as pioneer farmers cleared dense tree stands to plant fields, and subsequent development channeled surface runoff into the 700-square-mile watershed. The Tualatin got warmer still when two sewage-treatment plants were built in the 1970s and started discharging 70-degree effluent into its waters. Now, federal and state regulators are holding Clean Water Services, the multi-county district that serves the suburbs west of Portland, responsible for cooling the Tualatin down so native cold-water fish can swim upstream for spawning.

One solution would be for CWS to spend $150 million on refrigeration equipment to chill the treated effluent before it is released. But the agency recently received permission to try a cheaper, and quite possibly more effective, alternative: It plans to start paying local farmers $1.5 million over the next five years to plant Douglas fir, red alder, Pacific willow and other native trees along the Tualatin and its upstream tributaries. For the nation's water-pollution police, "it's really radical letting somebody plant trees instead of doing technology-based things," says Sonja Biorn-Hansen, of the Oregon Department of Environmental Quality.

In return for allowing Clean Water Services to scrap plans for installing the costly equipment, Oregon water-quality officials will require the agency to bring temperatures all along the river down twice as much as chillers alone would have accomplished. "Our regulators gave us 20 years for the trees to grow," but to meet that goal

From Governing, April 2004.

"we'll need somewhere between 15 and 40 miles of shade," says Bruce Cordon, the district's project coordinator.

In addition to reducing Clean Water Service's costs by better than 90 percent, the arrangement will help curtail soil erosion, control polluted farm runoff, replenish streamside habitat and help salvage the state's imperiled salmon and trout populations. This tree-planting approach is one of the nation's boldest experiments in relying on old-fashioned market incentives to control pollution as efficiently as possible.

In the past decade, full-fledged exchanges have developed for trading air-emissions credits to address acid rain from Midwestern power plants and more recently for greenhouse gases. The Tualatin River deal and other similar examples are generating interest in a systematic approach to swapping effluent credits—at least within individual watersheds—as a way of solving intractable water-pollution problems.

SHARING THE CLEAN-UP BURDEN

Despite enormous investments in cleaning up factories, sewage-treatment plants and other end-of-pipe pollution sources, more than half of the nation's 2,000 watersheds still don't comply with federal Clean Water Act goals for making waters fit for fishing, swimming and drinking. That's largely because pollutants running off farmers' fields, golf courses, parks and lawns are still clogging streams and lakes with sediment, raising their temperatures, and clouding waters with excessive loads of phosphorus, nitrogen and other oxygen-consuming nutrients. Landowners who release these widely dispersed "non-point" pollutants are exempt from the 30-year-old law requiring corporations and municipal sewage systems to obtain government permits that force them to clean up the effluent they release.

In an effort to fill in the regulatory gap, pollution-control agencies have begun the process of enforcing "total maximum daily loads," which impose contaminant limits and temperature standards for streams, rivers and lakes. They've also begun broadening the regulatory focus to take in entire watersheds, including contaminated non-point runoff as well as point-source releases, and designing strategies for spreading the burden of bringing pollutant loads down to TMDL limits.

> *"It's really radical letting somebody plant trees instead of doing technology-based things."*
>
> Sonja Biorn-Hansen, Oregon Department of Environmental Quality

Local sewage agencies and businesses will still be on the regulatory hook if tighter limits go into effect. But ratcheting point-source discharges down even more to comply with tighter TMDLs would be an expensive proposition. At the same time, farmers and other landowners can reduce their own "non-point" runoff much more cheaply by adopting sensible soil-management practices. The U.S. Environmental Protection Agency calculates that the nation could save $900 million and still meet water-quality goals with trading mechanisms that let big polluters buy marketable credits from landowners who can then use the cash to curtail "non-point" runoff from their property.

EPA has been backing trading experiments since 1996. Minnesota approved a prototype trading venture in a 1997 permit that allowed Rahr Malting Co. to start discharging barley-processing byproducts into the lower Minnesota River. To offset the 150 pounds of nutrients it releases daily, the company has spent $255,000 to keep twice that much out of the river by paying four farms within the watershed to plant native grasses, build livestock fences and adopt other measures to curb erosion that would otherwise carry nutrients into the system.

For the most part, however, trading proposals to cut the costs of controlling water pollutants have yet to catch on. In an analysis published last year of 37 pilot programs, a consultant and a University of Maryland professor concluded that "despite the compelling economic logic . . . very few nutrient-credit trades have actually taken place."

Connecticut has implemented a limited pollutant-trading scheme among 79 sewage-treatment plants to help them deal with steadily tightening limits on nutrient-laden effluent that reaches Long Island Sound. The state's sewage agencies must collectively reduce their nitrogen discharges by nearly two-thirds to reverse nutrient loads that are depleting oxygen levels in the sound's waters. Trading began in 2002, with the state setting the value of credits that plants must acquire if they don't meet discharge standards as the limits are ratcheted down; the state in turn buys excess credits that other facilities earn because they have already invested in tighter controls and therefore are reducing nitrogen discharges below the current standard.

Advocates of market mechanisms think pollutant trading will have to play a much more significant role for governments to supplement point-source controls by finally curbing non-point releases as well. Michigan, Maryland and Virginia have launched pilot trading efforts for controlling farmland nutrients that wash into the Great Lakes and Chesapeake Bay. North Carolina set up a nutrient trading system in 1991 for 14 point-source dischargers in the Tar-Pamlico Basin; the program finances state assistance for farmers to control phosphorus and nitrogen runoff, but no trading has taken place.

Around Colorado's Lake Dillon reservoir, resort towns have adopted phosphorus controls and sold credits to sewage systems. Outside Denver, a few small-scale phosphorus trades have been made along the Cherry Creek Basin, but a full-fledged market hasn't developed. EPA and Idaho regulators are backing the Boise sewage system's proposal for phosphorus trading on the Lower Boise River with local farmers, but the plan was stymied several years while federal and state officials debated setting TMDL levels for phosphorus downstream in the Snake River system.

Wisconsin's Natural Resources Department has conducted studies to assess the potential for similar arrangements between cities and farmers along three major watersheds. So far, however, just one municipality, Cumberland (population 2,400), has taken the plunge into trading with nearby farmers. The projected cost of installing phosphorus controls at the city's 450,000-gallons-per-day sewage treatment plant was $150,000, plus $35,000 a year for chemicals and operating expenses. For just $20,000 a year, the city is instead paying farmers to cover the cost of shifting roughly 1,000 acres to no-till planting. That has kept twice as much phosphorus from eroding into the Red Cedar watershed as retrofitting the treatment works would have accomplished. Cumberland and Wisconsin DNR officials acknowledge that trading works only because Barron County's soil conservation manager has been doing all the legwork to identify potential trades at no cost to city coffers. Other Wisconsin cities found trading doesn't make economic sense for meeting the state's phosphorus limit, at least at its current level.

THE TROUBLE WITH TRADES

To function, any market requires both willing buyers and willing sellers. The Bush administration is pumping money into new pilots, but EPA and many states have yet to follow through on imposing rigid TMDLs that would stimulate demand for effluent credits from factories and sewage systems. Meanwhile, controlling non-point runoff remains voluntary; and direct federal and state subsidies for best management practices make trading less attractive for landowners. What's more, enforcing trades requires considerable work by state regulators to make sure goals are met. "I like pollution trading," says James Klang, a Minnesota Pollution Control Agency engineer who monitors the Rahr Malting agreement, "but there is upfront knowledge of the watershed that you have to have before you enter into it."

Environmentalists, meanwhile, contend that trading in effect grants big point sources a right to keep polluting more than they should while rewarding farmers for improvements they should be making anyway. "The way we see it, there's nothing to trade, because their responsibilities are already there," says Brian Wegener, the watershed coordinator for Tualatin Riverkeepers, an Oregon conservation organization. Despite such doubts, Minnesota is working to renew the Rahr permit; and the planned trading efforts seem likely to come together in the next year on both the Tualatin and Boise rivers in the Pacific Northwest.

"You're never going to see a big market like you have in air," says Claire Schary, a former EPA acid-rain trading expert who now oversees the Tualatin and Boise proposals from the agency's regional office in Seattle. But, she adds, trading still makes sense for dealing with some pollutants in watersheds "if you have a big point source that's bumping up against a limit in its permit."

18

The E-mail Mess

Ellen Perlman

A new federal law is riding roughshod over tough state efforts to stop unwanted—and often indecent—spam.

Jason Heckel was a spammer. In 1998, he sent out between 100,000 and 1 million unsolicited commercial e-mails a week. Many of them were about how to spam people and used subject lines such as, "Did I get the right e-mail address?" At least he wasn't pushing prescriptions for Viagra or suggestions for body-part enhancements.

But he was a nuisance and, since many of the messages inundated computer users in the state of Washington, that state invoked its brand-new 1998 anti-spam law—one of the first in the country—and took Heckel to court. The 28-year-old found himself facing a judge and a steep penalty: a $2,000 fine for one violation plus $96,000 in state attorney fees and court costs.

That was five years ago. Since then, Washington has taken legal actions against four more spammers, and 35 other states, heeding the outcry from spam-stunned computer users, have also passed anti-spam laws. Some of the laws are more rigorous than others and details vary widely. Washington's, for instance, cracks down on deceptive e-mail that misrepresents the point of origin, has misleading subject lines, co-opts someone else's domain name or sends out messages that cannot be traced. Other states, such as California and Delaware, passed tougher measures aimed at stopping spam before it starts.

But now, the federal Can-Spam Act, which was signed into law in December, may scramble all or most of the state anti-spam statutes. Some of the strongest state provisions against spamming, such as those in Delaware and California, will be preempted. But some states—Washington among them—believe that provisions in their codes will help their laws survive and remain viable.

From *Governing*, January 2004.

STATING THE CASE

The federal action adds heft to the nationwide fight against spam mainly because it bolsters the rights of Internet users in the 14 states that didn't have anti-spam laws of their own. It also may help residents in states that had weak or ineffective laws against unsolicited commercial e-mail.

Elsewhere, however, dissatisfaction with the federal approach is rampant. Debra Bowen, a state senator in California, says that if Congress were truly interested in stopping spammers, it would have used California's new law as a model and "put a bounty on the head" of each person who sends spam. She is referring to California's provision allowing individuals to sue spammers. Although most people wouldn't file claims, ardent spam haters would, and their claims could act as a deterrent to other spammers. Under the federal law, individuals may not sue.

There are other places where state officials feel the federal law is weak. One is its "opt-out" feature. In both the California and Delaware laws, there was the reverse, an opt-in measure aimed at deterring spam messages before they arrived in e-mailboxes. The federal law's opt-out approach is much weaker, notes Tom Dresslar, spokesman for California Attorney General Bill Lockyer.

Under the federal opt-out provision, each business is allowed to send at least one unsolicited e-mail to a recipient, at which point the recipient has to make the effort to opt out of receiving any more. But even after a recipient does so, the sender still has 10 business days before it has to stop. "Under the federal law, everyone gets at least one free bite of the apple," Dresslar says. "Even after that, they basically have 10 days to bombard your mailbox with unlimited spam even after you ask them not to do it."

The opt-out provision is misguided from the start, says Ray Everett-Church, chief privacy officer for ePrivacy Group, a privacy and anti-spam technology company. Some states and several countries have determined that it

> *"In no other line of business does someone else get to dictate how much of your infrastructure they get to use and you're just stuck bearing the cost."*
>
> Ray Everett-Church, chief privacy officer for ePrivacy Group

doesn't work. "Even if every spammer in the world listened to your plea, there's a problem with scalability," Church says. For example, if the 25 million businesses identified by the U.S. Small Business Association decided in the next year to send just one e-mail with an opt-out option, e-mail recipients would receive on average more than 600 messages a day. The burden would be on them to clear out their mailboxes and beseech senders to stop. "If a bill says one opt-out e-mail is allowed, it's a terribly low threshold," Church adds.

Federal law also says that an e-mail sender must provide a valid return e-mail address that can receive opt-out messages for at least 30 days after the unsolicited e-mail is sent. However, senders would still be in compliance with the law if they are "unexpectedly and temporarily unable to receive messages or process requests due to a technical problem beyond the control of the sender, if the problem is corrected within a reasonable time period." The National Association of Attorneys General wrote a letter to six U.S. Representatives saying, among other things, that such a provision creates a huge loophole. "Spammers are always unable to receive messages right after their spam is sent out—their mailboxes are always full at that point," the A.G.s complained. "That is precisely when most opt-out requests are made."

BUSINESS ANSWERS BACK

State proponents of strong anti-spam laws agree that a national law could be more effective than 50 states trying to regulate spam coming from all corners of the globe. The concern is that this federal law weakens provisions that already exist. "Anything in state laws that would have accomplished anything would be eviscerated by federal law," contends David Sorkin, associate professor at the Center for Information Technology and Privacy Law at John Marshall Law School.

Companies that use e-mail as a legitimate business tool see it differently. They support the federal mandate and criticize California's law, which would have gone into effect this month, as burdensome to legitimate businesses. Because California's law provides for liability for a "single transmission or delivery to a single recipient," there would be many legal traps that lawful businesses could have fallen into quickly, says Walter Olson, a senior fellow at the Manhattan Institute.

Supporters of the federal law point to the merits of a "do not e-mail" registry that would be similar to the popular national "do not call" list targeting telemarketers. But the provision only requires that the Federal Trade Commission within six months set forth a plan and timetable for establishing a registry. It does not compel the commission to actually set it up.

Sorkin and others worry that the federal law is a road map for mass e-mailers to step up their activities. Right now, spam is the cheapest way to bombard people with sales messages. Television advertisers face costs for creating and running ads, forcing them to be judicious about how they do their ad placement. Direct mailers must pay per piece of mail and seal and stamp individual envelopes. Spammers pay next to nothing to send out millions of e-mails. The cost falls on recipients and Internet service providers who pay for service and bandwidth—and pay with their time. "In no other line of business does someone else get to dictate how much of your infrastructure they get to use and you're just stuck bearing the cost," says Church.

The Can-Spam Act allows for damages of $250 per spam up to a limit of $6 million. California's law allows for $1 million per spam. The size of the penalty makes a difference, anti-spam experts say. The lower it is, the more it becomes merely a cost of doing business. The higher, the less likely they are to send it, says Paula Selis, senior counsel in Washington State. One of the aims of Washington's law is to increase the costs for spammers by exposing them to costly court judgments.

Delaware, with a tough law that has been in place since 1999, has had some success in severing the rela-

---

Quantum Leaps

Percentage of e-mail traffic that's spam:

November 2002 _____ 40%
October 2003 _____ 50%

Source: Brightmail, Inc., a spam-filtering software company, based on 250 million e-mail users

---

tionship between credit card clearinghouses and spammers, particularly when the product being offered for sale is illegal. Prosecutors follow the money by going to the financial institutions identified as receiving payment and telling them that if they persist in aiding a spammer they could be liable for conspiracy. "That approach has been successful in several cases," says state prosecutor Steven Wood. But there hadn't yet been any successful prosecutions under the state's statute, although multiple investigations were underway.

Delaware's statute is vulnerable because it defined all bulk e-mails as illegal, not just those that used false information or routing. "It may well be that the federal legislation will preempt parts of Delaware's spam law," Wood says, adding that it seems like the portions of his state's law that deal with gaining access to someone else's computer in order to send spam and the ban on selling software designed to enable the falsification of routing information will hold up under the federal law. Can-Spam contains an exception from preemption for laws that prohibit "falsity or deception" in commercial electronic mail messages or the information attached.

As for Washington State, officials there also believe their law has slipped through the bounds of the federal preemption clause. Washington used provisions on falsity and deception to go after the five prolific spammers who were inundating e-mail boxes of Washington residents, even in the days before unsolicited messages on prescription medicines and mortgage refinancing flooded mailboxes.

Whether any law—federal or state—can stop the flood of spam is another question. Under the new law, those annoying e-mails for prescription drugs and mortgage refinancing could be considered legitimate. And there are enforcement issues. Although 36 states passed anti-spam laws, that has done little to stop unwanted e-mails, as most computer users can attest. The battle may have to be won through a combination of laws, technological fixes and education of e-mail users.

19

Who's Afraid of the DMV?

Jonathan Walters

For most people, motor vehicle offices are the face of government. It's not a pretty face.

South Carolina, like virtually every other state in the country, has long had problems at its Department of Motor Vehicles: frustrating renewal lines, bureaucratic mix-ups and terrible employee morale. Last year, top officials finally decided enough was enough. DMV horror stories were damaging the reputation of the entire state government. The system had to change.

And it did change. It got worse.

South Carolina's "Phoenix Project"—an effort to switch all vehicle owners over to a new computer-driven registration renewal program—crashed and burned last summer in spectacular fashion. It was plagued by inaccuracies in everything, starting with names and addresses of people who owned cars. In thousands of cases, drivers never even got a renewal notice. The long lines at the DMV offices got even longer.

Having taken office this year in the midst of this mess, Governor Mark Sanford is now pushing legislation to make the South Carolina DMV a stand-alone agency (for years it's been a branch of the public safety department), and to make basic changes in its function. That push includes both low-tech and high-tech initiatives. Sanford wants to place greeters in the state's 39 busiest offices and remove phones from the counters so clerks won't be interrupted while helping customers. More transactions will be pushed onto the Internet. The DMV, Sanford says, features "great people" working in a "flawed system."

At some point, virtually every state goes through a DMV meltdown similar to South Carolina's. New York went through one in the early 1990s. Citizens crawled along in line, waiting to register a car or renew a license, all the while trying to quell a gnawing feeling

From *Governing,* July 2003.

that the transaction would unravel when they reached the clerk's window. They wondered how it could have been any worse waiting in a bread line in Russia in the 1950s.

Ray Martinez, now director of the New York State DMV, remembers just what it was like as an ordinary citizen trying to get a license renewed a decade or so ago at any office in the state. "I used to go to the DMV and pack a lunch," Martinez says, "because you never knew when you were going to get out of there."

It wasn't much fun for the clerks at the counter, either. "It was almost a sweatshop mentality," says Karen Pellegrino, a union rep for New York State DMV employees. "It was about following the rules and making your numbers and nobody wanted to hear suggestions about ways to improve the process."

In short, New York's DMV was approaching the peak of frustration that exists right now in South Carolina. "We all knew we had a bad reputation," says Pellegrino, "and that something had to be done about it."

What New York did wasn't all that complicated. A labor-management initiative led to a host of customer-service improvements, from instituting "take-a-number" lobby management (something neighborhood bakeries had been doing since about 1910) to sprucing up the DMV offices themselves with new paint and furniture. Clerks were trained not only in customer service but also in basic problem solving, so they could actually help people rather than inform them that they'd have to come back later with more pieces of paper.

In the years since then, many states have made similar efforts in response to similar crises. "DMVs went through this extensive soul searching," says Bill Parent, a government innovation scholar at UCLA. "They did TQM and they put plants in the offices and they expanded their hours—knowing that a visit to the DMV was a miserable experience that everyone at some point just had to go through, and wait in line, and pay money, and deal with people behind the counter who hate the universe because it has to be the worst job in the world."

MORE THAN A SMILE

It would be a pleasure—as well as a relief to lagging states such as South Carolina—to be able to report that the customer service initiatives launched in most of the country in the past decade have proven effective at taming the DMV ogre once and for all. Unfortunately, that hasn't happened. New York and other states quickly discovered that ficus trees and cheerful clerks alone could not create smooth-running, effective motor vehicle departments. That's partly because the sheer volume of transactions that DMVs are responsible for has continued to grow at a staggering pace. And it's partly because DMVs have been forced to take on a new role as government gatekeeper, policing everything from immigration law to child support enforcement, and monitoring the fidelity and sanctity of citizens' very identities.

In response to all of these challenges, and in growing recognition that improving customer service by itself could not solve the problem, DMVs have begun a new round of changes, based much more on technology than on human relations. They have begun adapting information systems not only to smooth out internal functions but to roll back the number of transactions that require a trip to a DMV office. The more advanced states now allow most routine transactions to be handled over the Internet or at least by mail. This has taken people out of lines and all but eliminated the terrifying prospect of a half a day squandered while waiting to see a surly and overworked DMV clerk.

Some of the innovations have succeeded remarkably well. Minnesota, which recently switched from a paper-driven to a computer-driven renewal system, has seen the time it takes to issue a driver's license drop from 45 days to less than a week. Vehicle titles are issued in 10 days instead of a month. Registrations now take three days to process instead of nearly two weeks. With a PIN number, citizens in Minnesota can complete even high-security transactions, such as replacement of lost licenses, online. "Our overall goal," says Pat McCormack, who until recently was the state DMV's acting director, "is to get 25 percent of all transactions to be self-service." The state is about halfway there, McCormack believes.

Iowa has focused its IT innovations on making the job of the employees easier, in the belief that this is the best way to help citizens in the long run. At Iowa DMV offices, individual workstations now have direct connections to the central record-keeping center in Des Moines. Satellite offices no longer have to wait days for paper to pass back and forth; they can exchange documents and information immediately by keyboard.

These are logical improvements long overdue. But they are not necessarily easy ones to implement successfully, as officials in South Carolina and a few other places have learned, much to their embarrassment.

The District of Columbia DMV, an infamous bureaucracy long synonymous to local residents with maddening inefficiency, hoped to leap into the 21st century last summer by launching its "Destiny" computer system, aimed at moving virtually every transaction in the department away from paper dependence and onto computers. The goal was not merely to make the process less painful for citizens but also to ensure that anyone renewing a license or auto registration had "clean hands" when it came to unpaid fines or other outstanding legal obligations.

Destiny's launch was a disaster. Scores of residents trying to renew their driver's licenses and car registrations discovered they were being interrogated about incidents involving child support, bad checks and parking tickets, some of which were listed accurately—but had long since been resolved—and some of which had never occurred at all. The uproar caused by Destiny forced the city council to grant hundreds of clemencies and to rewrite the rules when it came to how far back the DMV could go in checking for dirt under residents' fingernails.

The system has been largely straightened out: Citizens are no longer getting dinged for ancient parking tickets, and the District actually offers a pretty impressive menu of online DMV transactions. "Obviously the first time you get a driver's license or register a car you have to come in," says Anne Witt, the interim DMV director, "but once you've been identified by our system you can do everything from renewing your registration to paying tickets to changing your address online."

Meanwhile, however, the agency continues to struggle with the classic personal service problems. Witt acknowledges that customer service remains inconsistent among the approximately 350 people who work for the department. She says one of her priorities is to refine policies so that they are as clear and simple as possible for clerk and customer alike, cutting down on the chances for misunderstandings and miscommunication.

"I want to come up with the simplest, legal way to say 'yes' to customers," she says. At the same time, she plans to focus more resources on staff training and morale. "I'm coming into an organization that has seen significant investment in systems and facilities," says Witt. "It's now time to make that same investment in our employees."

TOO MUCH TO DO

Once motor vehicle agencies around the country complete both phases of the revolution—once they improve their customer service and get their online systems working adequately—is it possible they could finally shed their longstanding image as the monsters of government bureaucracy?

Well, maybe—if we weren't continuing to pile more and more responsibilities on to a branch of government that still hasn't mastered the old ones.

Take, for example, the seemingly simple matter of a driver's license. Originally, licenses were meant to do just one thing, says Jason King, of the American Association of Motor Vehicle Administrators: document that somebody was old enough and fit enough to operate an automobile. "It was never meant to be anything more than that—a license to drive," says King. "But it has evolved into being what our society considers to be the primary, secure credential." This was quite a load to bear before 9/11. Now, the load is that much heavier. A driver's license is the first document a citizen is asked for upon entering a secure public building and the last one he is forced to show before boarding an airplane.

But it isn't just homeland security that's been placed—at least partially—on the shoulders of DMVs. In many places, they have been deputized to handle a front-line enforcement role in a host of other local, state and federal policy and program areas: tithing deadbeat dads, clearing up arrest warrants, policing citizenship laws and apprehending federal drug offenders.

Add to these the ever-growing list of more directly auto-related responsibilities that DMVs have no choice but to take on: licensing commercial drivers, issuing vehicle titles, making sure cars are roadworthy and insured, collecting sales taxes and other fees, and even, in some states, policing driving schools.

"It's been subtle and has crept in over the last 10 years," says Mark Wandro, director of the Iowa Department of Transportation. "We're now dealing with things like voter registration and organ donation and child support. Pretty soon it will be conscientious objectors." That isn't a joke. Wandro believes his state's DMV will soon be asked to keep track of whether or not kids in Iowa have registered for the Selective Service. No Selective Service card, no driver's license.

DEALING WITH EVERYONE

In other words, while accepting their reformist mandate to be friendly and responsive as they handle hundreds of transactions a day, DMV employees are being pressed harder than ever to ensure that drivers are in compliance with a host of local, state and federal laws. Every day, in every state in the country, DMVs are dealing with state and local courts, the U.S. Immigration and Naturalization Service and the federal departments of Transportation, Justice and Defense.

While his agency stresses customer service as a high priority, says Terry Dillinger, at the Iowa Office of Driver Services, "it's not uncommon for someone to be taken out of one of our facilities in handcuffs due to outstanding arrest warrants. We've had employees who have been hit by customers. It's a very, very small percentage, but there are always those people who've dug themselves into a hole as far as getting their driver's license and of course none of it is 'their fault' and they want it all resolved immediately."

So it is a constant dilemma for DMVs just how customer-friendly they can actually afford to be. Iowa has made it easier for those with black marks on their record to get things straightened out quickly, says Wandrow. It's a policy that doesn't compromise the DMV's role as front-line enforcer but helps ease conflicts between citizen and government.

Some states, though, have paid a high price for going overboard in the customer-friendliness department. In Virginia, for example, former Governor Jim Gilmore took office in 1998 determined to prove he could transform a churlish bureaucracy into a model of customer service. He transformed it so thoroughly that the state became notorious as a license mill for anyone who wanted to establish an identity, legitimate or otherwise. Among its satisfied customers were several illegal applicants with ties to the terrorists who crashed into the World Trade Center on September 11, 2001.

As they struggle to overcome the stigma of their inefficient past, the task for DMVs will not be merely to become technologically sophisticated or as customer-friendly as practicable—it will be to do both those things while at the same time figuring how to handle their rapidly growing and evolving role as front-line enforcer and identity gatekeeper.

One agency that seems to understand the complexities of its multiple tasks is the DMV in Washington State. After an information technology debacle of its own—the state poured tens of millions of dollars down the drain in a failed effort to impose a technological solution for the 10 million separate transactions it must handle each year—Governor Gary Locke appointed his own deputy chief of staff, Fred Stephens, to take over the state's Department of Licensing in 1999.

Stephens, who had extensive experience both in government and in the private sector's high-tech world, launched a New York-style joint labor-management approach. The result has been a sweeping overhaul that has moved on both fronts at once: a restructured organizational chart and beefed up technological capacity. "Our computer system had been frozen in time," Stephens admits.

As a first step, middle management was cut in half, and many of the positions moved back to the counters. Greeters began intercepting applicants at the door and steering them to one line or another, depending on the complexity of the transaction at hand. Front-line workers were trained and encouraged in the art of solving problems rather than processing paper.

Meanwhile, a successful technology overhaul was improving life on the front line by making office transactions smoother and faster and eliminating some lines entirely. Wait times at DOL offices statewide have plummeted from what used to be hours at the busiest offices to mere minutes in most cases. "Now," Stephens boasts, "citizens can do things in a period of minutes anytime day or night, with a credit card, that used to require a trip to the DOL office. To ensure the system's integrity, computer experts are regularly invited to try to hack in."

The investments in time and money that are taking place in Washington and Iowa and are being launched in South Carolina are ultimately based on a pretty simple premise, says New York's Ray Martinez: State DMVs are the one bureaucracy that virtually every constituent must deal with at some point. Why not try to make the experience as positive as possible. "We consider ourselves to be the face of state government," says Martinez. For quite a few citizens in an increasing number of states, it's a face that's becoming a little less frightening to behold.

20 Unscrambling the City

Christopher Swope

Archaic zoning laws lock cities into growth patterns that hardly anybody wants. Changing the rules can help set them free.

Take a walk through Chicago's historic Lakeview neighborhood, and the new houses will jump right out at you. That's because they're jarringly incompatible with the old ones. On one quiet tree-lined street, you'll find a row of old two-story colonials with pitched roofs. Then you walk a little farther and it seems as though a giant rectangular box has fallen out of the sky. The new condominium building is twice as high as its older neighbors and literally casts shadows over their neat flower gardens and tiny front yards. Angry Lakeview residents have seen so many new buildings like this lately that they have come up with a sneering name for them. They call them "three-flats on steroids."

Listening to the complaints in Lakeview, you might wonder whether home builders are breaking the law and getting away with it, or at least bending the rules quite a bit. But that's not the case. If you take some time and study Chicago's zoning law, you'll find that these giant condos are technically by the book. It's not the new buildings that are the problem. The problem is Chicago's zoning ordinance. The code is nearly half a century old, and it is an outdated mishmash of vague and conflicting rules. Over the years, it has been amended repeatedly, to the point of nonsense. Above all, it's totally unpredictable. In Lakeview, zoning can yield anything from tasteful two-flats to garish McMansions, with no consideration at all for how they fit into the neighborhood.

Chicago's zoning problem lay dormant for decades while the city's economy sagged and population declined. Back in the 1970s and '80s, not much building was going on. But then the 1990s brought an economic boom and 112,000 new residents. While almost everyone is happy that the construction machine has been

From *Governing*, June 2003.

turned back on, so many Chicagoans are appalled by the way the new construction looks that Mayor Richard M. Daley decided it was time to rewrite the city's entire zoning code. Everything about Chicago land use is on the table: not just residential development but commercial and industrial as well. It is the largest overhaul of its kind in any U.S. city in 40 years.

But while few communities are going as far as Chicago, many are coming to a similar conclusion: The zoning laws on their books—most of them written in the 1950s and '60s—are all scrambled up. They are at once too vague and too complicated to produce the urban character most residents say they want.

The zoning problem afflicts both cities and suburbs and manifests itself in countless ways. It takes the form of oversized homes and farmland covered in cookie-cutter housing developments. It shows up as a sterile new strip mall opening up down the street from one that is dying. It becomes an obstacle when cities discover how hard it is to revive pedestrian life in their downtowns and neighborhood shopping districts. And it becomes a headache for city councils that spend half their time interpreting clumsy rules, issuing variances and haggling with developers.

What urban planners disagree about is whether the current system can be salvaged, or whether it should be scrapped altogether. Most cities are not ready to take the ultimate step. Chicago isn't going that far. Neither did Boston, Milwaukee, San Diego and San Jose. All of them retained the basic zoning conventions, even as they slogged through the process of streamlining the codes and rewriting them for the 21st century. According to researcher Stuart Meck, of the American Planning Association, there's a cyclical nature to all this. He points out that it's common for cities to update their laws after the sort of building boom many have enjoyed recently. "Cities are in growth mode again," Meck says, "but they're getting development based on standards that are 20, 30 or 40 years old."

MYRIAD CATEGORIES

For much of the past century, if you wanted to find out the latest thinking about zoning, Chicago was a good place to go. In 1923, it became one of the first cities, after New York, to adopt a zoning law. The motivation then was mostly health and safety. Smoke-spewing factories were encroaching on residential neighborhoods, and the city's first ordinance sought to keep them out. By the 1950s, when more people drove cars, Chicago was a pioneer in rewriting the code to separate the places people live in from where they work and where they shop.

The 1957 zoning law was largely the creation of real estate developer Harry Chaddick, who proclaimed that the city was "being slowly strangled" by mixed uses of property. It classified every available parcel of land into myriad categories based on density. Residential neighborhoods, for example, were laid out in a range from "R1" (single family homes) to "R8" (high-rises). Land use rules were so strict as to dictate where ice cream shops, coin stores and haberdasheries could go. Chaddick's code was hailed in its time as a national model.

But over the years, one patch after another in the 1957 law made it almost impossible to use. Some parts contradicted other parts. Two attorneys could read it and come away with completely opposite views of what the code allowed. Finally, in 2000, the mayor tapped Ed Kus, a longtime city zoning attorney, to take charge of a full-scale rewrite. Kus thinks the law in the works will be equally as historic as Chaddick's—and more durable. "I hope the ordinance we come up with will be good for the next 50 years," Kus says.

Besides its rigidity, the old code has been plagued by false assumptions about population growth. Back in the 1950s, Chicago was a city of 3.6 million people, and planners expected it to reach a population of 5 million. Of course, it didn't work out that way. Like every other major city, Chicago lost a huge proportion of its residents to the suburbs. By 1990, it was down to fewer than 2.8 million residents. But it was still zoned to accommodate 5 million.

That's essentially how Lakeview got its three-flats on steroids. Had the city's population grown as the code anticipated, it would have needed a supply of large new residential buildings to replace its traditional two-flats and bungalows. The law made it possible to build these in lots of neighborhoods, regardless of the existing architecture or character.

For decades, this made relatively little difference, because the declining population limited demand for new housing in most of the city. Once the '90s boom hit, however, developers took advantage. They bought up old homes and tore them down, replacing them with massive condo projects. They built tall, and sometimes they built wide and deep, eating up front yards and side yards and often paving over the back for parking. "Developers are building to the max," Kus says. "We have all these new housing types and the zoning ordinance doesn't govern them very well."

There are other glaring problems. Although many people think of the 1950s as the decade when America went suburban, most retail business in Chicago was still conducted in storefronts along trolley lines, both in the city and the older close-in suburbs. The code reflects that mid-century reality. Some 700 miles of Chicago's arterial streets are zoned for commercial use, much more than the current local retail market can bear. Worse, the old code is full of anachronistic restrictions on what kinds of transactions can be conducted where. A store that sells computers needs a zoning variance to set up shop next door to one that fixes them. "If you're in a 'B1' district"—a neighborhood business corridor—"you can hardly do any business," Kus says.

All of these archaic provisions are quietly being reconsidered and revised on the ninth floor of city hall, where Kus heads a small team that includes two planning department staffers and a consultant from the planning firm of Duncan Associates. Their work will go to the zoning reform commission, a panel whose 17 members were picked by the mayor to hold exhaustive public meetings and then vote on the plan. The commission includes aldermen, architects, planners, business representatives and a labor leader. Developers are conspicuously absent, which may come back to bite the whole project later. But for now, the rewrite is moving remarkably fast. The city council is expected to pass the new code this fall. That will set the stage for an even more difficult task: drawing new maps to fit the changed rules.

In the past, Chicago's zoning reforms sought nothing less than to transform the face of the city. This time, however, there is more of a conservationist bent. What the reformers are trying to do is to lock in the qualities Chicagoans like about their oldest, most traditional neighborhoods. That's not to say they want to freeze the city in place. The building boom is quite popular. But it's also widely accepted that the character of Chicago's neighborhoods is the reason why the city is hot again, and that zoning should require new buildings to fit in. "Cities that will succeed in the future are the ones that maintain a unique character of place," says Alicia Mazur Berg, Chicago's planning commissioner. "People choose to live in many of our neighborhoods because they're attractive, they have front yards and buildings of the same scale."

MADE FOR WALKING

The new rules being drafted for residential areas are a good example of this thinking. Height limits will prevent new houses from towering over old ones. Neighborhoods such as Lakeview will likely be "downzoned" for less density. New homes will be required to have a green back yard, not a paved one, and builders will not be allowed to substitute a new creation known as a "patio pit" for a front yard. Garages will be expected to face an alley—not the street—and blank walls along the streetscape will be prohibited.

In the same spirit, the creators of the new zoning code are also proposing a new category, the Pedestrian Street, or "P-street." This is meant for a neighborhood shopping street that has survived in spite of the automobile and still thrives with pedestrian life. The new code aims to keep things that way. Zoning for P-streets will specifically outlaw strip malls, gas stations and drive-throughs, or any large curb cut that could interrupt the flow of pedestrians. It also will require new buildings to sit right on the sidewalk and have front doors and windows so that people walking by can see inside.

There are dozens of other ideas. The new code aims to liven up once-vibrant but now-dying neighborhood commercial streets by letting developers build housing there.

> "Predictability is important. The average person should be able to pick up the zoning code and understand what can and can't be built in his neighborhood."
>
> Ed Kus, city zoning attorney

For the first time ever, downtown Chicago will be treated as a distinct place, with its own special set of zoning rules. The code will largely ignore meaningless distinctions between businesses, such as whether they sell umbrellas or hats.

The new code also will recognize that the nature of manufacturing has changed. Light manufacturing will be allowed to mix with offices or nightclubs. But heavy industry will get zones of its own, not so much for the health reasons that were important in 1923 and 1957, but because the big manufacturers want it that way and Chicago doesn't want to lose them.

For all the changes, Chicago is still keeping most of the basic zoning conventions in place. It is also keeping much of the peculiar language of zoning—the designations such as "R2" and "C3" that sound more like droids from Star Wars than descriptions of places where people live, work and shop.

On the other hand, the new code will be different from the old code in one immediately identifiable way: It will be understandable. Pages of text are being slimmed down into charts and graphics, making the law easier to use for people without degrees in law or planning. An interactive version will go up on the city's Web site. "Predictability is important," says Ed Kus. "The average person should be able to pick up the zoning code and understand what can and can't be built in his neighborhood."

21 Murder Mystery

John Buntin

In the 1990s, New York and Boston achieved dramatic decreases in homicide. One of them is still improving. The other is getting worse again. Why?

From *Governing,* June 2002.

Two dozen young African-American men, wearing orange, blue and tan jumpsuits, are sitting in a semi-circle in a room at the Suffolk County House of Corrections in Boston. They are there because they are about to be released from prison, and because they are former gang members at high risk of returning to crime.

Sitting across from them is a whole battery of ministers, social workers, police and local and federal prosecutors. Each of them has something to offer the inmates. The ministers tell them about a mentoring program. The social workers say they can help arrange child support payments, get them IDs or driver's licenses, and find transitional living arrangements.

Then the prosecutors take over. Theirs is a different message: We're watching you, and if you return to your former lifestyle, we'll be there to make sure you regret it. "There are two messages," says Kurt Francois, who works for a program called the Safe Neighborhood Reentry Initiative: "It's time to change, and if you don't, you will bear the consequences."

There, in a nutshell, is Boston-style policing. It is based on an unusual collaboration between law enforcement agencies, social service organizations and local churches. It has given the city one of the nation's most admired police departments. Lately, however, local residents have been asking a blunt question: Does it really work?

Five years ago, the question would have seemed absurd. Between 1990 and 1999, as the Boston approach took hold, the city's homicide rate fell by 80 percent. Of course, other cities experienced big crime drops too, including some cities that did little in the way of innovative policing. But only two—Boston and New York—saw murder rates fall by double-digit figures year after year.

Both Boston and New York attributed the decline to new—and very different—approaches to policing. In New York, the police emphasized "quality of life" law enforcement, focusing on minor property and nuisance offenses as a key to serious crimes, and developed a high-tech mapping and accountability system to track police performance. Boston did some of that, but its emphasis was elsewhere: on the partnerships between police and parole officers, community leaders, "streetworkers," academics and ministers.

Because both systems produced impressive numbers, both departments became models for reform-minded policing across the country. But in the eyes of many, Boston had a clear edge: Whereas New York's reduced crime rate came at the cost of growing tension between police and minority activists, Boston accomplished the same result while police relations with the African-American community actually improved. U.S. Attorney General Janet Reno called it "the Boston Miracle."

It was almost too good to be true. And then the numbers started changing. Boston's homicide rate began creeping up again. It took a while for most of the country to notice, but New York noticed very quickly. Last December, in his nationally televised farewell address, Mayor Rudolph Giuliani made a pointed comparison. "In the last statistics put out by the FBI," the mayor said, "there has been a 67 percent increase in murder in Boston. During that same period of time, there was a 12 percent decrease in the city of New York. I don't know, which policing theory would you want to follow?" And then Giuliani answered his own question: "The reality is that the model that was adopted for dealing with crime in New York City is the very, very best way to assure that you can keep a city safe."

Officials in Boston wrote these remarks off as personal pettiness. "A shallow boast," sniffed the *Boston Globe* editorial board. "I can't tell you why he did it," said Boston Mayor Thomas Menino. "Maybe it was frustration because he wishes he could continue the job."

Whatever the motive, Giuliani's figures were accurate. In the past two years, Boston's homicide rate has increased by more than 100 percent. At the same time, the rate in New York City has continued to fall. Clearly, something must be going on. The question is what.

Does Boston's rising homicide rate reflect problems with the Boston model itself, as Giuliani charges, or is Boston suffering from new demographic trends that other cities can soon expect to see? It's a question whose answer has major implications for police departments around the nation. Looking at Boston and New York's divergent police styles isn't a bad way to begin studying this question.

Boston and New York began with a common problem. In the late 1980s and early '90s, both experienced a frightening epidemic of murder. In 1990, New York's homicide total hit the staggering number of 2,245—quadruple the figure in the 1960s. That same year, homicides in Boston reached 152—a number that sounds modest at first but in fact was almost identical to New York's on a per capita basis.

And the problem seemed certain only to get worse. "If there are two thousand murders this year," warned New York newspaper columnist Pete Hamill, "get ready for four thousand." A *Time* magazine survey found that 59 percent of New Yorkers would move out of town if they could. To many, it seemed the police had simply relinquished control of the streets to criminals.

The New York strategy was born in the waning days of Mayor David Dinkins' administration, when Commissioner Raymond Kelly publicly embraced the "broken windows" philosophy of policing, which held that "disorder and crime are usually inextricably linked." Kelly began with an aggressive crackdown on the notorious "squeegee men" who harassed the city's commuters.

The new approach wasn't enough to save Dinkins; he was unseated by Giuliani in November 1993. But Giuliani embraced "broken windows" and steadily built upon it. He replaced Kelly with William Bratton, the former Boston police commissioner, and Bratton added the critical innovation called Compstat.

The brainchild of Bratton's chief crime strategist, the late Jack Maple, Compstat married the idea of crime mapping with a new focus on precinct commander performance. Every week, precinct commanders from one of New York's eight patrol boroughs would come before the department's top brass to discuss the crime trends in their precincts. Commanders who failed to show sufficient familiarity with those trends, or who failed to come up with strategies for solving the problems, were quickly reassigned or demoted—two-thirds of the city's precinct commanders in all. The crime rate plummeted.

Criminologists continued to debate the effect of "broken windows" policing and Compstat, but the homicide rate continued to go down. It was 1,177 in 1995, 770 in 1997, 664 in 1999. Compstat quickly became one of the most admired innovations in American policing in decades.

But in the midst of the good news, some New Yorkers began to see a dark side to the aggressive style of policing that the New York system encouraged. Former Mayor Dinkins complained to the press that Bratton and Giuliani "seem more interested in 'kicking ass' than increasing peace." In 1999, when members of the elite Street Crimes Unit opened fire on Amadou Diallo, an unarmed African immigrant, much of New York's African-American leadership came out to protest against the NYPD.

Boston wasn't having those sorts of problems. And its murder rate was falling just as dramatically, from 152 in 1990 to 31 in 1999. Police officials there were quick to assert that the reason was their law enforcement philosophy, based on social service and neighborhood relations, not on the cold statistics and hard-nosed street tactics of the cops in New York. "It wasn't just tough enforcement," says Commissioner Paul Evans. "It was going out to the community, trying to prevent crime, trying to identify alternatives for young people, after-school programs, jobs." In short, he argues, it was the result of an extraordinary web of partnerships between local, state and federal law enforcement agencies, nonprofit organizations and social service agencies, and the city's African-American clergy.

The Boston strategy emerged, unlike New York's, not so much from numbers but from one horrifying event. In May 1992, a group of youths burst in on a funeral being held for a slain gang member at Morning Star Baptist Church in Mattapan. In the presence of 300 panicked witnesses, the youths repeatedly stabbed one of the mourners, whose presence they viewed as an insult to the deceased.

Boston responded to the Morning Star attack (and a string of youth homicides that followed) with a flurry of programs and partnerships, such as the 10 Point

> "[Boston's approach] wasn't just tough enforcement [like New York's]," says Commissioner Paul Evans. "It was going out to the community, trying to prevent crimes..."

Coalition, a group of African-American ministers who decided to reach out to kids on the street and put aside their distrust of the police. The homicide rate started going down, but rather slowly. Between 1992 and late 1996, it declined to 70 deaths per year—a big improvement from 1990, but more than twice as many as the city's historical average.

Then in mid-1996, Boston's police added something new to its network of partnerships—the idea of "focused deterrence." It was the inspiration of an unlikely coalition: front-line police officers from the Youth Violence Strike Force; a neighborhood probation office; the Department of Youth Services; the Streetworkers, a youth outreach program; the FBI and Drug Enforcement Administration; the U.S. Attorney and county D.A.; and researchers from Harvard University's Kennedy School of Government. "Focused deterrence" began not with social work but with the recognition that a relatively small number of hard-core gang members were responsible for most of the carnage in Boston.

At first, this was a discouraging finding: These hard-core offenders scarcely seemed the type who would walk away from drug-dealing and gun-running for a temporary summer job. But officers in Boston decided to turn these kids' very criminality against them. Because these kids were so criminally active, they could potentially be deterred or punished in a number of ways. As the officers put it, there were "a lot of levers to pull." Kids who were on probation could be supervised more closely; kids who had been referred to the Department of Youth Services could be taken into protective custody and even transferred to rural western Massachusetts; kids who were repeat offenders could be subjected to federal prosecution and sent out of state.

The Youth Violence Strike Force had achieved good results using a limited trial of focused deterrence on a gun-happy Cape Verdean gang on Boston's crime-plagued Wendover Street: not only had there been an immediate drop in gun-related incidents, but many kids gave up their weapons voluntarily. Now the same approach was employed citywide, with police, probation officers and prosecutors all warning gang members that gun violence would bring down on them the full attention not only of local authorities but of the U.S. Attorney's Office, the DEA and the ATF.

This marked a major change from the way Boston police had dealt with homicide "hot spots" in the past. "Years ago," said Commissioner Evans, "we'd have shootings in neighborhoods and we'd do saturation patrols and warrant sweeps and we were going after anybody and everybody. Now . . . we know what's going on; we know who's involved in the shooting; we call them all in; they're all on probation; we use the levers. We tell them, 'Fellows, the violence stops. . . . We're not going to let you kill each other.'"

In August 1996, Boston police and federal agents arrested 21 members of the Intervale Posse, one of Boston's most notorious gangs. Then, in a series of forums with other gangs in the city, the Ceasefire group quickly got the word out: If the shooting doesn't stop, this will happen to you, too. One notorious gangster found with a single bullet in his possession was sent to federal prison for 10 years. Soon the city's homicide rate was in a gratifying freefall.

Boston isn't the only city where this sort of intervention worked. Minneapolis, a city not normally associated with violent crime, experienced an explosion of gang-related violence in the mid-1990s. In 1997, it responded with a Ceasefire program. The same thing happened as in Boston—homicides fell dramatically. The city ended the year with 58 murders, down from 86 the previous year. In Stockton, California, gang-related killings fell from 20 to four with Boston-style tactics. Indianapolis and the city of Winston-Salem, North Carolina, reported similar results.

New York, meanwhile, was finding equal success with its different emphasis. Maple, the NYPD's chief strategist, stressed four guiding principles: "accurate and timely intelligence," "rapid deployment," "effective tactics and strategies" and "relentless follow-up and assessment." Partnerships and reeducation meetings were not at the top of his list of effective methods.

Nearly all the media coverage of New York's declining crime rate stressed Compstat and the constant use of computer data. But within the department, many believed that the key element in keeping crime down was the fourth one on Maple's list: follow-up.

"We're great at initiatives, but it's the follow-up that's crucial," notes Elizabeth Glazer, chief of staff of the New York City Department of Investigation. "What Compstat does is ensure that there's always follow-up."

And that may offer a partial clue to the puzzling discrepancy between Boston and New York crime rates in the past couple of years. Researchers who have studied Ceasefire-style interventions say they are weak when it comes to follow-up. They tend to produce dramatic initial results—and then fall apart. "They're hard to sustain," admits Harvard criminologist David Kennedy. "They take an awful lot of assembly. They're basically simple, but it takes a lot of moving parts to put it together. Some are so dramatically effective that there comes a time when there's really not much work to do. People gather around a table and ask each other, 'Has there been any violence?' People say, 'No,' and if that goes on long enough, the partnership weakens. Violence picks up and people move on, and the script has been forgotten."

As Boston's homicide rate was plunging in the late '90s, the Ceasefire group met less frequently. Key players were promoted or moved on to other tasks. The grant that had supported work on the program at the Kennedy School was phased out. While the Youth Violence Strike Force continued to hold an occasional Ceasefire forum, the gang members no longer received the sustained "focused deterrence" they once did. They didn't seem to need it.

In retrospect, it seems they may have needed it after all. By the spring of 2000, Boston's violent crime remission was over. After years of decreases, the number of gun incidents in the gang strongholds of Roxbury and Dorchester started to creep up again. The increased gunplay soon translated into a rising homicide rate. In 2000, Boston had 40 homicides. In 2001, the number jumped to 66.

There are plenty of explanations for that change that avoid the issue of police tactics altogether, and stress demographics. Many believe, for example, that the return of homicide is connected to convicts completing their prison terms and returning to their old neighborhood, settling old feuds and trying to regain control of the drug trade.

"You want my quick and dirty analysis for the jump in the numbers?" probation officer Billy Stewart told the *Boston Herald*. "Simple: They're b-a-a-ck! . . . and they're back smarter. They're back embittered. And that seasoned bitterness makes them extremely dangerous."

Some statistics do buttress this argument. A decade ago, the average age of the city's homicide perpetrators was between 20 and 25. Last year, the department says, it was 31. The average age of inmates released from the Suffolk County House of Correction in January 2001 was 32—considerably older than the prison population a decade ago. "When you look at the Boston Miracle or the Boston model," says Commissioner Evans, "it was really geared toward youth violence. Now what we've seen in the last year is a much older individual."

On the other hand, the release of prisoners back into the community is hardly a new phenomenon. The prisoner population at the Suffolk County House of Corrections peaked in 1999, when approximately 3,700 offenders were released. It's possible that these ex-cons are behind Boston's recent murder increase, but commanders in the field discount the notion. "I can look at some neighborhoods—Bowdoin, Geneva—a couple of guys got out of jail, and we saw things happen," says Captain Robert Dunford, "but in terms of citywide, no."

In contrast to the "ex-con" theory, some analysts say the explanation for increased homicide is exactly the opposite: a tough new batch of young kids. Back in the mid-1990s, criminologists such as James Alan Fox and John DiIulio were warning of a whole generation of "super predators"—teenage criminals more ruthless and more dangerous than any cohort that preceded them. "Although we would never use the term 'super predator,'" says the Reverend Eugene Rivers, co-chair of the National 10 Point Leadership Foundation, "this kid that we [have seen] emerging fits that description of that uncertain term. . . . A younger cohort of more violent young people [have been] surfacing."

There are problems with this explanation as well. Boston's youth population was growing steadily throughout the '90s, even as crime began to fall. In 1991, the percentage of homicide victims aged 24 and under (victim numbers generally track perpetrator numbers pretty well) was 48 percent. Last year, it was 41 percent. The story is much the same nationwide. According to a March report by the Urban Institute, a nonpartisan think tank in Washington, D.C., the youth population increased by 13 percent between 1990 and 2000. During that same period, the juvenile crime rate fell by a third, to its lowest level in two decades.

Given the inconsistencies in both of the demographic theories, it begins to seem more plausible to return to the issue of police strategy. And this is just what Boston is doing. However, rather than reinvigorating its efforts at "focused deterrence," the Boston police department seems to be redoubling its efforts at building partnerships, expanding social services and involving the community in the fight against crime.

This past January, the Boston police department laid out what it calls "Boston Strategy Part 2." It calls for redoubling the department's emphasis on "prevention, enforcement and intervention," for pushing more authority to the district commander level, and for creating a new law enforcement community coordinating group to direct the department's actions. "You can see with all of our strategies, we're not moving away from partnerships," says Superintendent Paul

Body Count

Number of homicides

	Boston	N.Y.
1985	87	1,384
1986	105	1,582
1987	76	1,672
1988	93	1,896
1989	99	1,905
1990	143	2,245
1991	113	2,154
1992	73	1,995
1993	98	1,946
1994	85	1,561
1995	96	1,177
1996	59	983
1997	43	770
1998	34	633
1999	31	664
2000	40	671
2001	66	642

Note: Data up through 1999 are from BJS, 2000-2001 are from PDs.

Source: Bureau of Justice Statistics, Boston Police Department, New York Police Department

Joyce. "You can't put the responsibility of dealing with crime issues on the police or on the probation officer; it's really too much."

That's the kind of sentiment that Giuliani and his police commissioners scoffed at. "I'm from the school of thought that the average citizen doesn't want to be engaged in patrolling their own neighborhood," says Bratton, the police commissioner who first introduced community policing to Boston in the early '90s, before becoming Giuliani's first commissioner in 1993. "When I come home at night, I don't want to be looking over my shoulder or coming upstairs to get my flashlight, my armband, and go out and patrol the neighborhood. That's what the police are for." Indeed, the idea that the police couldn't reduce crime on their own was one of the ideas that Giuliani and Bratton set out to demolish. When Bratton was appointed police commissioner, he promised Giuliani that under his watch the NYPD would reduce crime by 30 percent in three years—and it did.

The NYPD doesn't exactly repudiate the partnership idea. "It's critical," says Deputy Commissioner Michael Farrell, "that there be productive relationships with communities, particularly with cities that have as much diversity in their makeup as we do." On the other hand, Farrell acknowledges, the department's emphasis continues to be placed on those strategies it believes are working: Compstat and quality of life.

Boston police are hopeful that their new efforts will work, too. They say they're encouraged by early indications that the homicide increases are leveling off in 2002. They're optimistic that initiatives such as the prisoner reentry program and the ongoing efforts to provide more resources to district commanders will further depress crime rates.

Still, Superintendent Joyce doubts that Boston will soon return to the homicide levels of a couple of years ago. "Most likely, we've seen our best days," he admits. "Crime will move up. It's how you monitor that and how you deal with that as crime trends start to move up again."

Meanwhile, in the first quarter of 2002, the homicide rate in New York City was down another 29 percent.

22

Revising Sentences

Christopher Swope

State budget problems have sparked pragmatic, bipartisan debates about alternatives to incarceration.

In recent years, a "tough-on-crime" mentality defined corrections policies—for nonviolent drug offenders and murderers alike—nearly everywhere in America. Politicians in state after state voted for longer prison sentences, mandatory minimums and truth-in-sentencing laws. Despite its liberal leanings, Maryland was no exception. And the impact was predictable: Since 1988, Maryland's prison population has nearly doubled, from 13,600 to nearly 24,000.

Now, however, Maryland is ready to try a new approach. In April, the state legislature passed a law that will divert many convicted substance abusers away from pricey prison beds and into treatment instead. At the same time, the state is beefing up education and treatment programs for all inmates. Maryland is trying to put some correcting back into corrections.

If Maryland's shift from penal retribution toward rehabilitation sounds like something dreamed up by bleeding hearts, however, there's another surprise: Its leading proponent is a Republican. Governor Robert L. Ehrlich Jr. came into office last year pledging to get low-level drug offenders out of prison. "The war on drugs has been unsuccessful," Ehrlich says. "For Republican governors, that may have been an unsafe political statement to make 10, 15 or 20 years ago."

Maryland isn't the only state that's re-thinking the harsher sides of its punishment policies. In the past three years, about two-thirds of all states have lowered prison sentences or begun steering convicts into incarceration alternatives such as drug treatment or community corrections programs—and in many cases, Republican governors and/or legislators have been leading the way. Michigan recently

From *Governing*, July 2004.

repealed mandatory minimum sentences for drug crimes. Kansas last year mandated treatment for first-time drug abusers. And Connecticut this year loosened parole rules for nonviolent felons. There's a new shorthand phrase lawmakers of all stripes use to sell these policies to their constituents. Now they're getting "smart on crime."

Why the new attitude? The short answer is the states' recent budget crisis. After a decade of ratcheting up corrections budgets—states now spend nearly $40 billion on prisons—legislators suddenly found they had to prioritize whom they want locked up. It seems the budget crisis turned out to be a positive force for rational debate. "It allowed legislators and other elected officials to get past the partisanship that infected this issue," says Daniel Wilhelm, who monitors state sentencing policies for the Vera Institute of Justice in New York. "It broke that tough-on-crime/soft-on-crime dichotomy."

But money is not the only thing. The plunging crime rate since the early 1990s—due in part to tougher sentencing, many argue—means that crime isn't the volatile issue with the public that it was in 1994. Debate in statehouses today isn't as emotional and headline-driven as it used to be. Legislators are still toughening sentences for certain crimes—in particular, sexual offenses. But when it comes to low-level drug addicts and petty thieves, they're having genuine second thoughts about the efficacy and cost-effectiveness of prison as a correctional tool.

REFORM FROM THE RIGHT

Ironically, Republicans are best positioned politically to make that point. They've done such an effective job of branding Democrats as "soft on crime" that sentencing reform in many states had to come from the right, not the left. That's what happened in Texas, where Ray Allen, the Republican who chairs the House Corrections Committee, persuaded tough-talking conservatives to divert thousands of drug abusers out of prison and into treatment. "It opened up a real un-Republican can of worms

> "There's ample research showing that drug treatment is more effective at stopping crime."
>
> Republican Ray Allen, House Corrections Committee

for me," Allen says. "It was like Nixon going to China. Some of my colleagues said, 'Ray, what are you doing?' And I said, 'The only thing we can do.' We don't have the money to lock everybody up."

As in many states, the sentencing debate in Texas began with the budget. Facing a massive deficit last year, the legislature lopped $240 million from the two-year prison budget. As Allen scrounged for budget cuts, two facts jumped out at him. The first was that Texas had locked up more than 4,000 people on first-time drug-possession charges. That meant the state was spending millions of dollars, as Allen puts it, incarcerating people caught with less than a Sweet'N Low-size packet of cocaine or methamphetamine. The second fact had to do with the equity of sentencing around the state. It seems half of these first-timers were coming out of just one jurisdiction: Harris County. "What began as a budgetary search for expenses to cut," Allen says, "turned into some real questioning of what are we doing and why are we doing it."

Allen had seen members of his own family recover from drug addictions, and came to believe that first-time offenders deserved a shot at treatment before incarceration. His bill gave judges a range of sentencing options, from outpatient treatment to intensive inpatient care for the most serious addicts. The shift is projected to save Texas $117 million over five years. Allen is confident that it will also prove to be more effective public policy. "If we have to make choices, then low-level first-time offenders are the easy choice to make," Allen says. "There's ample research showing that drug treatment is more effective at stopping crime."

Some critics, however, argue that Texas and many other states are taking too simplistic an approach—making the same kind of mistake by diverting whole classes of criminals from prison that they did by putting them behind bars in the first place. "The pressure is there to free up beds," says Richard Kern, director of Virginia's sentencing commission. "But there's no sound methodology regarding how they're doing it."

Virginia was revisiting its sentencing priorities long before the fiscal crisis hit. It began switching to a data-driven approach to sentencing back in the mid-1990s. At the time, Virginia had just adopted a truth-in-sentencing law requiring violent felons to serve at least 85 percent of their sentences. Knowing that lockups would quickly fill with violent offenders, Kern's commission set out to free some space by reducing prison time for non-violent felons. Virginia still wound up building some new prisons, but not at the budget-busting rate that other states did.

What developed was a risk-based methodology in which judges set sentences much the way insurance companies set their rates. The sentencing commission analyzed thousands of criminal history records, looking for patterns of recidivism. What it found wasn't surprising—an unemployed, unmarried, 20-year-old drug offender is a greater risk than a working, married, 30-year-old drug offender—but for the first time that data is programmed into the judges' sentencing guidelines. High-risk convicts are more likely to do hard time. Low-risk felons are more likely to go into drug treatment or community corrections. "Judges can make a more informed decision on who they want to fill an expensive prison bed, and who they're willing to take a chance on putting into an alternative program," Kern says.

A THERAPEUTIC APPROACH

Maryland, too, is stepping up its individual assessment of criminals. The difference is that in Maryland the plan is for that to happen in prison, rather than in court. As part of a pilot program known as RESTART, all incoming prisoners will be evaluated for drug problems and mental illnesses. Case managers will tailor a treatment plan for each inmate, and begin making plans for housing, jobs and other transition issues nine months before release. Overall, it's a more therapeutic approach to hard time than Maryland has been accustomed to recently. "Guess what, 95 to 98 percent of inmates are coming out sooner or later," says corrections chief Mary Ann Saar. "We never asked ourselves what condition do we want these people in when they come out."

In Maryland's case, Saar insists, these changes aren't budget-driven at all. In fact, they'll cost at least $3 million more up front for expanding drug treatment services. If there's a cost savings, it will only become evident a few years from now—and that is only if the new philosophy actually stops ex-cons from becoming cons again. "The cycle has been addiction, offense, incarceration, keep the addiction, get out and re-offend," says Governor Ehrlich. "We didn't understand the importance of treatment behind the wall."

23

Deadly Strains

Christopher Conte

SARS, West Nile virus and bioterrorism are the big scares. But the greater threat is the gradual erosion of public health services.

From *Governing*, June 2003.

When Seattle received $2 million in federal money last year to prepare for a possible biological, chemical or radiological attack, public health director Alonzo Plough was relieved. Along with his counterparts around the country, Plough had watched new health threats multiply while public health budgets stagnated. Finally, he thought, the city would have funds to work out emergency procedures with area police departments, fire officials and other "first responders." He'd be able to hire new staff to help combat naturally emerging diseases as well.

Things haven't worked out as he planned. No sooner had he launched a terrorism-planning effort than he had to drop it because the federal government ordered its sweeping smallpox-vaccination program. That task tied up so much of Plough's staff that they were slow to detect a new outbreak of tuberculosis among Seattle's homeless population. As officials scrambled to catch up with that problem, SARS, or severe acute respiratory syndrome, emerged in China. Almost immediately, the mysterious disease started showing up in travelers returning from Asia. Plough had to divert staff from the unfinished smallpox and tuberculosis efforts and put them to work to keep the new disease from spreading in Seattle.

Plough's job has become a continuous exercise in triage. The reason: His department has too much to do and too few resources. "In my 20 years in public health, I have never seen such a layering of challenges, all with fairly equal urgency and all drawing on diminishing core funding," he says. "We aren't providing anything near the web of protection that's needed."

The problem isn't unique to Seattle. All over the country, local public health departments are struggling to keep on top of a growing list of health threats. Terrorism may turn out to be the least of their concerns. Changing patterns of land use are bringing people into contact with dangerous new microbes such as the West Nile virus and the coronavirus, which is believed to be the cause of SARS. Globalization is spreading these diseases more rapidly than human immune systems or modern science can build defenses. And many see a scenario in which the familiar influenza virus abruptly morphs into a deadly pandemic that the U.S. Centers for Disease Control and Prevention estimates could kill as many as 300,000 people. On top of that, old maladies such as tuberculosis have started appearing in drug-resistant strains; sexually transmitted diseases such as HIV and syphilis are on the rise because many people have become complacent about them; and chronic diseases such as asthma and diabetes are becoming more prevalent due to environmental and behavioral factors.

Local public health leaders widely agree with Plough that their tools and budgets haven't kept pace with these challenges. Despite the growing threat from communicable diseases, for instance, state health agencies employ fewer epidemiologists today (1,400) than they did in 1992 (1,700). When a professional association this fall and winter asked state health laboratory directors to rate their preparedness to handle a terrorist chemical attack, half scored their own facilities "1" or "2" on a scale of 1 to 10, with 1 being the poorest mark. And a Little Hoover Commission in California declared in April that the state's "public health infrastructure is in poor repair, providing less protection than it should against everyday hazards and unprepared to adequately protect us against the remote but substantial threats we now face." The commission noted, among other things, that only 20 percent of reportable diseases and conditions were actually reported to public health officials, and that at one key health laboratory, only 60 of 100 positions were filled.

As California goes, so goes the nation. Updating a 1988 report that concluded the country's entire public health system was in "disarray," the National Institute of Medicine said last fall that the system is plagued by "outdated and vulnerable technologies, lack of real-time surveillance and epidemiological systems, ineffective and fragmented communications networks, (and) incomplete domestic preparedness and emergency response capabilities."

STARVING THE SYSTEM

Policy makers are aware of the holes in the public health system. Last year, the U.S. Congress provided $940 million to help local health departments cope with emerging threats. Local health officials hoped to use the funds not only to prepare for terrorist attacks but also to improve their ability to conduct general surveillance and cope with natural outbreaks such as SARS.

The federal smallpox-vaccination program has absorbed nearly all of the funds so far, however, making "dual use" largely a chimera. Indeed, many local officials say the federal government hasn't even provided enough money for them to prepare adequately for possible terrorist attacks, let alone cope with naturally occurring diseases that already are killing people. In particular, the

---

No Simple Task

Washington State's public health system is trying to meet five basic standards:

- **Promote understanding of health issues**—by assessing community health and disseminating findings.
- **Protect people from disease**—by maintaining surveillance and reporting systems, developing plans for handling communicable disease outbreaks, and establishing procedures for disease investigation and control.
- **Assure a safe and healthy environment**—by educating the public, tracking environmental health risks and illnesses, enforcing health-related environmental regulations, and being prepared to respond to environmental disasters.
- **Promote healthy living**—by providing prevention, early intervention and outreach services, and involving the community in efforts to prevent illness.
- **Help people get needed services**—by providing information to the public on existing health services, analyzing what factors affect access to critical services, and developing plans to reduce specific gaps in access.

For more: www.doh.wa.gov/standards/default.htm

Is Information Technology The Answer?

Public health departments are harnessing computers to the task of identifying and tracking disease outbreaks, but they have a long way to go.

New York City and other jurisdictions are experimenting with "syndromic surveillance," which involves collecting information on symptoms from disparate sources—911 calls, emergency room visits, possibly even drugstore purchases—and using computers to search for patterns. A surge in drugstore sales of Pepto-Bismol, for instance, might indicate that the community has been hit by a new gastrointestinal disorder. "This could give us potentially an early-warning system," notes Dorothy Teeter, chief of health operations for the Public Health Department of Seattle and King County. But such fancy new computer systems may be unaffordable, especially at a time of tight budgets. Teeter estimates it would cost Seattle $10 million and take 10 years to create an effective system.

Costs aside, such ideas have their skeptics. "It's worth doing, but let's not put our eggs solely in the basket of automated systems," says Paul Wiesner, director of the DeKalb County Board of Health in Georgia. Wiesner argues that medicine is still an "art," and that there is no substitute for the judgment and instincts of health professionals. Moreover, he adds, public health departments need much more than new software: "We need to focus on all aspects of infrastructure, including training."

Meanwhile, health departments could take less costly steps to improve their technological capabilities. The Kansas Department of Health has developed a Web-based communication system that enables it to exchange information on emerging health issues with local health departments. That's a step in the right direction, but many health departments don't even exchange information across the hallway, let alone across the state. While many epidemiologists use geographic information systems to track diseases, for instance, public health departments rarely integrate their efforts. "Agencies in all 50 states are using GIS for disease tracking, but their efforts aren't coordinated," says Bill Davenhall, a manager for the software company ESRI in Redland, California.

—C.C.

preoccupation with smallpox has set back efforts to plan defenses against a host of other potential biological weapons, including plague, tularemia, botulism toxin, and viral hemorrhagic fever; chemical agents such as ricin and sarin gas; and a possible "dirty bomb" laden with radioactive materials.

Many public health officials such as Plough also say they lack secure communications networks linking them with other first responders. On top of that, public health officials have received no money to start educating the public about what people should do if there is a biological or chemical attack. "We are writing plans, but plans by themselves don't automatically translate into increased capacity," says Jeffrey Duchin, chief of the Seattle health department's Communicable Disease Control, Epidemiology and Immunization section. "We aren't committing the resources needed to turn them into living documents."

Federal officials counter by saying that state and local agencies would have trouble absorbing many more funds than Congress has provided. But the increased federal funding has had an unintended side effect: Fiscally strapped states and localities have seized on it to cut their own public health spending. In Colorado's Larimer County, for instance, a $700,000 slash in state funds for public health more than erased a gain of $100,000 in federal money. Even with new federal funds, the Boston Public Health Commission has been forced to cut scores of positions.

"Overall, we are losing money in the public health budgets in the 50 states, despite funds for terrorism preparedness," says Dr. George Benjamin, executive director of the American Public Health Association. Benjamin formerly was health director for Maryland, which has received federal funds to increase its epidemiological staff but has been forced to cut its state-financed food safety program.

Perhaps more troubling, public health departments have had to rely increasingly on revenues that come with many strings attached. For years, they have sought wherever possible to support programs with grants or with user fees, such as charges for restaurant inspections. But you can't charge a mosquito when you test it for West Nile virus, and while you can persuade public and private grant-makers to provide funds for programs aimed at recognized ills such as breast cancer, nobody seems to want to pay for ongoing operations or general preparedness. "There is a much greater investment in public health and public health programs now than there was a decade ago," notes Mary Selecky, Washington State's secretary of health and president of the Association of State and Territorial Health Officers. "But there is far less flexibility in how the dollars are spent. We are driven by categorical funding."

Seattle's health department, considered by many to be dynamic and forward-looking, illustrates the problem. Its overall budget has grown impressively, reaching $187.9 million this year from $77.5 million in 1993. But almost all the increases have been in programs supported by user fees and grants. County government gives it $28 million to run its emergency medical services; a federal program provides $5 million to support AIDS victims (but not to help prevent spread of the HIV virus that causes AIDS); and the Robert Wood Johnson Foundation donated money for the development of a program to deal with asthma.

None of these funds pay for basic public health operations, including surveillance to detect new disease outbreaks, investigators to track the spread of diseases and a host of prevention-oriented activities. This year, funding for "core" activities totaled $30.9 million, barely up from $30.1 million 10 years ago. The current West Nile virus and TB outbreak alone would more than eat up that increase this year. And that doesn't take inflation or Seattle's substantial population growth into account. Per capita, core funding has dropped from $21.34 in 1997 to $16.67 today.

WAITING TIME

Behind those numbers lies a slow deterioration in the department's ability to address long-term problems or react quickly to changing conditions. When SARS hit this

> "Overall, we are losing money in the public health budgets in the 50 states, despite funds for terrorism preparedness."
>
> Dr. George Benjamin, executive director of the American Public Health Association

spring, for instance, the department couldn't follow up on a number of hepatitis B cases. The rate of childhood immunizations has fallen since 1998, while cases of measles and pertussis (whooping cough) have increased, and new TB cases are at a 30-year high.

When a team belatedly began combating the TB outbreak, it moved ahead in fits and starts. The key to stamping out such an outbreak is painstaking detective work: Investigators interview known victims, identify places they frequent and other people with whom they have come in contact, and then follow up those leads with additional screening and information-gathering. Eventually, such searches enable them to track a disease's movements, isolate it and stamp it out. By this spring, investigators had collected more than 50 pieces of information on each of some 528 actual or potential carriers. But the information lay unanalyzed for precious weeks because the outbreak team couldn't find an epidemiologist to work on it.

"Somewhere in there is the answer to where and how this got kicked off, and where it's going next," says Linda Lake, a consultant who leads the outbreak team and also chairs the Washington State Board of Health. "But the department is too busy dealing with SARS or other things. When you find somebody to help, it's always part-time, it's always for a short period of time, and it always takes them away from something else."

Outbreaks don't occur on a neat schedule, and there inevitably will be times that are busier than others. Even the most ardent public health advocates don't expect voters to pay to have public health workers waiting around for the next outbreak the way firefighters are paid to be available at all times. But there's a backlog of tasks that could keep the public health workforce busy when there are no emergencies.

Currently, the Seattle department can afford just 10 public health nurses for an intensive counseling program called "Best Beginnings," which has been proven to reduce a wide range of health problems affecting children of first-time teenage mothers. That's enough to reach only about one fourth of the mothers who need the service. Meanwhile, a strategy for working with schools to encourage teenagers to drink less soda and get more exercise—keys to reining in a near epidemic of juvenile diabetes— remains on the drawing boards for lack of funds, as does a major initiative to help Seattle's health providers incorporate ideas about safer behavior, better diets and exercise into their daily interactions with patients.

Although public health departments could make good use of additional funds, public skepticism about government and taxes usually trumps proposals to increase their resources. In Washington State, public health advocates were optimistic early this year after the Republican and Democratic leaders of the Senate cosponsored a bill that would ask citizens to vote on whether to raise property taxes by $151 million to support local public health agencies. But health advocates lost heart after a poll commissioned by the Washington State Association of Counties and others showed the idea was far from assured of winning voter approval.

The lack of support demonstrates, in part, how reliance on categorical funding has become a political trap for public health agencies. Victims of specific illness often lobby tirelessly and effectively for funds to address their afflictions, but it's hard to find citizens who feel the same degree of passion for quiet government activities that keep people healthy. Public health workers have the passion, but it doesn't get them very far. "People think they're just asking for a handout." says Pat Libbey, executive director of the National Association of County and City Health Officials.

REALITY CHECK

Clearly, voters expect more than they are willing to pay for. The Association of Counties poll showed, for instance, that 96 percent of Washington voters believe the services public health agencies provide are "very important." Yet the state Department of Health estimates that total public health spending in the state— about $507 million annually—amounts to only one third of what public health agencies need to do the job they currently are expected to do. The department says only one half of local public health agencies are doing reasonably well in meeting 202 performance measures developed for them.

For Carolyn Edmonds, a member of the county council for Seattle's King County and a former state legislator, the disparity between expectations and reality represents a political quandary. On one hand, she wonders whether advocates should present the budget situation in starker terms—by warning voters, for instance, that the current stringency is forcing public health officials to put fighting infectious diseases ahead of making sure children are immunized. "Public health has shied away from doing that," she says, "but maybe we're going to have to be more blatant" about what the trade-offs are.

On the other hand, Edmonds fears that voters won't believe leaders who say current budget and tax policy require such decisions: "People go to restaurants expecting that the food will be cooked properly. They go to a drinking fountain expecting that they won't get sick from the water. There is a built-in assumption that they will be taken care of."

Eventually, she says, the assumption will be disproved—maybe not in dramatic ways but slowly and less noticeably. "Response times will be slower. There will be fewer prevention measures," she says. "More people will get sick. People will die."

The end result, in Edmonds' view, may not be as shocking as, say, terrorists detonating a dirty bomb in a baseball stadium. Nevertheless, it will be very real and might have been avoided.

24

Maine's Medical Gamble

Penelope Lemov

Can broader insurance coverage bring health care costs under control? One state is betting on it.

The tiny business district in Blue Hill has all the quaint little shops you'd expect in a small Maine town: pottery studio, art gallery, even a white clapboard "take-out" lobster shack. It looks idyllic. And if you're a tourist, it is charming. But if you work on Main Street in Blue Hill, life isn't quite so carefree. The odds are your job won't give you health insurance. Few of the small businesses—and Blue Hill is, like much of Maine, a town of mom-and-pop enterprises—offer their employees any significant coverage at all.

"I used to, but I don't anymore," says Tina Allen, who runs Fairwinds Florist with the help of three employees. "If it were more affordable, I would. It's important. But I can't even do it for myself."

It's the same story at Blue Hill Books, where Nicholas Sichterman says he can't offer coverage to his one employee because of the expense. Out of his own pocket, Sichterman buys a very limited form of coverage—catastrophic coverage—for himself, his wife and son. It costs him $6,500 a year. He'd like to have a comprehensive policy and offer it to his employee, but it's beyond his reach.

That is a situation that the administration of Governor John Baldacci is aiming to change. Last year, Baldacci and his health policy adviser, Trish Riley, persuaded the legislature to pass a multifaceted health care program, known as Dirigo (Latin for "I lead," the state motto). Dirigo has as its goal universal health care for Maine residents, and it is the most far-reaching attempt at such coverage that any state has attempted.

Dirigo is a complex plan with interdependent parts that touch on everything from hospital costs to chronic disease management and fitness education. "What Maine has said, and they are right in say-

From *Governing,* November 2004.

ing it, is that you have to address access, quality and cost simultaneously," says Alan Weil, executive director of the National Academy for State Health Policy. Weil points out that little in Dirigo is new, that most of the bits and pieces have been tried before by others. "What's unique," he adds, "is pulling them all together and making them fit."

All of which makes for an admirable piece of legislation. But will it work? Since the legislation was signed into law in June 2003, Riley, the Dirigo staff and the seven commissions and boards that form the backbone of the program have been struggling to implement some of the interlocking parts. With a program so massive and all-encompassing, it will take years to put all the pieces in place—to get hospitals to sign on to cost containment; to see what health services the people of Maine are willing to have regionalized; to educate the never-before-insured to make use of wellness programs. It will take even longer to take the measure of overall success or failure.

INSURANCE FIRST

At the moment, one piece of the program is attracting the bulk of the attention, in Maine and in the rest of the country: securing health coverage for workers in small businesses, such as the ones in Blue Hill. "There are a lot of bells and whistles on this legislation that are important to pay attention to," says Andrew Coburn, director of the Institute for Health Policy at the University of Southern Maine, "but insurance is what everyone is focused on right now."

In fact, many health experts believe that Dirigo as a whole will fail or succeed based on its acceptance or rejection by small-business owners. That may or may not be true—controlling hospital costs is also crucial—but there's no disputing that insurance for small businesses is key to the overall program's well being. At the moment, 14 percent of the Maine population lacks basic health coverage, and four out of five of the uninsured work for small businesses, which employ 70 percent of the state workforce. In 2004, the cost of health insurance premiums paid by employers increased nationally by an average of 11.2 percent—the fourth consecutive year of double-digit growth—but premiums for some small businesses leaped by as much as two or three times that rate.

Small-business owners are reacting to inflation the only way some of them can: They dump coverage, never pick it up in the first place or muddle through and try to make ends meet in other ways. Speaking as a businessman, Christopher St. John, the executive director of the Maine Center for Economic Policy, says it is "very daunting to the enterprise's budget to sustain premium increases of 15 percent to 20 percent over the last several years. It impacts our ability to do our work—whether we hire or not hire, use consultants or part-time people." The center is a small nonprofit business that employs four people.

The coverage gap for workers in small business reverberates throughout the entire health care system. Hospitals, required to deliver services to all Maine residents regardless of ability to pay, get stuck with the bad debt and charity care bill for the uninsured. They make up that cost by raising rates on other consumers who have insurance policies. Insurance companies, in turn, pass on their increased costs by raising monthly premiums, creating a vicious cycle that leaves even more Maine families and businesses unable to afford coverage, and making the underlying problem that much worse. "Bad debt and charity care is a hidden tax," Trish Riley says.

The cost to hospitals of treating uninsured patients is about $40 billion a year across the country, according to Urban Institute health researchers Jack Hoadley and John Holahan. In Maine alone, it is $270 million a year, an amount equivalent to 20 percent of insurance premiums.

Dirigo's strategists know that if they can create a workable system for financing the coverage of small-business employees, they will have taken an important step toward solving the other pieces of the puzzle. Under the terms of the law, the state is mandated to work with insurance companies to develop an affordable product specifically for the small-business market. The businesses themselves must pick up 60 percent of the premium for individual coverage of each employee; the employee pays the rest. For those whose earnings are too low to make the 40 percent share affordable, the state offers a subsidy—not just the 40 percent individual portion but, in the case of married workers with children, subsidized premiums that cover the entire family.

In the first year, the money to pay these subsidies will come from a state appropriation. After that, they are supposed to be paid for by savings that hospitals will realize as a result of lower charity-care and bad-debt costs and by assessments on insurance premium revenues. The assessments are supposed to be levied only if the health care cost savings materialize.

It took the state a year to find an insurance company to underwrite a small-business insurance plan. Only one firm, Anthem Blue Cross Blue Shield of Maine, bid on the job. But on October 4, health coverage for small-business employees went on sale under the Dirigo Choice umbrella for the first time.

MEASURING SUCCESS

In the first week of Dirigo Choice's appearance in the market, Anthem and the Dirigo office fielded thousands of calls for information and price quotes. Whether those inquiries will turn into enrollment is anyone's guess. But Dirigo is not leaving anything to chance. The program has been holding small business forums and consumer information sessions and will continue the effort through the end of November. "We're trying to educate people and make them aware of the insurance," says former legislator Charlene Rydell, one of the program's original sponsors.

An informal survey of a dozen or so small businesses in and around Blue Hill and nearby Ellsworth, conducted just before the start of the enrollment period, found that most had heard about Dirigo but few were sold on it. Nick Sichterman of Blue Hill Books thought the premiums still sounded too high for him. Tina Allen, the florist whose family is now covered by a plan her husband pays for, said she had heard the governor talking about Dirigo and might look into it. Several business owners said they planned to check it out, but others either didn't see that the employee subsidy would help them or expressed resentment at the intrusion of the state. "The entire thing smacks too much of socialism for my taste," said one small-business owner.

The state won't have a final count on the number of policies sold until January 1, 2005, when the coverage actually takes effect. But even those numbers won't provide a definitive evaluation. It is far from clear how "success" can even be measured.

For example, there is a real possibility that many business owners who say yes to Dirigo will be ones who are already covering their employees and are simply looking for a better deal. "They will find the subsidy attractive," predicts health economist Christopher St. John, "but only in comparison to other comprehensive-benefit packages. People who want barebones coverage won't be interested." If St. John is right, then the only achievement might be a slowdown in the number of businesses that give up coverage due to escalating premiums. That would be a plus but wouldn't do much to alleviate the rising bad-debt and charity-care costs.

THE BOSTON FACTOR

If the insurance plan is a key to Dirigo's overall success, containing hospital costs—which the insurance piece is supposed to help do—is at the heart of the matter. Maine's hospital costs are significantly higher than national and regional averages, and it's not just because of the bad-debt and charity-care problem. Maine also has more hospital beds per capita and higher utilization rates than the rest of New England. Although the state is 40th in the country in median household income, it is 11th in health care spending per capita. "The people of Maine," says St. John, "have Arkansas-level incomes with Massachusetts-level health care tastes."

There is, in fact, something of a "Boston factor" at work in Maine. Residents have access to Boston's internationally renowned hospitals and want to have in Portland or Kennebunkport the top-of-the-line care they've seen there.

It's hard to argue with excellence, but the result of Maine citizens' high expectations is a considerable amount of costly duplication of service. That duplication is certain to be a major target of the drive to cut overall health care costs. "We could safely slow down investment in high-end stuff and pick and choose more carefully," St. John says. "It's a matter of fierce debate."

Part of that debate is coming to a head over whether Maine's hospitals will agree to a certificate-of-need program that lim-

Bookstore owner Nicholas Sichterman thinks the premiums in the state program may still be too high to insure his family and one employee.

its the use of scarce health resources to create additional hospital beds and treatment centers. Riley is putting a lot of effort into establishing criteria for acceptable capital investments by health care institutions—in other words, a budget for approvable projects. So far, Maine hospitals have been chafing at the idea of a strict cap on improving capital structures and keeping current with technology. "We don't want to see Maine's excellent health care system deteriorate relative to contiguous states," warns Scott Bullock, president of MaineGeneral Health, a hospital in Waterville, who also sits on Dirigo's hospital study commission.

While Dirigo and the hospitals struggle with the capital investment issue, the hospital study commission is looking at proposals to reorganize hospital care on a regional basis and recommend consolidation or elimination of services where appropriate—again, to help tamp down health care costs. During legislative debate on Dirigo, the state's business community let lawmakers know it wanted action taken to slow the rate of increase in health care costs. But whether businesses will press for regional solutions is uncertain. Some companies that have argued forcefully for lower insurance premiums tend to become less enthusiastic when the idea of restricting hospital expansion comes up. "Now that we're doing things," says Trish Riley, "we get, 'Whoa, wait a minute. We didn't mean do that.'"

But the creators of the program intend to keep trying. This winter, Dirigo will run a series of town meetings called Tough Choices. Citizens will be called together to talk about what kind of health care they want, where they need what kind of services and where the health care system should be investing money.

The Tough Choices agenda underlines how complicated an undertaking Dirigo is. "Health care is a big, messy place to work," says NASHP's Weil. "Any state faces a lot of hurdles if their goal is universal coverage with cost containment and quality improvement. It's too early to say where Dirigo will end up. But the pieces are the ones you'd want to try."

25 The Left Behind Syndrome

Alan Greenblatt

The federal government is telling school systems exactly what they must accomplish. It isn't doing much to help them accomplish it.

By almost any measure, Montgomery High School, located in horsey Somerset County, New Jersey, is a tremendous success. The school boasts the third-highest average SAT scores in the state, and ranks in the top 3 percent in both reading and math. The federal Department of Education has named Montgomery a U.S. Blue Ribbon School. "I went to private school and considered it for my children, until I found Montgomery to be of similar caliber," says William Middlebrook, who has sent two daughters to the school.

Yet Montgomery High failed its attempt to meet the requirements of the federal government's No Child Left Behind education law. That 2002 statute demands a 95 percent participation rate on testing day, so that schools won't somehow discourage weaker students from taking the tests. Montgomery has 29 students signed up for special education, and two of them didn't show up on the day standardized tests were given out, making for an unacceptable 93 percent participation rate. The U.S. Department of Education has since softened the requirement slightly so that schools can average 95 percent over two years, but even under those rules, embarrassments like the one in New Jersey are certain to keep happening.

Making sure that virtually all students in a given area are tested equally is a legitimate goal. But as the Montgomery example attests, sometimes what looks good on paper doesn't play out too well in the real world. Under No Child Left Behind, any failure is a complete failure. And there are lots of ways a school can fail, even if it is doing its day-to-day job extremely well.

One of the major innovations of the law is to force schools to break down test results by numerous demographic subgroups,

From *Governing*, September 2004.

reflecting race, income level and proficiency in English. There are as many as three dozen different subgroups in all. Individual kids cut across the subgroups. A special education student who is a Latino from a low-income home is counted in 10 different subgroups across the NCLB grid. If she can't pass muster, she'll throw the school into jeopardy 10 different ways. As Montgomery High found out, even having her stay home sick on test day can cause real problems. Perverse results of this sort aren't playing too well with teachers, school administrators, parents or state and local officials. "This whole system is punitive," says David Shreve, an education specialist at the National Conference of State Legislatures, "and designed to identify problem schools without really dealing with the problems that are being uncovered."

CONSERVATIVE DOUBTS

The No Child Left Behind law, promoted by President George W. Bush and approved with bipartisan support in Congress, has given the federal government a huge new say in public education, at relatively little cost to the U.S. Treasury. The law has prompted some states to recalibrate their curriculum and educational efforts in positive ways. But those who have been stuck with both the expense and the job of making the law work are starting to wonder whether it's worth the attempt, if even a high-performing school ends up failing anyway.

This year, more than half the states considered legislation protesting No Child Left Behind, including resolutions calling on Congress to change or repeal it, bills to take schools out of the federal testing regimen (forfeiting federal dollars in the process), and others to block the use of state and local money to support the tests. "Everybody will fail," predicts Jim Rosborg, superintendent of schools in Belleville, Illinois, about 20 miles southeast of St. Louis. "Why have a penal system if you're going to throw everybody in jail?"

That school administrators and state officials are starting to push back hard against the new law and its strictures is a surprising turn of events, in many ways. No Child Left Behind grew out of the state-generated accountability movement in education, based on the idea that regular testing would allow teachers and schools to be judged by measurable criteria. In the 1990s, virtually every state passed requirements for new standardized tests. NCLB simply went further, requiring more ongoing testing and higher standards for teacher qualification.

To those who believe in this approach, the important issue is not whether teachers and school administrators find NCLB disturbing to budgets and to the status quo, but whether the law promises greater opportunity to kids who need it the most. "The basic idea was that all kids can learn, and if all kids can learn, schools should be held accountable for their progress," says William L. Taylor, chairman of the Citizens' Commission on Civil Rights and a leading liberal supporter of the law. If NCLB is abandoned or seriously weakened, he warns, "we will see more and more people leaving public schools."

Despite the complaints, no state has so far decided to opt out of the requirements. Vermont has come the closest, passing a law that allows individual districts to make that choice for themselves. But the concerns are serious in much of the country, and especially in conservative states, among them Virginia, Utah, Nebraska and Oklahoma, where the law is being viewed as the worst sort of federal bullying. "The entire conversation about this has gone from an education conversation to a political conversation," says Doug Christensen, commissioner of education in Nebraska. "Every state legislator, whether they like the idea or not, ought to be angry that the evolution of No Child Left Behind absolutely excluded them."

Those favoring No Child Left Behind tend to argue that the intensity of the criticism is itself a sign that the law is strong, appropriate medicine for a serious malady. When the president of the National Education Association called No Child Left Behind a "formula for failure" at the union's annual meeting—the group is considering a lawsuit challenging it—attorney Sandy Kress, who was a top adviser to Bush during NCLB's formulation, says he took it as evidence that the law is working. "It was the

> *Fear of flunking*
> *'Everybody will fail.'*
>
> Jim Rosborg, superintendent of schools in Belleville, Illinois

intention of this law to challenge the status quo," Kress says. "This is proof positive that it's succeeding."

That may be overly hopeful. With state legislators, school superintendents, teachers unions and many parents and media organs complaining so regularly and so loudly about the law's perceived flaws, including its betrayal of federalism, it's suddenly become a real question whether the law can retain enough support to survive.

HIGH HURDLES

The clear intent of No Child Left Behind is to make sure that school districts instill the same mastery of basic skills in minorities and the disadvantaged as they do in middle-class white children. Currently, almost half of all Hispanic and African-American students fail to graduate from high school. Those who do graduate, on average, trail several years behind white and Asian peers in basic skills. "Those are the kids whose needs are most likely to be swept under the rug," says Andrew Rotherham of the Progressive Policy Institute, a moderate Democratic think tank. "In a lot of states, what you're talking about are tests about pretty basic reading and numeracy. It's what middle-class parents expect and demand of their schools and would not tolerate for a moment if their schools were not imparting to their children."

It's an unquestionably noble idea. But is it feasible? Over the next decade, the law's requirements will toughen until schools will be asked to lift 100 percent of their students over the testing hurdles. Given the data so far, it's hard to see how anything close to that number could possibly be achieved.

During the past school year, for example, only 23 percent of Florida schools met NCLB requirements, even though 68 percent of the schools received grades of A or B from the state's own Department of Education. In Illinois, 44 percent of the schools have failed to meet the law's requirement for at least one year, while 15 percent have missed it two years running. A good number of the failures are due to statistical quirks, like the one in Somerset County, New Jersey, but so far, at least, all schools that fall short are being treated the same under the law.

NCLB formally describes schools that don't meet its requirements for any subgroup as being "in need of improvement," yet the media have latched onto a more contentious term: "failing schools." Whatever term one embraces, schools in that category face real penalties. If they don't meet the requirements for two consecutive years, they must allow any student to transfer to another school within the district. In the next year, they have to provide increased tutoring. In the year following that, if they are still deficient, the state has to step in and help them.

These penalties, along with the testing procedures themselves and the reformulation of curriculum to prepare for the tests, account for the huge cost estimates that have been associated with the legislation. This year alone, federal funding is expected to fall more than $6 billion short of the level promised at the time of passage in 2002.

TAKING THE LONG VIEW

NCLB opponents have won an important battle in the public relations war by arguing that the law should be operating smoothly already. Supporters insist that is asking too much. Michael Kirst, an education professor at Stanford University who was involved in the creation of the 1965 Elementary and Secondary Education Act, recalls that it took "three or more reauthorizations" and more than a decade before they'd gotten most of the bugs out of a law that was a lot less complicated than NCLB. "One of the things, rhetorically, the opponents have done well is set up the expectation that this law is supposed to work well immediately," Andrew Rotherham agrees. "You have to take the long view."

As was the case with No Child Left Behind, the 1965 law was pushed through Congress quickly by an ambitious president. The difference was that Lyndon Johnson had a consensus-building strategy that stretched beyond passage. "In our era," Kirst says, "we spent a lot of time building up grassroots support groups—parents groups, school site councils and others. We created a bottom-up constituency that was able to provide political counterweight to the existing organizations."

The Bush administration has operated a little differently, seeking mainly to dismiss or keep a lid on the NCLB opposition. Education Undersecretary Eugene Hickok has publicly dismissed the complaints of state legislatures against the law as "dinner conversation." Hickok charges that critics "would like to revisit the statute to gut it." Both the department and the White

House worked hard this year to make sure that bills protesting the law wouldn't survive legislative action, with some state legislators receiving calls from Karl Rove, Bush's political adviser.

The administration has run a fairly sizable public relations operation in support of its views, sending Hickok, Education Secretary Rod Paige and others on regular tours around the country, and holding workshops for teachers to try to drum up support for the law from skeptical state and school officials. Still, the administration remains vulnerable to criticism that its efforts at persuasion have been more cosmetic than substantive. "I told a couple of high-level people in the department, 'You guys get criticism and treat it as a marketing problem,' " says NCSL's David Shreve. " 'This is like the New Coke—you keep shoving it down people's throats and they don't want it.' "

States have made some progress in winning flexibility from the Education Department in how they are permitted to adapt to the law's requirements. In response to their complaints, some of the rules were tweaked this year, offering more ways for teachers to meet the definition of "highly qualified," slightly increasing the percentage of special-education and limited-English students who can be exempted from a school's score, and allowing the participation rate to be averaged over time. But the department hasn't been as flexible as some states would like. And the new rules don't apply retroactively, meaning that some test scores yet to be released are going to count against schools, despite the fact that they would be acceptable under the revised guidelines.

There's a reason the feds have been reluctant to make significant changes in the law. A decade ago, the Improving America's Schools Act anticipated many of NCLB's goals and standards, and more than 8,000 schools were identified as needing improvement. But the feds proved eager to give in to state complaints, and granted so many waivers that the law was rendered practically meaningless.

"The 1994 act was far less effective than it should have been because the department moved, in my view, too aggressively to make it easy" to comply, says Sandy Kress, the Bush adviser. He says states that sincerely want

> *What critics really want to do is 'Gut the law.'*
>
> Eugene Hickok,
> Education Undersecretary

to comply with NCLB, such as Michigan, Massachusetts and Ohio, are not only finding it practical to do so but seeing test scores improve as a result.

There remains, however, the indisputable fact that the law has not been funded at anywhere near the level that was originally promised. The Bush administration insists there is plenty of money to pay for the required testing, but financially distressed school districts, unable to attract much money from Washington, have been tempted to opt for the cheapest, least diagnostic "fill-in-the-bubble" tests, and to practice "drill and kill"—rote memorization teaching techniques—in order to get their scores up.

Ironically, these tactics may be most harmful to the disadvantaged students that the law was written to help. In some places, educators say, special-education pupils who had been receiving vocational help are now engaged in academic drilling and practice that, arguably, will be less useful to them as adults. Bill Mathis, school superintendent in Brandon, Vermont, says poorer schools in his area are concentrating on reading and math exercises, forgetting about music, arts, civics and just about anything else that isn't on a federally prescribed test. "The so-called failing school," he says, "is having a failing curriculum."

EXTRA CREDIT

Many educators say that of all the demands No Child Left Behind puts on schools, the hardest one to accept is the notion that schools can overcome all the environmental factors that keep some children from being ready to learn as easily as their peers. No pedagogical strategy or initiative, they argue, is a strong enough weapon on its own to overcome the long-term effects of poverty.

So far, the state that has worked hardest to supplement NCLB with its own broad-based programs is Michigan. It has gone so far as to place social workers in the more troubled schools in order to address problems of housing and hunger so that students stand a better chance. "If you look at the schools that are failing, they obviously tend to be in districts with higher rates of poverty and have families that are facing difficulties," says Marianne Udow, director of the Michigan Family Independence Agency.

Udow concedes there is little hard data after a year to prove that this particular effort is helping boost test scores significantly. Still, she says, there have been some notable success stories—a hearing-impaired child whose condition was spotted by social workers; a student whose performance improved after stable housing was found for his family.

Michigan will double the number of schools with social workers on site, from 19 in the last school year to 39 in the current one. But even if that proves sufficient to make a tangible difference in test scores, it will be much too costly to implement on an extensive basis statewide. Social work adjuncts are not underwritten by any federal education dollars, and state funding for such programs, in Michigan as in most places, has been decreasing in the past couple of years.

In addition to the social work experiment, the Michigan Department of Education is stepping up other efforts, providing direct assistance and training to those schools labeled as "High Priority" because their students have struggled for several years. The result has been an encouraging short-term change in some of the numbers. In May, Michigan School Superintendent Tom Watkins announced that math scores for African-American students in the 8th grade were up by 13 percentage points over the previous year.

But that only lifted the percentage of those students passing the tests from 21 percent to 34 percent. Michigan doesn't have enough money to make all schools a "High Priority." Meanwhile, further spending pressures loom on the horizon, there and elsewhere, as more and more schools turn in failing scores and as parents opt to transfer their children out of those schools, which will require paying for buses and finding seats at other facilities. Money for tutoring will be spread thin as more schools stand "in need of improvement," with states unable to send all of them enough money to make much difference in their numbers. "What you're left with," says Daniel Losen, an education scholar at Harvard University, "is a very highly charged political football where you don't have all the resources necessary for these schools to be successful."

26

Edge-ucation

Rob Gurwitt

What compels communities to build schools in the middle of nowhere?

There can't be many people in Ohio who have heard of Henry Linn. But they're certainly becoming familiar with his work.

Ohio is four years into a massive $10.5 billion school-building program, which is expected to leave very few communities untouched. For many school districts, the prospect of millions of dollars in state aid has been enormously appealing; faced with the question of whether to renovate existing schools, or to abandon them and build anew—often out on the edge of town—they're opting for the new.

There's a reason for this, and that's where Linn comes in. A half-century ago, the Columbia University education professor wrote an article for a trade magazine, *American School and University*, in which he suggested that if the cost of renovating a school was more than half what it cost to build new, school districts should swallow the extra expense and build new. It's unclear how Linn arrived at this disdain for the old, but until recently, his thinking appeared to hold the force of scripture within school facilities circles. "If you track the literature," says Royce Yeater, the Midwest director for the National Trust for Historic Preservation, "it starts to appear in footnotes, then one study refers back to another. . . . But still, it all comes back to one man's opinion. If you look at the original article, there's no studies, there's no nothin' behind this. It is clearly an old wives' tale."

Perhaps, but it's an old wives' tale with legs. Many states, Ohio included, use what's now known as the "percentage rule" in deciding whether schools should be renovated or replaced. The actual percentages vary from state to state, but the rules all amount to the

From *Governing*, March 2004.

same thing: a preference for creating new schools over preserving old ones. In Ohio's case, until a few years ago, a school district couldn't get state money for renovation if it cost more than two-thirds of building new. These days, the "two-thirds rule" is just a guideline, but many school districts, with the encouragement of the state, follow it anyway. Officially, the Ohio School Facilities Commission is neutral on the question. Still, it has a clear, if unstated, preference. "There are a lot of advantages in building new," says spokesman Rick Savors. "You can get into situations when you try to renovate where you have no clue what the actual costs will be; just ask anyone who has renovated a kitchen or bathroom." Which is a part of the reason why, of the 1,300 schools the commission has looked at so far, 790 will be abandoned.

Six of these are in the town of Galion, Ohio, which is giving up its four neighborhood elementary schools, its middle school and its high school, built in 1917 and housing a pipe organ believed to be one of only two of its kind left in the world. An old industrial town about 60 miles north of Columbus, Galion is crawling back from a series of plant closures that began in the 1970s and, by the mid-1990s, had left its downtown largely vacant. In recent years, a revitalization program has generated new life there. But although most storefronts are occupied, the future is still tenuous. As Pauline Eaton, a member of the city council, puts it, "We still have a long way to go, because we were in really bad shape."

Now downtown Galion is about to lose the high school and middle school that sit at its very heart. "Renovation," says school board president Ken Green, "is completely out of the question." The school board has come to this conclusion, he says, in part because the state encouraged it to do so, and in part because of a sense of "what we had versus what we could have." The board is hoping it can build the new schools on 29 acres not far from downtown that were given to the school district last year, but the site presents some challenges, so there is also a strong possibility that the schools will end up outside of town, at one of two new highway interchanges planned for Galion. That prospect galls Eaton. "Our whole revitalization program is built around smart growth and historic preservation," she says. "We also know that the area around the interchanges will become our sprawl area. So we've tried to come up with a plan for how the growth will take place, so that it doesn't suck everything out of downtown again." The problem, Eaton notes, is that where schools go up development inevitably follows.

This seems an obvious point, but it has been only within the past few years that the issue has taken wing around the country. Driven in part by concerns about stemming urban sprawl, in part by movements promoting smaller, neighborhood schools as antidotes to ailing educational quality, and in part by burgeoning concern over keeping community cores intact, many people are asking whether it makes sense to keep putting up large new schools on the edge of town.

It would be a stretch to say that this "anti-school-sprawl" movement has swept the nation. "I would bet that 60 or 70 percent of the time," says the National Trust's Yeater, "we find the bureaucracy and prevailing attitude immovable; we're losing more schools than we're saving." Yet the issue is picking up steam, from local planning boards to legislatures and governors' offices, and the attention has had two notable effects: It has turned a spotlight on the assumptions that are embedded in state school-building guidelines; and it is beginning to call into question the relatively free hand that school systems have enjoyed in shaping community development patterns.

BIPARTISAN CONCERN

If the national effort to get a handle on school sprawl had a single catalyst, it was the publication in 2000 of a report by the National Trust called *Why Johnny Can't Walk to School*. "We were getting more and more desperate requests for help from community groups who were finding that due to state policies, as well as misperceptions about what they could do with older buildings, they were losing neighborhood schools," says Constance Beaumont, its author.

The report was careful to cast the issue as reaching far beyond preservation for preservation's sake. "Schools that hold the memories of generations are disappearing," it commented. "Handsome school buildings—landmarks that inspire community pride—are being discarded for plain, nondescript boxes that resemble factories. Increasingly, a stressful drive through congested traffic separates parents and children from ever-more distant schools. Like the movement of post offices and other public buildings from downtowns to outlying commercial strips, the migration of schools from settled neighborhoods to middle-of-nowhere locations is one more factor weakening the ties that once brought people together."

The report served its purpose, drawing national attention to the issue, and winding up in the hands of countless citizens standing up before school-board meetings called to consider plans for a new school. Yet even without the Trust's report, it's likely that the growing size and on-the-fringe location of schools would have become an issue. For what's striking about the various state and local efforts to address school sprawl is they were not sparked by a single set of political concerns.

In Michigan, for instance, the matter is being spurred by a growing understanding that even while the state's economy and population are holding steady, land is being eaten up at a ferocious rate. "What's happening," says Mac McLelland, of the Michigan Land Use Institute, "is parents move to good-quality school districts around urban areas, they expand and grow and then have to expand more to meet the demand. At that point, they can take an incremental approach and add on, or they can build a new facility because they figure they'll need the space in the future, so they hopscotch development out toward the rural area. And then people say, 'Hey! They've got a nice new school, let's move there.'"

In response, Democratic Governor Jennifer Granholm has launched an initiative to promote denser development and preserve open space, and MLUI and the state's Chamber of Commerce have joined forces to tackle school sprawl. The two organizations don't always see eye to eye, but in this case, the Chamber's concern with how tax dollars are being spent and MLUI's focus on land use have brought them together. Indeed, says Bill Rustem, senior vice president of Public Sector Consultants in Lansing, the very breadth of the political ground covered by the two groups makes it likely that their proposals—which were due out last month—will get attention. "Anytime you get a group on one end of the spectrum and one on the other saying, 'This is a problem,' the inclination of legislators and agencies is going to be to deal with it," he says.

In South Carolina, the matter has gone beyond the talking point—and has led to the most far-reaching legislative effort in the country. The issue first surfaced in a 1998 study of how difficult it was for children to walk to school, sponsored by the South Carolina Coastal Conservation League. The study found that schools built before 1973 had far larger percentages of children able to walk to them than schools built later, simply because they were placed within neighborhoods or other central locations.

For a few years, only the League seemed to care much, but then, in 2002, Republican Mark Sanford won the governor's race. Before taking office, Sanford convened a task force to examine quality-of-life issues in the state; its

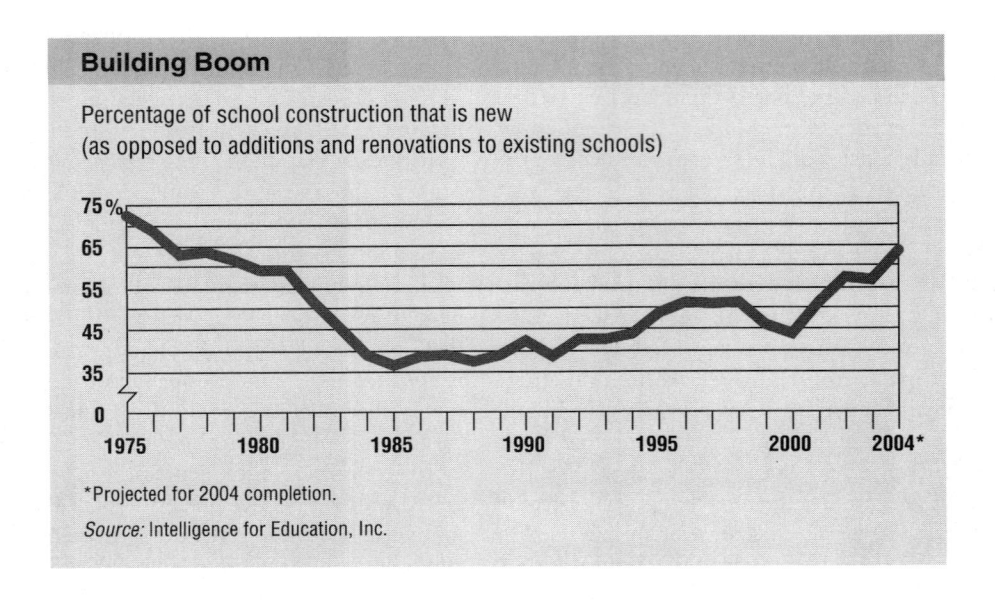

Building Boom

Percentage of school construction that is new (as opposed to additions and renovations to existing schools)

*Projected for 2004 completion.
Source: Intelligence for Education, Inc.

members found themselves agreeing that school-building decisions needed attention. "What they said," recalls Michelle Sinkler, director of the League's land-use program, "was that they were all seeing an alarming trend of mega-schools built far from population centers, and because of that they were seeing a degradation in the quality of education as well as exacerbation of growth-management issues."

Sanford didn't wait long to respond. In his State of the State address last year, he launched a campaign to promote smaller, neighborhood schools, decrying the "construction of massive, isolated schools" and their tendency to "accelerate developmental sprawl into our rural areas and what comes with it—increased car trips, lengthened bus routes and a disappearing countryside." Sanford and a small, bipartisan group of legislators worked together to come up with a bill to attend to several of the forces driving school sprawl: the state's requirement that new schools sit on large lots; a variety of building codes that made it difficult to convert existing commercial sites into school buildings; and a lack of limits on how large schools would be allowed to grow. In the end, only the first two were addressed in last year's legislative session; Sanford's bid to cap school size died in committee.

Even so, eliminating the so-called "acreage standard" is a significant step. Like Henry Linn's percentage rule, it's a longstanding part of the armature of school-building regulations that push school districts to consider older schools outmoded, since they tend to sit on smaller parcels; instead, minimum-acreage standards encourage districts to look for new-school sites outside settled areas. And like the percentage rule, these standards have no clear roots. "We never could find a definitive answer as to where those acreage standards came from," says Constance Beaumont. Many states have simply adopted the standards established by the Council of Educational Facilities Planners International, which suggests 10 acres for elementary schools, 20 for middle schools, and 30 for high schools, plus additional acreage depending on the number of students at the school. These numbers were developed in an era when most school building was taking place on suburban sites, where land is more plentiful.

BIG VS. SMALL

The truth is, there are any number of guidelines, regulations and concerns that convince school districts they're better off building large new schools on large sites. In the Cincinnati suburb of Glendale, for instance, school administrators are considering abandoning the town's 1901, Spanish-style elementary school, which sits in the heart of the village, despite clear opposition from residents and a school board that seems to prefer renovation. Glendale is a wealthy community, so the state isn't contributing any money; instead, the issue seems to be coming down to school design.

"The big thing now is 'adjacencies,' " says Albert Slap, the PTA president and a local lawyer. "We've gotten past the fact that there's enough square footage on the current site—they can build behind the school. But now they're talking about the 'important adjacency' of the gym, the lunchroom, the music room and the playground. The argument goes that it's important for kids to be able to do all these things grouped in one area and not have to go through the building, with all the noise and the disruption and how far it might be for them to walk."

Similarly, school districts often make the argument that, given their financial pressures, they can offer the full range of educational opportunities to students only if they can build large schools on large parcels in order to reap the benefits of economies of scale. This is one of the reasons it's not unusual to find high schools and even middle schools—such as the one containing 4,000 7th- and 8th-graders that recently opened in Cicero, Illinois—that are larger than many colleges.

For proponents of renovation or those who favor the construction of smaller, more centrally located schools, these various arguments all have counter-arguments. Is putting the lunchroom next to the gym, for instance, really more important than holding on to a school that has defined its community for more than a century? As for size, "Small alone doesn't make for a good school," says Michael Klonsky, who runs the Small Schools Workshop at the University of Illinois in Chicago, "but in a big school you can't do the things that good research shows are needed: personalization; building a professional community among the educators; making the curriculum relevant to the lives of the students and the teachers; making the school safe. These big schools have 10 to 20 times the level of serious violent incidents as smaller schools."

Indeed, driven by these considerations and others, some school districts are opting for smaller, centrally located schools. This is the thinking behind one of the more striking neighborhood schools efforts in the country—the ambitious school-building program launched by the Los Angeles Unified School District. Facing the prospect of a 200,000-seat shortfall over the next 10 years, L.A. Unified has two phases of construction underway—the first, costing $3.8 billion, will deliver 78,000 new seats in 80 new schools and 60 major additions; the second, approved by voters last November, will add another $1.5 billion to build or expand some 40 schools. A third bond measure is on the ballot this month; it would add another $1.7 billion for new construction.

Many of the first-phase schools, which were planned three or four years ago, will be large, albeit in neighborhoods with a lot of students. But in the past few years, led by school superintendent Roy Romer, the former governor of Colorado, L.A. Unified has rethought its plans, and now intends to build smaller schools, although some will share a campus with others. "When the program started," says Jim McConnell, the district's chief facilities executive, "we were facing a compelling imperative to get seats built. But now, we have a small-school philosophy. We gained confidence that we would satisfy the most severe overcrowding, and Governor Romer came to believe that he needed to improve secondary education, and the way to do that was to move away from huge high schools to smaller learning academies."

CATALYST FOR RENEWAL

Just as schools going up on the periphery of a community can promote sprawl, so a decision to build or renovate in the central city can generate revitalization. In Omaha, Nebraska, the public school system will open a 650-student elementary school on the edge of downtown, which Omaha Public Schools decided was warranted because of the number of students living in the area. Students who will go to the school are already in temporary space nearby, and the impact on the neighborhood has been dramatic, notes Mark Warneke, the public schools' director of buildings and grounds. "There's been more involvement of parents around that school now," he says, "and fewer problems in that community because parents are walking their children to school and there are more activities in the evening. Also, now that the school is being built, you're seeing more renovation going on around it."

Downtown Spokane, Washington, saw a similar impact after officials decided to renovate Lewis and Clark High School. The school system bought the entire block next to the high school in order to give it room for expansion, and the renovation—finished in 2001—has been so successful that the school's population has grown since it reopened, as students from other areas opt to go there instead of their local school. Just as important, says Michael Edwards, president of the Downtown Spokane Partnership, the renovation has stabilized a part of town that badly needed the help. "If LC had left downtown," he says, "I don't know what would be going on down at that end. It would eventually be eaten up by [the nearby] hospital, but in the meantime it would just be parking lots and derelict buildings. LC showed a certain commitment to downtown, and it's been part of the renaissance going on here."

COORDINATED PLANNING

For all the debate over percentage rules and acreage guidelines, adjacency requirements and economies of scale, cases such as Galion, Glendale, Omaha and Spokane serve as strong reminders of one overriding fact: School building decisions have an impact that stretches far beyond the education of a community's students. Which is why those concerned about stemming school sprawl are beginning to focus on one key consideration: Not *how* decisions get made, but *who* makes them. They're questioning the freedom that school boards and administrators have had to weigh their own criteria separately from the wishes of other public bodies.

You might take as an example a high school built about four years ago in Mount Pleasant, South Carolina, a suburb of Charleston. The 3,000-student school went up at the edge of town, within walking distance of none of its students, on land that developers made available to the school district in anticipation that the school's presence would spark demand for development. Which is exactly what the county recently approved. As the Coastal Conservation League's Michelle Sinkler puts it, "Those 2,000 acres around the school, it's going to be big-box nightmare hell."

What's most striking about all this, though, is that the school is there despite the fact that Mount Pleasant imposed an urban growth boundary designed to limit growth precisely where the school sits and the new development has been approved. In other words, the school district simply ignored the town's effort to get a grip on how it develops.

That has sparked a bill in this year's legislative session by the local state representative, Republican Ben Hagood, that would require contiguous municipalities, local transportation authorities and school districts to coordinate their land-use planning. "Growth is happening, and I'm not anti-growth," says Hagood. "But I'm for better planning of the growth. The idea is to plan where you build and build where you plan."

The state that has gone furthest in encouraging school districts to pay attention to overall planning priorities is Maryland, where former Governor Parris N. Glendening's "Smart Growth" initiative made it hard for districts to get state support for building projects that would promote sprawl. These days, although schools no longer have to be in a so-called "priority funding area" to get state financing—a move the state made in an effort to help out rural schools—proposed projects do score higher on the state's point system if they're in established neighborhoods or within corporate limits.

Elsewhere, getting school districts to play ball with other public agencies is likely to be difficult. The attitude of many state school board associations is pretty well summed up by Ed Dunlap, who runs the North Carolina School Board Association. "Our position is very clear," he says. "It is the responsibility of the local board of education to make decisions about where schools are sited. Period."

Even so, in states such as South Carolina and Michigan, where policy makers are starting to take a hard look at school sprawl, it may just be a matter of time before school districts' planning independence comes up for review. "I think there is increased understanding that much of this whole land-use issue relates back to government decision making," says Michigan's Bill Rustem. "The rules of the game are set by public agencies. And, of course, school boards are public agencies."

> "Our position is very clear. It is the responsibility of the local board of education to make decisions about where schools are sited. Period."
>
> Ed Dunlap, North Carolina school board association

27

Politics and Promises

Christopher Logan

Rhetoric meets the reality of a slowdown in homeland security funding.

Donald Plusquellic has been the mayor of Akron, Ohio, for nearly two decades. He knows what the city's vulnerabilities are, what it needs to do to prepare itself for disasters—natural or manmade—and how much that preparation is going to cost. What he does not know is where he's going to find the money to pay for it.

Grants from the federal government will help, but the rules require cities to spend their own money first and then wait for reimbursement checks from the U.S. Treasury. And even in Akron, which Plusquellic acknowledges has weathered recent tough economic times better than many cities its size, fronting the money for multimillion-dollar equipment can be difficult.

"Our finance administrator has to certify that there is cash on hand before we can purchase anything," Plusquellic explains. "We need an 800 MHz radio system that costs $15 million. How are we supposed to do this?"

Akron, population 217,000 and growing, has its share of potential terrorist targets. The city, once known as the "Rubber Capital of the World," is still home to the Goodyear Tire & Rubber Co. and its fleet of world-famous blimps. The city now touts its leading role in polymer research, centered at the University of Akron's Polymer Science Institute. It also boasts a minor league baseball park, the 8,500 seat Canal Park Stadium.

Plusquellic, who was elected president of the U.S. Conference of Mayors in June, says he doesn't think terrorists would stage a 9/11-style assault in Akron. His worries tend to less-conspicuous but equally devastating plots, such as chemical or biological attacks in public places. He is more worried about the water-treatment plant,

From *CQ/Governing*, October 2004.

which serves 220,000 people in Akron plus about 150,000 in the surrounding area, than about terrorists downing the city's trademark Goodyear blimp.

The mayor says that, nearly three years after the 9/11 terrorist attacks propelled local preparedness to the top of the national agenda, the process of obtaining federal funding to purchase new equipment or train public safety workers is frustratingly slow. Ohio officials and their federal counterparts spent months approving Akron's plan for the new $15 million radio system, even though it was developed quickly and with the cooperation of surrounding jurisdictions. "In places where there may be legitimate problems with coordination and planning," Plusquellic notes, "they're going to be way down the line in terms of getting their funding."

Indeed, city officials across the nation have been complaining loudly and often that federal homeland security dollars are not reaching them. A June 2004 report from the Conference of Mayors, for example, found that more than half of the 215 cities surveyed have not received funding from the $1.5 billion fiscal 2003 Federal First Responder/ Critical Infrastructure program. And nearly a quarter of those surveyed said they have not received any money from the $556 million fiscal 2003 State Domestic Preparedness program.

Since the 9/11 attacks, the Bush administration and Congress have set aside roughly $6.3 billion in terrorism preparedness grants for state and local governments. Another $3.5 billion is on tap for fiscal 2005. But a review earlier this year by the House Select Committee on Homeland Security, chaired by U.S. Representative Christopher Cox of California, found as much as $5.2 billion of that money is stuck in the funding pipeline—caught up in the bureaucracies of the Department of Homeland Security and state governments.

"Cities are being pinched, states are being squeezed and add to that calls from the FBI about threats that mean overtime for police, which is not reimbursable unless the administration raises the threat level," Plusquellic says. "The federal government has to have a role in providing the levels of security that federal officials are recommending."

Several recent studies, including a review by Cox's committee, trace the funding delays to all levels of government. Despite the rhetoric of blame emanating from Capitol Hill, state houses and city halls, the real question is not who is at fault but whether the wheels of government can turn quickly enough to get the money flowing to where it's needed most—before terrorists can strike again.

AN OUTDATED SYSTEM

A task force on state and local homeland security funding, created by Homeland Security Secretary Tom Ridge last March, couldn't put its finger on who was to blame for the funding delays. But Massachusetts Governor Mitt Romney, who co-chaired the task force with Plusquellic, lays out the problem plainly. "The standard grant process and purchasing procedures that exist in our country at all levels of government don't work terribly well if your objective is speed," he says. They were set up to avoid fraud and waste and abuse. Which means, Romney points out, that "they have inherent within them a slow, methodical process."

The task force also noted that, in addition to the reimbursement requirements, which are set out in the federal Cash Management Improvement Act of 1990, state and local government rules also hamper officials' ability to quickly purchase homeland security-related equipment. And the lengthy process of developing federally mandated state homeland security strategies and long-term operational plans at times conflicts with urgent security needs such as overtime reimbursement.

The basic problem, says Gerard Murphy, director of the National Governors Association's homeland security and technology division, is two-fold. First, the grant programs, some of which were in place before the 9/11 terrorist attacks, were not designed with immediacy in mind. Approvals are required by legislative bodies at the local and, sometimes, at the state levels before money can be spent. Then there are time-consuming procurement procedures that must be followed. And often, orders back up at equipment suppliers

> "We need an 800 MHz radio system that costs $15 million. How are we supposed to do this?"
>
> Akron Mayor Donald Plusquellic

because so many states and localities are relying on a limited number of vendors.

In addition, state and local officials often misunderstood how the federal grant programs worked. "Some government officials thought they were going to get a check, that the money was going to show up in their bank account and they could simply draw on it, but that's not the way it works," Murphy says. "It's a reimbursement program."

FEUDING FORMULAS

The speed at which the money to fight terrorism is moving from the U.S. Treasury to local governments is taking a back seat right now to a broader debate: Is the money going where it is needed most? Politicians from rural states argue that their low-population states deserve at least a modicum of funding to prepare for all kinds of disasters—that agricultural operations are as likely targets for terrorists as skyscrapers. Opponents argue that the existing funding formula, in which each state and U.S. territory receives a base amount of funding, with the balance distributed based mainly on population, is an inefficient use of scarce resources that deprives areas considered to be at the highest risk of terrorist attacks of the funding they need to protect themselves.

The Cox committee report concluded in part that the existing system "has provided small counties across the country with relatively large awards of terrorism-preparedness money, while major cities such as New York, Los Angeles, Washington and Chicago struggle to address their needs in a near-constant heightened alert environment." One rural Wyoming county with a population of 11,500, for instance, was awarded $546,000 in grants in 2003, while Jefferson County, Kentucky, which surrounds the city of Louisville, has a population of nearly 700,000 and has been designated by DHS as a high-threat urban area, received $783,000.

The Homeland Security Department has attempted to address that problem through the Urban Area Security Initiative, which is slated to send about $720 million in grants directly to the nation's 50 largest cities and to public transportation systems in those cities in fiscal 2005.

Criticism of the base-funding approach for other grant programs remains, however. New York City Mayor Michael Bloomberg, for example, calls the present funding system "irrational," "tragically misguided" and "creating grave hazards not just for New Yorkers but for all Americans." In response to Bloomberg's complaints and others like them, several legislators have proposed basing the distribution of funds on the terrorist threat faced by a particular locality. Cox is leading that effort in the House. His Faster and Smarter Funding for First Responders Act (HR 3266), introduced in October 2003, would base grants to state and local governments primarily on risk. "Terrorists are not arbitrary in their selection of targets," Cox says, "and we shouldn't be arbitrary in how we prepare to deal with them."

TIME LIMITS

Cox's bill also attempts to address the issue of how quickly funding reaches local governments by reinforcing an existing 45-day limit for states or regions to pass grant money on to local entities. The legislation would impose financial penalties on states that fail to meet that deadline, and it would allow DHS in some cases to bypass state and regional government agencies and award money directly to local governments.

In the Senate, Susan Collins of Maine, who chairs the Governmental Affairs Committee, is also concerned about the rate at which grant money is flowing to the local level. Her bill, the Homeland Security Grant Enhancement Act (S. 1245) would require DHS to provide 10 percent of its grants directly to local governments, by-passing state bureaucracies. Like the Cox legislation, Collins' bill also would keep in place a requirement that states pass on 80 percent of their grant funds to local governments and distribute the funds to localities within 45 days of receiving their grant awards. Her committee approved Collins' bill unanimously in June 2003, but the Senate leadership still had not brought the legislation up for a vote by the full Senate.

Congress has imposed time requirements in earlier legislation, including the fiscal 2003 homeland security appropriations bill, but with only limited effect. While nearly every state met the statutory 45-day deadline for passing through funding to local governments, the statistic "can be misleading with respect to the actual availability of funds for expenditure by localities," Cox notes. The Ridge task force reached a similar conclusion, finding that "while statutory deadlines for 'obligating' or making these funds available for use by county, municipal and tribal governments were met, it is important to understand that 'obligation' is not synonymous with 'expenditure.' Significant obstacles stood in the way of these funds being quickly spent and therefore 'drawn down' from the federal treasury by state, county, municipal and/or tribal entities."

Those obstacles included administrative and procurement policies at the state and local level, lack of personnel to administer the grants, the reimbursement provisions of the 1990 Cash Management Improvement Act and the absence of up-to-date and accurate data about the status of grant performance at all levels of government. In addition, the task force found that the "extraordinarily complex" grant-distribution system "was not designed to coordinate and monitor the huge amount of funding that was now being made available to every state and territory as well as thousands of local governments in the nation."

Plusquellic says there is not a lot local governments can do on their end to fix that problem. "The federal government has to change the rules that were in place prior to September 11," he says. "The Cash Management Act is a strategy the federal government uses to hold on to its money, to keep the interest flowing into the federal treasury." In effect, it forces cities to spend their own money first—and sometimes they don't have it to spend. Both Cleveland and Pittsburgh, for instance, recently announced layoffs in their police and fire departments. "So at a time when cities are laying off first responders, they're being forced to spend their own money on homeland security upfront," Plusquellic says.

Josh Filler, director of the DHS's Office of State and Local Government Coordination, says the federal government is taking steps to alleviate some of the upfront burdens state and local governments are being asked to carry. For instance, the rules say that states can draw money directly from the Treasury, without waiting for a reimbursement, only if they spend it within three to five days. Because state and local governments often are required to have cash on hand before even beginning a

> *"Half the money set aside for state and local governments is stuck in the funding pipeline, caught up in state and federal bureaucracies."*
>
> Rep. Christopher Cox

procurement, the three- to five-day limit doesn't provide enough time for the often-lengthy purchasing processes.

The Ridge task force recommended that Congress allow funds to be provided to state and municipal entities in advance of expenditure for up to 120 days. That, Filler says, should give them enough time to carry out a procurement.

Language in the House version of the fiscal 2005 Homeland Security Appropriations bill would extend the expenditure window. The Senate version of the bill does not have similar language, but Filler says senators are aware of the House language and understand the need to include the provision in the conference bill.

But state and local officials can't rely solely on the federal government to remove the blockages in the funding pipeline. "Local officials should look closely at their own processes when they're considering how to improve the system," Filler says. "Those rules and regulations have a significant impact on the speed at which the money moves."

The March 2004 inspector general's report also found the process slowed down by state and local jurisdictions that had delayed spending funds pending the completion of state-wide risk assessments and homeland security strategies and the development of detailed spending plans. "Spending the funds wisely," the report said, "was more important than spending them immediately."

That's good news to NGA's Murphy, who served on the staff of the Ridge task force. "The silver lining is that the deliberate process allows states and regions to engage in planning across levels of government and disciplines, and to guard against frivolous or inappropriate expenditures," he says.

CHECKS AND BALANCES

Adding to the speed-of-funding difficulty is that the grants in question are for homeland security, a policy area that did not exist until 9/11. A significant percentage of the grant programs apply to a number of different agencies: law enforcement, emergency management and public health. That means there are a lot of officials in the planning process, including agencies that do not have a strong history of working well together.

While that makes simple or quick solutions difficult to come by, progress is being made. The task force report found that DHS's Office for Domestic Preparedness, now part of the OSLGC, has streamlined its processes so that it requires less upfront paperwork from state, local and tribal governments. That should expedite the distribution and expenditure of grant funds.

The paperwork involved filling out detailed budget worksheets explaining exactly how the grant money was going to be spent. Lifting the requirement gives states greater responsibility to oversee how the money is being spent at the local level while Homeland Security retains after-the-fact audit capability.

The department's program guidance for fiscal 2004 also required states to work with federal, county, municipal and tribal governments to develop strategies to guide the use of DHS funds. States also are taking steps to improve their systems and cooperative efforts. Nebraska's Emergency Management Agency, for example, launched an "awareness, education and training" program so that state, city and county officials fully understand the grant process.

In South Carolina, a Counter-Terrorism Coordinating Council was created in 2003 to improve cooperation and coordination among governmental and private entities. The council also formed a grants committee to make recommendations for funding priorities based on the state's homeland security strategy.

In an effort to streamline the flow of money or equipment down to the local level, several states have reorganized their procurement systems, in some cases by developing statewide contracts that allow local governments to purchase equipment and services at pre-negotiated rates. In Kansas, for example, state officials set up a password-controlled Web site that allows municipal officials to view their grant-allocation balances and place orders for equipment until the allocation is exhausted. In effect, the state retains the funds and the locality receives the equipment. And in Louisiana, state officials also are establishing a statewide procurement contract, modeled after the federal General Services Administration's list.

The overall effect, according to William O. Jenkins, director of homeland security and justice issues at the Government Accountability Office, is that "the process is becoming more efficient and all levels of government are discovering and institutionalizing ways to streamline the grant distribution system." But Jenkins told the House Subcommittee on Economic Development, Public Building and Emergency Management in May that "These increased efficiencies . . . will not continue to occur unless federal, state and local governments each continue to examine their processes for ways to expedite funding for the equipment and training needed by the nation's first responders."

While the push for reform is gaining momentum, mayors like Plusquellic say time is not on their side. "There needs to be a balance between the urgency that we feel and the careful planning that the state and federal officials want," he says, noting that the arrest in June of Nuradin Abdi, a 32-year-old Somali accused of plotting to blow up a Columbus, Ohio, shopping mall, is a case in point. "Even in middle America, there are potential targets," he says. "We have places where people come to be entertained, to see events, and we can put extra police there. But we just don't have the manpower to protect everything."

28
Breaking and Entering

Ellen Perlman

Protecting government networks against terrorists requires being relentlessly vigilant.

A Delaware state employee receives a "chain letter" via e-mail that promises $100 and lunch with Bill Gates—if the user forwards the message to 20 friends. The question is, should she forward the message to a few close friends, send it to everyone in the office or ignore the message? Even though the correct response may seem apparent, it is part of a 20-question "responsible computing" quiz that Delaware employees take as a reminder of the rules of accepted computer use. "The intent is to make it obvious what the answers are," says chief technology officer Elayne Starkey.

The state wants to knock into people's heads that the Internet, which can be a huge boon for government efficiency, can also wreak havoc with the state's ability to secure itself against terrorism. If the state is to keep its networks and information uncompromised by malicious intruders entering via cyberspace, state employees who use those networks have to stop doing risky things, such as opening attachments from strangers, keeping their passwords on a yellow sticky note affixed to their computer monitors or using personal software on state computers. Delaware officials hope state employees will answer "false" when the quiz asks if it's okay to e-mail around a good joke because it will "reduce stress and lighten things up in the office."

State and local technology officials have a huge job trying to secure cyberspace, and it requires cooperation from users, good technology and some luck. "It's a big ocean to boil," says Larry Kettlewell, chief information security officer for Kansas, and vice chair of the National Association of State CIOs' security subcommittee. The volume of threats has increased substantially in the past year, while the amount of time to respond to attacks has shrunk

From *CQ/Governing,* October 2004.

markedly. "You really have to be proactive insofar as you can be," Kettlewell says.

Trespassers can be terrorists intending to disrupt homeland security. They also can be teenage hackers and disgruntled employees. The Department of Homeland Security doesn't distinguish among sources, says Amit Yoran, director of the National Cybersecurity Division. While the motives may be different depending on who is striking the system, the disruptive and sometimes destructive results are the same.

Cybersecurity has so many facets that governments are attacking the problem from a variety of directions—from providing employee training and education to implementing technologies that can secure networks to sharing cyber-threat information nationwide.

ATTENTION DEFICIT

The constant is that governments have to be relentlessly vigilant. "One hundred percent security is never attainable," says Will Pelgrin, director of the Office of Cybersecurity and Critical Infrastructure Security in New York State, which has one of the most progressive cybersecurity operations in the country. Because funding is tight, governments also must look creatively at the resources and methods for protecting vital information. "The things that can be done and the things that are being done are in two different universes," notes Michael Corby, director of META Group Consulting, a technology research and analysis firm.

Funding is an ongoing issue. So far, Department of Homeland Security monies have not been targeted at protecting information technology infrastructure. That is a mistake, Kettlewell points out, since IT networks are a modern-day utility, just like electric power, railroads and telephones. If an IT network is compromised, "your state government is frozen in a moment in time in which it cannot conduct business," he says. "Until now, it's been given short shrift in terms of homeland security."

Most local governments are aware of the need for cybersecurity and are trying to address it. For the most part, however, there isn't a concerted state-local effort to protect data or the federal funding to encourage it. Then again, the Department of Homeland Security faces its own cyber-protection problems. In a report released in July, the department's inspector general found that the department's networks lack coordination, suffer from poor communication and have failed to set priorities to fight cyber attacks.

Local governments also have problems with employee training and awareness. Pelgrin, who interacts with many local governments, explains that few have money for technology staff. When the state puts out advisories about vulnerabilities to systems, they land on the desk of the person responsible for technology—who may very well be the town clerk or recorder and often is not technologically savvy. Pelgrin says his office will put out an advisory about "patching a system" and will get a call back from someone who is, in effect, looking for duct tape rather than figuring out code.

Part of paying attention is keeping up to date on firewalls and virus protection. Schoharie County, in upstate New York, learned a lesson about that the hard way. The county created two listservs for e-mail correspondence—one for local government records managers and another for an association of towns. Unfortunately, participating governments either had no firewalls or no virus protection, or the virus protection software was so old it was useless. Both listservs "were floating viruses all over the place," says Stan France, Schoharie County's director of central data processing. "We had to knock both of them off."

While the Schoharie municipalities are attempting to set up a coordinated process to protect themselves, many of the smaller ones have almost no technical support. There is talk about developing a strategy for working together, but more help is clearly needed. "State agencies do a lot of business with municipalities

> *"The things that can be done and the things that are being done [for government cybersecurity] are in two different universes."*
>
> Michael Corby, director of META Group Consulting

and counties," France says. "If local governments are not protected, it raises the issue of all those viruses shipping off to the state. It behooves state agencies to do something."

A DOSE OF ANTIVIRUS

The national cybersecurity picture is not all bleak. Technology officials are making efforts to ensure that information remains confidential, accurate and available. The chief focus is on trying to prevent or reduce the potential for virus and denial-of-service attacks, which result in depriving users of normal computing services. Governments have done a pretty good job in the past by installing antivirus software and educating users not to open an attachment from someone they don't know. Still, Corby says, the public sector tends to be "half a step behind hackers."

Where it's doing a more effective job is with data classification—identifying which data, if compromised, lost or incorrectly modified, would pose the greatest risk to the proper functioning of government. Many governments are using their scarce resources to protect sensitive data, such as credit card information, that would be vulnerable to identity theft or information crucial to the operations of government.

States are not going it alone. When a cyber threat lurks and one state becomes aware of it, that information is passed along to 48 other states and the District of Columbia through the Multi-State Information Sharing and Analysis Center. The ISAC was established in January 2003 to provide a way for states to share security intelligence and information, both on a monthly basis through teleconferencing and as needed when problems arise.

The ISAC issues color-coded alerts and helps with triage. If 10 alerts are sent out about potential threats to networks, information also will be sent about which threats deserve the greatest attention. Information will be included on how to handle software patching and threat mitigation. "We used to have a lot of time to take care of these," says Pelgrin. "Now it's close to zero-day exploits."

Kansas is the lone state that has not joined the multi-state ISAC. Kettlewell says the ISAC doesn't have the technical depth he's looking for. He has chosen to rely on other sources of expertise. "I need more technical details when it comes to an event or incident coming down the pike." He counts on three or four trusted sources and doesn't want duplicate information that would need to be evaluated to see how it fit with the other information.

STANDING GUARD

Educating users is a key strategy in the battle against network breaches. New York asked the vendor commu-

---

Three Steps to Security

Larry Kettlewell, chief information security officer for Kansas and vice chair of the National Association of State Chief Information Officers' security subcommittee, lists three keys to a solid security program:

1. **An automated asset-management system.** The state should know what technologies it has and the status of software patches and anti-virus software at any given time.

2. **Knowledge of the latest technology.** Many governments, for example, have intrusion-detection systems so a live body no longer has to watch a console. These automated systems provide alerts, but the next step is intrusion prevention and some states are putting that into operation.

3. **A layered system that has "defense in depth."** If one layer is penetrated, there are plenty more to go. If an intruder manages to get beyond perimeter security as well as other initial defenses and gets into the network, he or she will be stymied by defensive measures at the desktop and elsewhere.

nity to provide pro bono security presentations via the Web, and Pelgrin insisted that they be solely informational and not end with "buy me, hire me." Twenty vendors responded. The Webcasts last an hour or less and offer concrete suggestions for participants to apply to their systems. About 850 people from 40 states registered for the first one this summer. The presentations are taped and archived for others to view into later, but Pelgrin says "attending" original Webcasts is most useful because they are interactive—taking impromptu polls of attendees, for example.

Several states have created the position of state chief information security officer, hiring someone to "stand guard" over networks. As Nevada's CISO, Randy Potts' job is to get the message out about how important it is to set standards and priorities and fund the protection of cyberspace—otherwise, all the information a government gathers into databases is vulnerable. "It's really difficult to explain that intangible to lawmakers and budget makers when they're just starting to grasp the understanding of desktop applications," Potts says. "It's difficult for them to fathom how important that information we're storing is." And how widespread that data collection is.

Much of Nevada's physical infrastructure, for instance, has an IT component. Dams, which used to have manned control rooms, mostly have electronic operations centers, and those could be turned against the state if hacked into. Electronic systems connect the state to hospitals that feed information to the Nevada health department. "I don't think awareness has risen to the point where everyone understands how reliant we've become on technology," Potts says.

Delaware also stresses the importance of keeping the governor and other top officials aware of potential dangers. The IT department relays information to the governor's office regularly, using an activity graph that "explains in English" how much spam is coming in and how many viruses the network is being hit with. "We quantify it so they can understand that we're not immune and that this is a constant battle," Starkey says.

To keep data safe, most states have set up firewalls, purchased intrusion-detection software and worked with security firms to try to keep hackers from doing harm. The Delaware technology office is also engaged in a project that allows it to segment pieces of its network so that if there is an attack that breaches the firewall, it can be isolated and won't float around the whole network.

Technology officials are resigned to the fact that systems diligence is a full-time, never-ending task. That was true before 9/11, and now it is even more critical. "It's one of those things that has no finish line," says Starkey. "It's not like Y2K when we could all breathe when it was finished and stop funding it. We have to stay one step ahead of the evildoers."

29
Enemies of the State

Alan Greenblatt

State-versus-local tension is getting worse. Locals fear state budgets will be balanced at their expense. They may be right.

From *Governing*, June 2002.

Imagine yourself watching a sexy television ad about municipal finance. If you're having a hard time with that, imagine trying to write one. That's Mike Madrid's job. A longtime Republican political consultant, Madrid is working on a campaign to persuade voters in California to protect the finances of cities, counties and special districts from poaching by the state. His polls suggest voters are sympathetic—most of them believe local taxes should stay in the hands of local governments. But the complexity of the financial machinations involved makes it very hard to get their attention, let alone persuade them to support an initiative on the subject. "When we would break the money out into different, specific revenue streams," Madrid says, "the voters' eyes would glaze over in focus groups."

The League of California Cities, the major force behind the initiative campaign Madrid is running, wanted at first to place its initiative on this year's state ballot. Now it has backed off and is trying for March 2004. The whole process has been frustrating for the league—even many local officials are dubious about the ultimate prospects for passage. But then, feelings of frustration are something that California's cities and counties have grown used to.

A quarter-century of prior initiatives and policies have left localities here at the financial mercy of the state. Cities control less than half of their discretionary spending—the state tells them what they can do with the rest. The situation is even more desperate for counties, which have final say over less than one-third of the money they spend. The League of Cities initiative wouldn't change any of that. It would simply lock into place those revenues that localities still do control, using the year 2000 as a baseline.

Whatever happens with the initiative, localities in California don't expect things to break their way significantly anytime soon. All the many billions of dollars that the state has taken from them over the years, they figure, are gone for good. The state government, for instance, has shown little inclination to return to localities the property-tax dollars it has shifted to the K-12 education budget over the past decade. So the locals, at this point, simply hope that no more is taken away.

But the threat of further losses is all too real. The state of California is facing a deficit in the neighborhood of $20 billion. Localities know they are going to get hit again. The only question is, how hard. "The governor and legislature have said that they are not going to balance the budget on the backs of local government this time," says Steve Szaley, executive director of the California State Association of Counties. "Of course, none of us are buying that."

What the localities fear most is that when the moment to balance the budget actually comes, the legislature will stiff them on car-tax revenue. Back during the flush days of 1998, the state decided to slash vehicle license fees, promising to make good the lost dollars this tax cut would mean for local governments. But the state has to appropriate that payback each year. This year, that gesture would cost $4 billion. The suspicion that the legislature ultimately will refuse to pay up haunts city and county officials all over the state. "They have their budget to balance," says Jake Mackenzie, a city councilman in Rohnert Park, a small Northern California town. "It's sort of tough luck in terms of local government."

If localities in California are starting to flinch, they are not alone. Forty-three states are grappling with revenue shortfalls this year, which leaves governors and legislatures with three choices: cut state spending, raise taxes or shift the burden onto somebody else. Given the political unpopularity inherent in the first two options, it's no wonder many states are looking to squeeze as much money out of local government as they can.

Last year, as a candidate for governor, New Jersey's Jim McGreevey criticized his predecessor for stinginess in offering state aid to towns and school districts. But he froze that aid in his own budget this year. Wisconsin Governor Scott McCallum went much further—he proposed to end the state's 90-year tradition of sharing revenue with localities, a move that would eventually have cost the localities $1 billion a year. North Carolina Governor Mike Easley is withholding $209 million in payments owed to local governments in shared tax income and reimbursements.

"It was painful," says Fred Terry, an alderman in Winston-Salem, which lost $7.2 million out of its $200 million budget. "It may not sound like that much, but when you're counting on that money and it doesn't arrive, it puts you in a pinch."

There have been some victories for localities in state capitals this year. Most notably, the Virginia legislature voted to allow the Washington-area suburbs to hold a referendum that would raise local sales taxes to pay for more roads, ending the state's decades-old stranglehold on transportation policy. For the most part, though, the state legislatures have been looking at localities as if they were ATMs.

It's not that local officials quarrel with the need to freeze aid payments or make one-time cuts to grapple with a gaping deficit. Their worst fear is that such short-term fixes won't do much to solve chronic budget problems next year, or the year after that. If the red ink continues to flow another two or three years, locals worry, the cutbacks inflicted on them won't be quick or simple ones. They are likely to be deeper structural cuts with the potential to cripple the capacity of local governments for a long time to come.

No doubt some of the fears are exaggerated, but what they reveal is that many years of heavy-handed treatment, in California and other places, have left localities wary of the legislatures and governors they must report to. It's a wariness that spreads beyond the fiscal arena, into such areas as transportation and land use, in which any state needs the full cooperation of localities to put its policies into place. The requisite goodwill is no longer there. "The state has, from our point of view, been such an unreliable partner that it's hard for us to trust them," says Chris McKenzie, executive director of the League of California Cities.

California's local strategists, as they search for ways to win sympathy and support for their cause, might want to examine the successful public relations campaign waged by localities in Wisconsin against McCallum's budget proposal. That state has a shared-revenue system that is a remnant of the Progressive Era, designed to equalize payments across the state on a per capita basis, so that even residents of property-poor areas can count on a minimum level of services. It's separate from money the state grants to localities for roads, computers or other specific programs.

McCallum threatened earlier this year to do away with the entire system, and not just because Wisconsin was looking at a $1.1 billion deficit. The governor said his ultimate purpose was to get rid of wasteful layers of local government. He complained that there were 54 units of government within a 10-mile radius of where he stood in downtown Madison. McCallum figured if he cut off one of their major funding sources, some of those units would be forced to consolidate, thus reducing duplication. "People here agree there ought to be consolidation," he says. "It's just that they want to have control after they consolidate—not the other guy."

Wisconsin cities used a number of tactics to challenge McCallum, attacking the honesty of his numbers and describing services they would be forced to cut if the governor's plan went through. For weeks, those budgetary horror stories seemed to turn up in the lead of just about every newspaper story about the controversy. Then the stories were featured in a series of television ads the League of Wisconsin Municipalities ran knocking McCallum's ideas—the first such direct-to-voter ads that the league had ever run.

The strategy worked spectacularly, aided by the governor's own failure to recommend specific steps that would help towns to merge. The plan reached the legislature "dead on arrival," in the words of one legislative aide.

But while Wisconsin's shared-revenue system may have survived McCallum's assault this year, its long-term prognosis is still shaky. One portion of the program has not been granted an increase in seven years (it's due for one this year), while the other major portion has been frozen since 1981. The fact that it shuttles money from one unit of government to others with few strings attached puts it at risk politically. "People don't like to run for office to be a tax collector for somebody else," says Dan Thompson, executive director of the Wisconsin municipal league. "That's always a hard sell."

The shared-revenue system is certain to face renewed attacks in coming years, and local officials will spend a considerable amount of time trying to repel them. "When the livelihood and survival of your community depends on the funding of state shared revenue," says Jane Wood, city manager of Beloit, "that becomes your consuming priority."

Beloit, just north of the Illinois border, receives the most shared revenue in the state on a per capita basis. Its local government has produced a brochure suggesting that if that state money were taken away, it would be able to meet its bond obligations and retiree health insurance payments, but then would have only $4.6 million left to fund nearly $30 million worth of current services. Beloit, in other words, would go broke.

Perhaps the most important lesson of this year's state-versus-local war in Wisconsin was the ability of the local forces to turn the public argument around, suggesting that instead of accusing cities and counties of waste, McCallum should get the state's own house in order first—getting rid of the swimming pools and planes that it owns before cutting off funding to localities for the parks, libraries, police and fire service that everybody loves.

It is a tactic that local officials in other states are likely to turn to as they become more desperate. In California, local governments are already starting to train their ammunition on the state's management problems, from the electricity deregulation debacle to the fact it managed to dig itself a $20 billion hole.

There is a historical irony in all this, because California used to be one of the strongest home-rule states in the country. Communities can enact charters and ordinances, change their names and annex their neighbors without the permission of the legislature. They used to have control over their own budgets and property taxes as well. All that changed in 1978, when the statewide Proposition 13 ballot measure not only cut property tax revenues roughly in half but also gave the state authority over their distribution.

> "The state has, from our point of view, been such an unreliable partner that it's hard for us to trust them."
>
> Chris McKenzie, executive director of the League of California Cities

This became a crucial power in the 1990s, following passage of another ballot initiative requiring the state to devote 40 percent of its general fund to elementary and secondary education. The property tax that had once funded basic county services became, in essence, a state tax used to finance K-12 education. "Since 1993," says Alameda County Supervisor Keith Carson, "when the state started shifting more dollars into the Department of Education, just our county alone has lost $1.48 billion in revenue."

Several legislators have proposed giving back to the localities a portion of the money the state has transferred to education, but even those proposals would put strings on almost all the dollars involved. Tom Torlakson, chairman of the Senate Local Government Committee, concedes that his bill, which would give localities transportation money if they build more affordable housing, has no chance to succeed in a deficit year.

As a candidate for governor in 1998, Gray Davis sounded pretty friendly to the local cause. "We will give the money back," he said, "because it wasn't ours to start with." Two years later, however, when the state was enjoying a surplus of more than $12 billion, Davis vetoed a measure, passed unanimously in both legislative chambers, which would have allowed localities to keep the increased property tax revenue they received because of rising home values.

The state did compensate for much of the money it had shifted to schools, but provided most of that money in the form of grants tied to a specific purpose and unavailable for other needs. Sacramento has been making decisions about funding priorities in communities located hundreds of miles away. Meanwhile, the more mundane and sometimes less visible costs of local government receive scarcely any state help at all. "We can't stop putting out fires and filling potholes just because the state decides it wants to spend money on something else," says Margaret Clark, a member of the Rosemead City Council in Southern California.

It is California's counties that fare worst under this system of earmarked grants: Counties provide more than $13 billion worth of state services annually, but the money the state sends them does nothing to help fund many less glamorous programs and services they are expected to handle purely as a local matter. "What we have in California," says Marianne O'Malley, of the state Legislative Analyst's Office, "is local administration. We don't have real local governance."

Home Rule in California

Percentage of total revenues that are self-controlled

	1978	1981	1988	1992	1995
Counties	50%	18%	19%	19%	20%
Cities	66%	36%	43%	45%	43%
Special Districts	59%	37%	49%	39%	38%
School Districts	54%	7%	5%	5%	6%
Higher Education	30%	15%	18%	21%	24%

Source: Public Policy Institute of California

Cities have things a little easier, in large part because they still have a dedicated funding stream they can count on, namely, the sales tax. Of the 8 cents or so that the state collects on every dollar of sales, one penny of purely discretionary money makes its way back to the city of purchase. Naturally, this has led to a mad rush on the part of cities to land major retailers within their borders, notably big-box stores and car dealers. More than in any other state in the country, local planners court retail business in preference to residential development, and even to new industry.

The textbook example is Monrovia, a Southern California town that passed up a Kodak plant a few years ago, even though it would have brought several hundred manufacturing jobs to the city. All those employees, Monrovia's government reasoned, would cause wear and tear on the local roads, while the tax benefits from the plant would go largely to the state. The city wanted the site used instead for a Price Club discount store, even though it would generate far fewer jobs at much lower salaries, because a reliable portion of the sales-tax dollars generated would stay in Monrovia.

Other communities have been making the same seemingly perverse decision. "It may not be best from the perspective of smart growth and creating high-paying jobs," admits Jake Mackenzie, the city councilman in Rohnert Park, which recently sold some city land to attract a Costco warehouse store. "But we tend to act rationally under these circumstances." What's rational for a city in the short term, though, obviously can be irrational for the state as a whole.

An obvious solution to this problem would be some sort of revenue-sharing agreement between the locals and the state. But local governments in California are increasingly wary of such an agreement: They fear that their financial dependence leaves them in a weak negotiating position. They also worry that the legislature and the governor will change the terms of any deal after the fact. "There's not in this state the sense that we're all in this together," says Diane Cummins, fiscal adviser to state Senate President John Burton. "It's 'I don't trust what you're going to do to me.'"

This year, however, a bill to force some limited tax sharing within six counties in the Sacramento area did pass the Assembly. The bill, sponsored by Assemblyman Darrell Steinberg, would force localities inside the area to divvy up a portion of their future sales tax revenue growth. The city of sale would be guaranteed one-third of the money, and would be eligible for another third if it met stated housing and planning goals. The remaining third would be redistributed throughout the Sacramento area on a per capita basis.

Steinberg argues that since a limited number of Wal-Marts and Costcos are going to locate within the region anyway, it doesn't make sense for the local communities to fight over them, wooing developers with subsidies that they don't need and the communities can't afford. His critics counter that it is merely a backhanded way of transferring funds from Sacramento suburbs to the central city, where Steinberg himself once served on the city council.

But the real significance of the bill could be as a possible precedent for future statewide action. Steinberg's proposal has attracted support from diverse elements within the state but also has been derided by dozens of cities, many of which are lobbying hard against it even though they are located far from the affected area. "Any formula contained in state law to change the allocation of local revenues could easily be changed by a new state law," says Matthew Newman, director of the California Institute for County Government, "and that makes the locals nervous."

So the most important obstacle in the path of Steinberg's bill may simply be the mutual suspicion that hovers over the entire state-local relationship at this point. "Local government has good reason not to trust the state," says Patricia Wiggins, who chairs the Assembly's Local Government Committee. "The pressure on these communities to build housing without being able to use the property taxes from the housing is almost like an unfunded mandate."

The heated reaction to Steinberg's fairly modest bill suggests that any wholesale change to the state-local fiscal relationship may be a long time coming. In a climate of distrust, sweeping changes usually don't occur until the crisis is imminent.

There's one other factor, of course, that prevents a more rational distribution of funds between state and local government in California. That is the fact that the state benefits from the present arrangement. When times are good, the legislature can afford to be generous to localities, as it was in the immediate aftermath of Proposition 13. When times are tough, it can turn off the spigot, forcing the locals to take the blame for any resulting cuts in services. There is little incentive for state policy makers to abandon a system that grants them power through control of the dollars.

30

Made in Sacramento

Christopher Swope

California is using its clout to fill what officials there view as a national policy void on key issues. Is the state overstepping its boundaries?

On July 1, a sweeping government mandate on consumer privacy takes effect, impacting thousands of businesses across the country and perhaps around the world. The order has to do with security breaches, or more specifically, what happens when names are stolen out of a database along with Social Security or credit card numbers. It used to be that when a company's computers got hacked, whether by an insider or an intruder from the outside, the company could keep it a secret. Not anymore. Now, because such personal information can be used for identity theft, that company will almost certainly have to disclose such an infringement to anyone whose data is accessed by an unauthorized person.

Although this mandate reaches across state and international borders, it wasn't passed by Congress, written by federal regulators or handed down as an executive order from the president. Rather, it was passed by the California legislature. Any civics textbook will note, of course, that laws made in Sacramento apply only to Californians and that national policies are set in Washington, D.C. Lately, however, those clear lines of authority are blurring as regulated parties feel they have no choice but to apply California's standards in a larger forum.

The disclosure law is a good example of how Sacramento, on certain issues, is setting de facto national policy. Say a shop in Atlanta sells T-shirts via the Internet to all 50 states, storing customers' names and credit card numbers in a database. And say a hacker plunders that database. Technically, the law only kicks in if data on Californians is revealed, requiring the T-shirt shop to notify those customers by e-mail, postcard or through newspaper advertise-

From *Governing*, July 2003.

ments. Yet Californians in the database are most likely jumbled together with people from every other state. Not only might it be difficult to pick out the Californians from everyone else but doing so would inevitably raise the ticklish question of why people in only one state are being told about the incident. As a practical matter, the T-shirt shop would probably want to notify all customers nationwide.

This privacy law flies in the face of a new conventional wisdom that says the Golden State, long the national trendsetter, is growing increasingly irrelevant. In April, *The Economist* called California the "left out coast," citing its power crisis, the technology bust and the war on terrorism's focus back East. Add to that the state's crippling $35 billion budget deficit and you may well wonder whether California has lost its edge. Yet, in fact, it seems that California is asserting itself more than ever before. On a number of national issues, Sacramento sees a void in Washington that it is trying, for better or for worse, to fill on its own.

When President Bush pulled the United States out of the Kyoto accord on global warming, for example, California came up with its own alternative. A state law passed last year intends to force automakers to build cars and SUVs that emit less in greenhouse gases. Since California accounts for more than one-tenth of the American car market, the move could eventually alter the cars all Americans drive.

Another example is stem cell research. When Bush put strict limits on federal funding for research using cells derived from human embryos, Sacramento shot back with a law that explicitly encourages all kinds of stem cell research. The law doesn't set a national policy per se, but California is home to so much of the U.S. biomedical industry that it could, in time, render Bush's decision moot. Since the "safe haven" law passed last year, private donors have already pumped $17 million into California universities (much of it specifically for embryonic stem cell research), and the state is toying with the idea of selling $1 billion in bonds to fund even more.

Even California's public pension funds are sticking it to Washington. The fund for state employees, known as CalPERS, and the fund for teachers, known as CalSTRS, are the largest and third-largest pension funds in the country and are well known for boardroom activism. But as Washington responded lethargically to the recent corporate scandals, both funds stepped up their efforts on corporate governance, especially in the area of executive compensation. Meanwhile, both funds acted when it became clear that a bipartisan plan to stop U.S. corporations from avoiding taxes by setting up an offshore mailbox was dead in Congress.

Teaming up with labor groups and other pension funds, they've publicly campaigned for offshore companies in their portfolios—including Tyco International, McDermott International and Ingersoll-Rand—to "come home to America." They earned surprisingly favorable votes on the matter from shareholders at Tyco and Ingersoll-Rand, although none of the companies has yet agreed to repatriate. "This is something the federal government should've cracked down on," says California Treasurer Phil Angelides, who sits on the board of both pension funds. "But the Republicans in Congress and the Bush administration keep blocking the effort. So we say to ourselves: If they won't, we will."

SHADOW CAPITAL

In many ways, Sacramento, a modest town on the flat green plains of California's central valley, is emerging as Washington's shadow capital. Not that there's any coordinated effort going on to poke the feds in the eye. But whether you read the *Los Angeles Times*, the *New York Times* or the London *Times*, you've probably noticed that the political gulf between Sacramento and Washington is huge and only growing wider. The recent tensions started with California's power crisis, when policy makers in Sacramento complained that Washington turned a blind eye to market manipulation by energy companies.

Since then, on one issue after another, cocksure Californians have circumvented the Washington policy juggernaut, which they see as firmly in the grip of business interests and senselessly slowed by abortion politics. Especially on environmental issues and consumer protection, California is increasingly comfortable using its clout as the nation's largest state to force changes in the way companies around the country—and around the globe—do business.

Meanwhile, critics in Washington note that California might want to fix its own problems before exporting some more. Whether the issue is greenhouse gases, privacy or corporate governance, industry lobbyists are especially wary of California, or any other state for that matter, setting different standards than Washington's. "If a government is going to take a position on climate change, it has to be done at the national level or even international level—not by individual states," says Eron Shosteck, spokesman for the Washington-based Alliance of Automobile Manufacturers.

Regardless of whether people in Washington policy circles think California is acting bravely or foolishly, they're finding they have to take Sacramento seriously. Business lobbyists who are scoring touchdowns in the nation's capital are getting trounced in California's. On flights between the two capital cities, they coordinate their offensive game with their defense. "The metaphor of the 800-pound gorilla doesn't come close to describing California," says Mark Bohannon, public policy chief for the Software & Information Industry Association in Washington, D.C. "It's the 800,000-ton gorilla because of the economy's size, the population and the fact that California is such an important customer base, even for companies that don't operate there."

If you ask policy makers in Sacramento why they and Washington are drifting apart, most will tell you it's because a conservative president is more or less getting his way with a Republican Congress. If it's true that Washington has moved markedly to the right, however, it's equally true that California is in the midst of a long, wide turn to the left. In the wake of last November's elections, Democrats now hold California's governorship and all of its statewide elected offices for the first time since 1882. Democrats control both houses of the legislature by nearly two-thirds majorities. Even at CalPERS, the 13-member board of directors is composed entirely of Democrats and labor leaders.

What's more, the current tension between Sacramento and Washington is a dynamic that may prevail for some years to come. California's GOP is in shambles and the latest round of redistricting locked in the Democrats' lopsided majorities. Even if a recall vote in September forces Governor Gray Davis out of office, that's not likely to alter the political environment that makes it easy for elected Democratic officials such as Attorney General Bill Lockyer and Angelides, the treasurer, to score political points by harping on Washington.

California's bullishness could also be viewed another way: as part of a growing power struggle between the federal government and the states. The sentiment in Sacramento is shared by the likes of Eliot Spitzer, New York's attorney general who challenged corruption on Wall Street while federal regulators sat and watched. Spitzer sees the current wave of state activism as a progressive twist on "New Federalism," the idea long pushed by conservatives that Washington's power be devolved to the states. People in Sacramento are thinking about things in exactly the same way. "It's ironic," says Fran Pavley, the Democratic assemblywoman who pushed California's global warming law through the legislature. "In Washington, the Republican leadership generally supports states' rights and less federal intrusion. Unless the states are doing something they don't like."

> "It is left to California, the nation's most-populous state and the world's fifth-largest economy to take the lead," Governor Davis said. "We can now join the longstanding and successful effort of European nations against global warming."

THE WORLD STAGE

In the marble halls of California's capitol building, you cannot discuss these issues with lawmakers, staff and lobbyists without being constantly reminded of the same fact. California is not only the nation's largest state, they will say over and over again, but the world's fifth-largest economy, just behind the United Kingdom and just ahead of France. It's an interesting statistic, although not an altogether meaningful one since California, like North Dakota, is still just one of 50 states. But it does give a sense of the importance California assigns itself and how it sees its role in the country and the world.

On no issue is this clearer than with global warming. Since Pavley's bill on greenhouse gases came up last summer, California environmentalists buzz about the European Union more than they do about the American one. As they see it, President Bush and Congress have checked out of an important international debate on global warming. Governor Davis himself initially wavered on whether to sign Pavley's bill, but once he made up his mind, he used it as a chance to draw new lines between Sacramento, Washington and Brussels. "It is left to California, the nation's most-populous state and the world's fifth-largest economy, to take the lead," Davis said. "We can now join the longstanding and successful effort of European nations against global warming."

When it comes to regulating air pollution, California has always had a somewhat unique place in the country. The state enacted its own motor-vehicle standards years before Congress did, and when national lawmakers got around to it in 1970, they let California keep its stricter standards. Congress later gave the 49 other states the option of ditching the weaker federal standards for California's. Although only a handful has done so, regulators around the country, when they discuss vehicle emissions, talk about two separate systems: Washington's and California's. Currently 22 percent of the nation's population lives under air pollution rules made in Sacramento.

The greenhouse-gas law isn't California's first foray into prodding Detroit to build cars differently. Past efforts inspired the use of catalytic converters and onboard diagnostic computers. But with global warming, the board is on new regulatory ground. Typically, when California cracks down on air pollution, the problem is smog and the target is local, or possibly regional, in scope. Greenhouse gases, however, are a global problem. "We're aligned with the rest of the world on climate change," says Alan Lloyd, chairman of the California Air Resources Board, the agency in charge of implementing the climate-change law. "We can't control what happens in Washington, but we can control what happens here."

How will California exercise that control? CARB has two more years to figure this out. It's an important question, because it speaks directly to the power struggle between Sacramento and Washington. The main culprit in global warming is carbon dioxide, and the best way to reduce CO_2 emissions is to build more fuel-efficient cars.

Regulating fuel efficiency, however, is a power that Congress, by law, explicitly reserves for itself.

The automakers have played this federalism card against California before. Last year, General Motors and DaimlerChrysler successfully argued in court that CARB illegally stepped on federal turf when it asked Detroit to make zero-emission vehicles. In fact, the Bush administration joined that suit on the side of the automakers, signaling a likely federal stance should the greenhouse gas law also land in court. Everyone involved expects it will.

There's another argument that the car manufacturers sling at Sacramento. For all its size, California cannot by itself make a dent in such a worldwide problem as climate change. "Even if you abolished all motor vehicles in California, the level of greenhouse gases in the world would be unaffected," says Phil Isenberg, Detroit's lobbyist in Sacramento.

Lloyd insists that CARB's rules will "lead to real reductions" in gases that cause global warming, although he is elusive about how CARB will do that. His hope is that other states will copy California's rules for greenhouse gases, as they have for smog, and that Washington will be surrounded by world capitals on one side and state capitals on the other. "There's no action—or, in fact, questioning—going on at the federal level," Lloyd says. "California is again in a leadership role on the environment, a role we're accustomed to."

PRIVACY PIONEER

California is also emerging as the nation's primary battleground on privacy issues. On one level, this reflects the state's historically strong leanings toward consumer protection. That culture is now converging with the new realities of the Internet economy, much of which, despite the tech bust, is still based in California's Silicon Valley. As personal information flows ever more freely through computer databases and across borders, California more than any other state and more than Washington has sought to address privacy problems and identity theft, often with national reverberations.

For example, California passed a law in 1997 that helps identity-theft victims clear their credit reports; at least one of the three credit bureaus has decided to apply the rule nationally. Another California law, which takes effect 18 months from now, may change the way consumers around the country log into the Web sites of insurance companies. California doesn't want people to have to type in their Social Security numbers unencrypted, and since so many of the insurers' customers are in California, they'll likely make that change for everyone.

The database-breach disclosure law was conceived in the same spirit. Early last year, it seems, a hacker broke into a government computer system, compromising the payroll data of some 250,000 California state employees. While no actual cases of identity theft or economic damages were traced to the incident, the political damage was significant. As news of the infraction dribbled out, frustrated state workers wanted to know what data the hacker had gotten to, and on whom. Only months later did the state tell them. Lawmakers responded with the disclosure law, knowing full well that it would force businesses located in other states—and perhaps other countries—to comply. Companies that ignore the law risk facing class-action lawsuits in California courts.

High-tech businesses think California is taking a dubious approach. They would much rather see this sort of issue handled in Congress, not just because it affects national and international commerce but because their chances of either killing it or at least shaping it to their liking are better in Washington. "We're constantly telling legislators the Internet doesn't stop at the California border," says Roxanne Gould, a Sacramento lobbyist for the high-tech trade association known as AeA. "We regularly argue that it makes no sense to regulate these issues state by state when they should be dealt with at the national level or even the international level. That doesn't carry much weight in this legislature."

Joe Simitian, the bill's sponsor in the Assembly, sees it differently. Simitian is a tech-savvy legislator who represents part of Silicon Valley. He also chairs the legislature's select committee on privacy. He agrees that interstate issues of this kind should be handled in Washington. But he's tired of waiting. "I sympathize when the industry says it doesn't want 50 state standards," Simitian says. "But that's not an excuse for inaction. Many of the folks who testify in Sacramento for a single national standard are the same folks who testify in Washington for no standards at all."

31

Squeezing the Federal Turnip

Alan Greenblatt

This isn't the easiest time for localities to get money out of Washington. But they aren't about to quit asking.

Alan Autry, the mayor of Fresno, California, steps out of his Washington hotel into a bright, cold winter morning. "It's a great day to beg," he declares.

Today he will be begging at high levels, pleading with his state's congressional delegation for money. Autry takes this part of his job seriously, both in D.C. and in Sacramento. He's hired a lobbyist to work the California legislature for Fresno, after the city went a decade without one, and he's rejoined the U.S. Conference of Mayors after an even longer absence. In Washington, he's retained the services of Leonard Simon, one of the many lobbyists who specialize in guiding local governments through the federal policy thicket.

Autry understands that cities come to Washington for the same reason Willie Sutton robbed banks—because that's where the money is. Fresno, a fast-growth city that's now up to almost half a million people, is burdened by a long list of problems, including a 15 percent unemployment rate, air quality that's among the worst in the nation and enough crime to justify spending three-quarters of the city's general fund on public safety. That anti-crime concentration doesn't leave Autry much money to fund economic development efforts, or any other policy innovations, for that matter. In his quest for new revenues, Autry is hoping that Washington will help.

As it happens, the federal government is not in a particularly generous mood toward cities or counties just at the moment, with war and tax cuts dominating its agenda. Local officials complain that Washington is involving itself intrusively in issues such as public safety, education and election procedure, normally the province of state or local government. Moreover, the feds are mandating costly changes without offering sufficient help to enable the localities to pay

From *Governing*, March 2003.

for them. Autry and his counterparts around the country worry that further changes in federal health and welfare programs might lay more responsibility at their feet.

It appears that the agenda of cities and counties is more at odds with that of the federal government than it has been for a long time. "You get the feeling sometimes that the feds are just not on the same map as state and local governments," says Lynn Cutler, who worked in the White House intergovernmental affairs office during the Clinton administration and now lobbies for the city of Cleveland. "And—hello—I thought they all represented the same people."

But if states and localities are finding the feds unresponsive to the larger items on their agendas, earmarked funding for local programs remains a growth industry in Congress, with members eager to support projects that can earn political credit for all involved. If only the strongest dogs are going to get scraps in the present budget environment, it may be more important than ever for local governments to hire their own lobbyists if they want to stay in the hunt.

Fresno has been averaging more than $3 million a year in earmarked appropriations, which is pretty good, and as Autry makes his rounds on Capitol Hill, he takes pains to sound grateful. He thanks the city's three U.S. representatives—Fresno is split into three districts—for their help in securing money for transit and an industrial park. Autry is thrilled when Senator Barbara Boxer looks him in the eye and pledges her support for a half-million dollar study that may lead eventually to a major mass transit system in the San Joaquin Valley. "When you sit face to face to get a commitment, that's huge," he says.

Fresno's mayor has some advantages in working Capitol Hill that other mayors do not possess. When he walks down the hall with a congressman, Autry is the one guards and tourists recognize. Not many recall that he was a backup quarterback with the Green Bay Packers, but nearly everyone seems to remember his role as Lieutenant Bubba Skinner in the TV series, "In the Heat of the Night." While dining at his Washington hotel, in fact, Autry is recognized by the ambassador from Uganda, who says after the ice is broken that he'd like to come study the cotton fields outside of Fresno.

DOUBLE TEAMING

While the mayor shakes hands, poses for pictures and compares notes on football games, Simon stays in the background, checking appointments on his portable Web device. ("I have a deep passion for anonymity," he says.) But Autry plays up the veteran lobbyist's connections in an effort to score points himself with members of the delegation. He tells Devin Nunes, Fresno's 29-year-old freshman congressman, that Simon (who spent a decade lobbying for the U.S. Conference of Mayors and has been in private practice 15 years) will be available to help explain the players and the process on Capitol Hill. Over lunch, Simon points out some of his new congressional colleagues to Nunes and advises him to play pickup basketball in the House gym as a way of making contacts.

However helpful a service this may be, the fact remains that Autry, not Simon, is the city's most effective lobbyist. So why does Fresno need to pay Simon $24,000 a year to advance its interests? The answer is fairly simple: The money buys persistence. Autry will fly home the next day, but Simon will be walking the corridors over and over again, reiterating the same points to the same members, staff and executive branch bureaucrats. It is an article of faith on Capitol Hill that members of Congress respond to repetition—they believe that if a city keeps asking about a project, it must really want it. The more visits, phone calls and e-mails from Simon that are logged into a congressional office computer, the better Fresno's chances of seeing its projects through to completion. "I make a good pitch, then I go back and run a city," Autry says. "Any endeavor's going to take a sustained effort to push things through."

Or so everyone believes. "If you leave it just to the members and the senators," says Cutler, "they've got a whole lot of folks they have to take care of, and they're picking among their children in a way,"

Only the largest cities—Chicago, New York, Los Angeles—have their own Washington lobbyists on staff, but hundreds of cities, counties and transit authorities contract out such services. Most of them rely on small-shop lobbyists such as Simon, Carolyn Chaney (who, like Simon, represents several cities in the West) and Virginia Mayer (who works for Boston), or big law firms with municipal practices, such as Patton Boggs or Holland & Knight (where Cutler works). It's impossible to guarantee results, however, and some mayors question whether the expense is worth it. Cincinnati, for example, recently cut its Washington lobbying budget by 17 percent and may eliminate such spending altogether. "I don't think we're getting the kind of service we should for that amount of money," Mayor Charlie Luken, a former congressman, complained to his local newspaper recently. "I plan to do a lot more of the lobbying for the city myself."

Other mayors are just as convinced, however, that the money is well spent. The city of St. Joseph, Missouri, shares a federal lobbyist's time with the local college, hospital and chamber of commerce, an investment that Mayor David Jones says has paid off in additional highway money. "They know how to play the game better than us," Jones said during a recent visit to Washington. "Within an hour of a vote, we know how it affected St. Joseph. Having them up here to inform us is a huge benefit every day." Alan Autry agrees. "If you had to pick one or the other, an active mayor or a lobbyist," he says, "you better pick the lobbyist."

STRAINED RELATIONS

These days, hiring a friend in Washington may be about the only way a city can ensure that it will have one. Local officials are coming to town with low expectations and then finding even those too optimistic. Issues of the greatest importance to cities and counties barely register as a concern in the capital, even among members of Congress who used to be mayors or county commissioners themselves. When the problems do register, the first instinct often is to punt to the states, who can act as middlemen with the locals. The federal government has a constitutionally based relationship with states, and policy makers find it easier to keep an eye on how programs are doing in 50 states than tracking them through 19,000 local entities.

There is a widely stated notion that Republican control of both the White House and Congress makes federal relations even tougher for cities, whose political leadership is heavily Democratic. But municipal-federal relations seem to ebb and flow in ways that have more to do with institutional roles than with which party is in power. "Our membership is about half Democrats and half Republicans," says Larry Naake, executive director of the National Association of Counties, "and I don't think the Republicans are getting any more help than the Democrats from the federal level."

Bush administration officials, from Homeland Security Secretary Tom Ridge on down, have offered repeated assurances to local officials that Washington will send them billions of dollars for police, fire fighters and other so-called first responders. But those checks have yet to be put in the mail. Meanwhile, according to the U.S. Conference of Mayors, localities are out $2.6 billion in additional security costs for the year following the attacks of September 11, 2001. If the feds refuse to pay for a heightened state of alert for foreign terrorism, mayors complain, what would they pay for? "The perception is, here we come again with tin cup in hand," says Carol Kocheisen of the National League of Cities. "The other side of the equation is, we wouldn't be here again if you didn't want us to do X, Y and Z by yesterday."

There are other complaints as well. Because of accounting problems, the U.S. Department of Housing and Urban Development plans to cut aid to public housing by 10 percent from the amount promised earlier. That figure was itself a reprieve of sorts; the reduction was originally supposed to be 30 percent. New federal education testing and reporting requirements are going to cost state and local governments billions, and the hopes of additional federal funding for that purpose are becoming ever more dim. Last year's federal election law allotted $4 billion to help pay for new voting machines and other improvements, but local officials doubt that much money will actually be appropriated.

Cities, meanwhile, are suing the Federal Communications Commission to reverse a ruling last March that declared cable modem service to be an "interstate information service." That means that cable companies providing this service don't have to pay fees to cities, as cable TV franchises do, or reimburse them for tearing up rights of way. The loss in fees to local governments could add up to about $200 million a year. Ken Fellman, the mayor of Arvada, Colorado, and chairman of an FCC advisory committee on intergovernmental relations, says his state's congressional delegation is sympathetic to the cities' plight in the matter. But, he says, it's simply not an issue that distracts their attention from matters such as Iraq and homeland security. "Public safety and transportation are much higher on their priority level than consumer privacy or local revenues," Fellman says.

BANDING TOGETHER

To cope with the FCC ruling and other telecommunications matters, more than 100 cities have formed a lobbying alliance. That kind of response is necessary, they say, because of the generally poor coverage of communications issues: Of four federal lobbyists at the National

League of Cities, only one-third of the time of one of them is devoted to communications. The industries that cities are competing against, meanwhile, maintain some of the best-funded lobbies in Washington.

Local officials often feel outgunned in lobbying competition with private industry on many issues besides communications. For instance, cities and counties have not succeeded in several attempts at persuading Congress to pass legislation allowing them to force garbage haulers to take some of their waste to local facilities. (The Supreme Court ruled such requirements illegal in 1994.) "All the counties in the country couldn't defeat waste management companies," says one former city lobbyist who now works for Congress. "They don't pass out $100 bills."

Anyone who lobbies for local governments in Washington will tell you it's difficult right now to win any policy change aimed at helping cities in general. Decisions once made at the Cabinet level are now under strict White House control in the Bush administration. Where once the HUD secretary, for instance, was an internal advocate for more public housing funds, now he is more likely to toe the line in support of White House policies. "For all Andrew Cuomo's faults, he did have a relationship with the White House, one that was characterized by a robust debate with OMB over funding levels," says Kurt Creager, head of the Vancouver, Washington, housing authority, referring to Clinton's HUD secretary. "We don't have that anymore."

And—mostly under cloak of anonymity—local officials and lobbyists say that within the White House, the Office of Intergovernmental Affairs, which was never terribly powerful to begin with, has further diminished in importance. Director Ruben Barrales has been moved out of the West Wing and split off from the domestic policy operation. Barrales' role is to be a facilitator, presenting local concerns to federal policy makers and explaining consequent policies to cities, counties and states. Barrales says he's doing just that. "We spend a lot of time advising the president and others in the White House about concerns of mayors and local officials at all levels," he says. "In many ways, a lobbying effort is always involved in wanting more."

Many local officials, however, complain that communication flows only in one direction, with the administration handing out marching orders and not listening to their arguments. "Ruben was given less resources to engage with local officials than were provided to me," says Mickey Ibarra, who ran the Office of Intergovernmental Affairs during the second Clinton term and now lobbies for cities and corporate clients. "In the current administration, they have lost their place. There's no pretense of involving them." For all of his insistence on White House openness to city and county concerns, even Barrales has a hard time listing many Bush administration programs or policies of specific benefit to localities.

LOCATION AND LUCK

And so the best thing for a mayor to do in Washington right now may be to avoid the broader policy questions and instead focus on specific projects, coming up with a strategy for converting them into earmarked dollars. Then he or she can present that strategy on the Hill and work the phones until it bears fruit.

It's a cliché that much success in life springs from the mere act of showing up, but it's a lesson that cities far from Washington forget at their peril. A few weeks ago, Autry and Simon sat in the office of U.S. Representative George Radanovich, hoping to persuade him to keynote a regional clean air summit in Fresno in April. Local governments from eight counties, along with farmers, environmentalists and business leaders, will be gathering to formulate a plan for cleaning up the stagnant air in Fresno and California's San Joaquin Valley, which the EPA is about to downgrade from "severe" to "extreme," a move that will do nothing to burnish the city's image. Autry hoped Radanovich, who represents parts of Fresno, would lend his congressional imprimatur to the resulting plan.

As it turned out, he got more than that. While Autry and Simon were talking to Radanovich, four officials from the federal Environmental Protection Agency were cooling their heels in the congressman's cramped reception area. Radanovich brought them into the meeting, and won a promise that a top-level EPA official would attend the summit. That was important because it would tacitly link the Bush administration to whatever plan might emerge, which in turn would help assuage the concerns of corporations looking for a place to locate.

It was a small but significant victory—and one that was achieved essentially by coincidence. The right people turned up in the right place at the right time. "We plan everything meticulously," says Leonard Simon, "and then let life take over. Location and timing are just extremely important."

32

HUD the Unlovable

Christopher Swope

The federal housing agency changes its focus every couple of years. The only constant is local frustration.

Last year, shortly after taking over as President Bush's secretary of Housing and Urban Development, Mel Martinez cut off funding for "drug elimination" grants, a $309 million program aimed at providing drug treatment and beefing up law enforcement for residents of public housing projects. It wasn't either of these things that Martinez opposed—it was the fact that under his HUD predecessor, Andrew Cuomo, some of the money from the program had been used to buy back guns from tenants willing to turn them in. The National Rifle Association was fiercely opposed to the buy-backs, and the NRA had been strong supporter of Bush. So Martinez wasted no time in putting an end to the practice.

The move enraged local officials, especially since most of them were putting the money into security patrols, not gun control. But furious as they were, the locals weren't sure whom to blame: Martinez or Cuomo. Some saw Martinez selling out to a powerful interest group. Others faulted Cuomo's insistence on using a popular grant program to promote a cause for which it had never been intended. "Housing authorities got dragged into the desert of ideological warfare," says Kurt Creager, who heads the local agency in Vancouver, Washington, and leads the association of housing officials known by its acronym, NAHRO. "Very few of us were using the money for gun buy-backs, but now we're all scrambling to replace the lost funds."

If the locals felt they were caught in a federal crossfire, it was a familiar feeling. All through the past decade, they had grown accustomed to getting trapped by the ever-changing agendas and political ambitions of HUD's leadership. The 1990s were an era of

From *Governing*, December 2002.

passionate and politically driven secretaries, from Jack Kemp in the first Bush administration to Henry Cisneros and Andrew Cuomo under Bill Clinton. Each brimmed with ideas for reinventing, revamping and revolutionizing the agency and the federal housing program, prodding the nation's 3,300 housing authorities, who carry out HUD's policies at the local level, to change course over and over again.

Kemp sought to sell public housing to tenants, "empowering" them, as he liked to say, through the magic of homeownership. Cisneros set out to demolish the nation's worst public housing projects and create new ones, where the poor and the middle class could live side-by-side. Cuomo pushed an ambitious agenda to transform HUD's notorious bureaucracy, ending some of the inefficiencies that had plagued it since the its founding in the 1960s. In the middle of all that came Newt Gingrich and a Republican Congress that had very different plans for HUD. They wanted to shut down the agency altogether.

Martinez, who joined the current Bush cabinet from a county executive post in Orange County, Florida, promised that he would slow things down and give local authorities relief from all the upheaval. But since the episode with drug-elimination grants, the locals have been wary of expecting too much. "The current administration gives great lines about ending the Cuomo era of micromanagement," says Robert Rigby, housing director in Jersey City, New Jersey. "But that stated desire has not yet hit us. They haven't yet changed the environment."

40-DAY PLAN

In fact, housing authorities have watched the whole decade-long spectacle at HUD with a mixture of hope and dread. They knew from their own experience that the agency badly needed fixing. If all the ideas and agendas floating around the capital would improve public housing, so much the better. Yet they also knew their place at the bottom of the policy totem pole. With all the reinventing and political jockeying going on, they feared they would inevitably get squeezed in Washington's power games.

HUD's internal management did improve, slowly but steadily. By the time Cuomo left, the agency as a whole had worked its way off the government's watch list for waste, fraud and abuse. Congressional critics backed down on their threats to eliminate it. In fact, as HUD's managerial credibility has risen, Congress has increased its budget, so the local authorities have had more money to work with.

But those improvements have come with a cost. The more HUD has reinvented itself, the more sour its relationship with housing authorities has become. Tensions peaked under Cuomo, who slammed through a system for assessing the condition of the local projects. Housing authorities found the system both unfair and irrelevant. "Andrew came in and promised to change the world in 40 days or kill everyone trying," says Frederick Murphy, executive director of the housing authority in Syracuse, New York. "The assessment system was a disaster. It totally destroyed any positive relationship between the industry and HUD."

Martinez is much quieter than Kemp, Cisneros and Cuomo, as well as more sympathetic to the housing authorities. Mostly, he has kept HUD out of the news. He's declined to stake out titanic new visions for public housing and seems, so far anyway, uninterested in using the agency as a stepping stone to higher office. Shortly after taking over, Martinez put his aims this way: "One thing I don't want to do," he said, "is reinvent HUD."

YEARS OF TURMOIL

The fact is, however, that after what happened in the 1990s, just leaving the agency in peace amounts to a minor revolution.

The years of turmoil began in the first Bush administration, when Kemp promised to wage a "progressive conservative war" on poverty, with the emphasis on privatizing public housing by helping tenants purchase the units they were living in. Kemp made passionate speeches about how this would give them a greater stake in their communities and help lift them into the middle class.

The idea never gained much traction, however, within the Bush administration or with Congress. It also turned out that not many residents had the money or desire to buy homes in run-down or crime-ridden projects. Kemp's larger impact occurred inside HUD. Corruption had scandalized the agency during the Reagan years and Kemp successfully cleaned house. HUD's budget, after years of decline, was gradually built back up.

By the time Cisneros took over as President Clinton's HUD secretary, in 1993, the privatization effort had all but subsided and been replaced by concern for the physical condition of the nation's most deteriorated projects. A congressional commission found that 86,000 public housing units were in bad shape and isolated in pockets of poverty. Congress funded a program to begin demolishing some of those units, but Cisneros grabbed on to it and made it his own.

Cisneros, a former mayor of San Antonio, set the goal of blowing up America's most distressed projects, including many high-rises. He would replace them with something drastically different: townhouse communities where poor tenants lived next door to families paying market-rate rents, thus deconcentrating the poverty that had haunted public housing for decades.

But after the 1994 elections, when Republicans swept into power in Congress, Cisneros had to devote much of his energy to just keeping HUD alive. As an alternative to the agency's elimination, Cisneros suggested drastic reforms. One idea was to eliminate traditional public housing entirely, replacing it with a dramatic expansion in the number of housing vouchers residents could use on the private rental market. Other ideas included significantly downsizing HUD's staff, and reducing some 60 separate programs into three block grants.

While much of Cisneros' reform agenda never went anywhere, it did stave off HUD's critics. Congress left the agency alone, although not without slashing its budget. "HUD could have lost its seat at the cabinet table," Vancouver's Creager says. "Cisneros recognized that and mobilized to solve the core problems."

Then came Cuomo, in 1997. He had served as an assistant secretary to Cisneros, and he knew that HUD's credibility with Congress was still low. He forced through another round of reinvention that came to be known as the "HUD 2020" reforms. Management of many programs was turned over to private contractors, allowing staff levels to be reduced from 10,500 to 9,500. The first-ever assessment of the condition of the nation's assisted-housing stock was completed. And there was a new "enforcement center" to take action against negligent housing authorities and private landlords. By one measure, the changes seemed to pay off. In 1999, HUD's financial statements got their first clean audit ever.

Cuomo also had more traction with the White House than Cisneros or Kemp did, and his advocacy began to pay dividends. In 1999, Clinton's budget asked for new housing vouchers—and for the first time in four years, the Republican Congress gave him 50,000 of them. The pattern repeated itself the following two years, with 60,000 new vouchers for 2000 and 87,000 for 2001.

Unfortunately, the Cuomo reorganization was so drastic that it created a personnel crisis. Two in five remaining HUD staffers are eligible to retire within the next five years. "That was cutting muscle," says Michael Stegman, an assistant secretary under Cisneros.

STAFFING UP

It has put Martinez in a strange place for a Republican. He now finds himself staffing up the very agency that many in his party once wanted to eliminate. But aside from that relatively low-profile effort, and a non-controversial plan to increase minority homeownership, the agenda is short. "Martinez is less visible than any HUD secretary since the Reagan administration, but his message is very salient," Creager says. "He believes in ethical public administration, he believes in homeownership and he expects people to run local housing authorities in an effective manner. I can't argue with any of those. It may fall short of a vision, but in retrospect, the people with a vision often brought personal and political pain."

It's not as if all the fads and enthusiasms that have taken hold at HUD have disappeared without a trace. Kemp's strategy of selling public housing to tenants didn't go far, but years later, under Cuomo, it re-emerged in the form of Section 8 homeownership. Tenants can now use vouchers—normally reserved for rental housing—to make mortgage payments. The program is mostly a hit with housing authorities, and Martinez embraced it as part of his homeownership agenda.

In a similar way, Cuomo cut the ribbons at many of the projects rebuilt according to Cisneros' plans, and came to embrace their neo-traditional style of development. Another Cisneros proposal—vouchering out public housing altogether—was too controversial to be adopted on its face but continues to echo in Washington. Lawmakers are more willing to pay for housing vouchers than they are to pay for more public projects—and the balance shifts more and more toward vouchers with every high-rise that comes down.

What all the HUD regimes have had in common, despite their ideological differences, is a lack of discretionary funds. Despite a deepening affordable-housing crisis, housing is fundamentally off the national agenda. There hasn't been a national housing production program since the 1970s, and none is currently envisioned. While HUD's budget has risen over the years—from $19 billion in 1988 to $31 billion in 2002—most of that is out of the secretary's control. The cost of renewing housing contracts rises from year to year, for example, and now consumes more than half of HUD's budget. Most of the rest, including billions in community development dollars, is allocated to state and local governments by pre-set formulas.

Indeed, in the current environment, even activist housing secretaries can only hope to nibble at the edges. "The challenge any HUD secretary faces, be it Kemp, Cisneros, Cuomo or Martinez, regardless of their personal motivations, objectives, politics and influence, is that the HUD budget is basically pre-committed," says Conrad Egan, policy director at the National Housing Conference. "By the time you add in salaries and expenses, there's nothing left. It makes you wonder. Why be a HUD secretary? You may as well stay home and not come into the office in the morning."

INVADING ARMY

This is not to say that local officials don't feel HUD's impact every day. Most would say they feel it too much.

That opinion has grown since the Cuomo management reforms, and especially since the assessment of assisted housing. This was something HUD clearly needed to do. Each year, the agency was handing local housing authorities billions of dollars to fix roofs and do other maintenance. But when Congress asked HUD officials what they were getting for that money, they were unable to say. Cuomo finally got the answers but at the cost of HUD's remaining goodwill among its local partners. "I personally credit Andrew Cuomo with torpedoing the relationship that existed," says David Morton, head of the Reno Housing Authority and president of the Public Housing Authorities Directors Association.

> *HUD's budget has risen consistently over the years, but most of that money is outside the secretary's control.*

"He escalated friction between HUD and the housing authorities to a degree I've never seen in 30 years."

The annual public housing inspection program launched under Cuomo came to be known as PHAS. Hundreds of men and women toting wireless computers began fanning out into every public housing project in the country. They hiked through developments and peered into residents' homes, looking for signs of damage: cracks in walls, leaking pipes, broken fire detectors. The checklist ran 800 items long. Each time they found a problem, they punched away at their keypads, zipping the bad news back to HUD's offices in Washington. The procedure was an effective way to counter HUD's longstanding national reputation for waste, fraud and abuse.

But local housing managers had a much different view of PHAS. They saw Cuomo's inspectors as an invading army. The tiniest flaws sent the inspectors typing away. A closet door off its hinge could cost points, even if the tenant had never called in a work order. So could a weed growing through a crack in the sidewalk. Even well-run housing authorities felt they were doomed to fail the test. "It was a Gestapo approach," Morton says. "The attitude was 'you're all playing games and we're going to catch you.'"

What local officials found offensive about PHAS wasn't the fact that HUD was rating their performance. They agreed this was necessary and good. It was the absence of any local input into how the system should work. The housing authorities had no idea what they were being graded on or how that information would be used.

The current regime at HUD sees PHAS as a good idea, but one executed with HUD's traditional bureaucratic excesses—both in the top-down approach and the obsession with minutiae. "There were five or six different scoring factors related to holes in walls," says Michael Liu, Martinez' assistant secretary for public housing, "How many different elements related to holes in walls do you really need to determine whether or not there's a problem with the basic livability of that unit? It raises questions of basic common sense. How far do you need to go?"

Still, like so many other experiments of the past decade, PHAS has not disappeared; Martinez and Liu have asked the locals for advice on how to improve the inspections and make them more meaningful. HUD rules are due out soon that will specify changes in the system. "We've attempted to inject a clearer notion of what we want and a clearer way of measuring which gets away from the minutiae," Liu says.

Inevitably, however, all the years of frustration have taken their toll. In fact, they have generated something of an independence movement among local housing authorities and the associations that represent them. NAHRO hopes eventually to overthrow PHAS and institute its own assessment system. That project, which is still in early stages, is a collaboration with Standard & Poor's. The idea is not only to assess the physical condition of public housing but also to link the data with measurements of the authorities' financial condition. Proponents think this would give a better view of the locals' performance, and would be useful not only to HUD but to local housing managers and private investors as well.

Meanwhile, the PHAS fiasco has sparked discussions among some big city housing authorities about finding a way to get out from under HUD's oversight entirely. Some are pushing for a third-party accreditation system, similar to one used for hospitals. Others, increasingly entrepreneurial in their approach, are looking at ways to lessen their financial dependence on the agency by dipping into tax credits and other sources for cash, while partnering with private firms, nonprofits and foundations to fix up old housing and even build some new units. Creager's housing authority in Vancouver, for example, now depends on HUD for less than half of its assisted housing. "We've developed a diversified funding base," Creager says. "That makes us less vulnerable to the whims of federal policy makers."

33

The Avengers General

Alan Greenblatt

State AGs have accumulated an enormous amount of power. Too much, some people think.

Tom Miller, the attorney general of Iowa, is a genial sort of fellow, with sandy hair, a guileless face and a soft-spoken manner. But when he talks about suing corporations, he can sound a little menacing. Miller is convinced that, on many issues, attorneys general have become an almost unstoppable force. If the AGs get wind of a company engaging in illegal activities and join together against it, he boasts, there is nothing that company can do to head them off before justice has been meted out. "There's no political fix," he says. "They can't hire the right lawyers, they can't hire the right lobbyists. They can't go to the governors."

Few would dispute that, in the past five years, state attorneys general have altered the dynamics of corporate regulation in this country. They have taken on Microsoft and Merrill Lynch, Philip Morris and Household Finance. They have sued the manufacturers of compact discs and lead paint, footwear and George Foreman grills. And most of the time, they have won.

"In some ways, they're more powerful than governors," says Bob Sommer of MWW Group, a lobbyist for major corporate clients. "They don't need a legislature to approve what they do. Their legislature is a jury. That's what makes them frightening to corporate interests."

And most attorneys general have not been shy about acknowledging their influence. Last fall, when a coalition of AGs reached a $484 million settlement with the parent company of Household Finance, Miller called it a "basis for reforming the [lending] industry." New York Attorney General Eliot Spitzer made similar claims about changing the behavior of Wall Street financial firms when he announced settlement deals with them last year in a conflict-of-interest dispute.

From *Governing*, May 2003.

That a backlash against this power would ultimately emerge is no surprise. What is interesting is where the backlash is coming from—a dissident bloc of the attorneys general themselves. Four years ago, a group of Republican AGs created RAGA, the Republican Attorneys General Association, to stop what they called "government lawsuit abuse" and redirect state legal efforts away from national tort cases and back to traditional crime fighting. RAGA may not have slowed down the litigation process very much, but it has brought the office of state attorney general back into political play around the country. There were only 12 Republican attorneys general in 1999, when RAGA was founded; today, there are 20.

One of the RAGA recruits is Phill Kline, who was elected attorney general of Kansas last November on a platform that accused his predecessor of presuming corporations to be guilty and treating justice as a revenue source. Kline says today's activist AGs have gotten "dangerously close" to an "addicting" cash-prize legal system reminiscent of the old territorial practice of paying judges for convicting defendants.

Like several of the other RAGA rookies, including Mike Cox of Michigan and Brian Sandoval of Nevada, Kline feels it is a mistake to spend too much time and energy pursuing consumer cases at the expense of criminal prosecutions. He says he will pursue any case where there is clear wrongdoing and will join with other states when a case warrants it. But, in general, he favors a less confrontational approach, hoping that his fellow AGs will be more willing to talk things through with a company before filing a suit. "There's a different threshold that has to be met," Kline says. "You have to prove legal violations, not just an unfortunate policy result."

RAGA has received generous help in its bid to rein in the activists. Last fall, the U.S. Chamber of Commerce ran its own television campaigns against aggressive Democratic candidates for attorney general. So did the Law Enforcement Alliance of America, an arm of the gun lobby. In some states, these efforts generated million-dollar ad campaigns. In Texas, the Alliance's estimated $1.5 million late-season ad campaign helped keep the attorney general's office in Republican hands. This was an expanded version of the Chamber's effort in Indiana in 2000, when a $200,000 ad campaign was widely viewed as a leading factor in driving an incumbent Democrat out of office.

To some of the conservative AGs who are active in RAGA, winning elections is the one sure way to change the culture of the office. "Any time you've got more Republicans in any organization, it tends to be more conservative, more business-friendly and more anti-regulatory," says Virginia's Jerry Kilgore, the current RAGA chairman. Kilgore cites the issue of pharmaceutical pricing as one that would likely have been pursued by state AGs through the courts just a few years ago but is being addressed in much more quiet negotiations today. "Everything will be looked at more closely," Kilgore says, "to keep the balance between protecting consumers and allowing business to grow."

NO LETUP

Despite RAGA's successes, however, it is not at all clear that the activism of recent years is about to crumble away. Even the Republican attorneys general who have been most critical of the multistate cases have been happy to share in the wealth once a nationwide settlement agreement has been reached. True, they are less likely to generate such cases themselves. But there remain more than enough activist Democrats in office to keep the litigation going. "Even five to 10 AGs, if they have the resources and drive, can go ahead if they have a good case," says Tom Miller. "It was always a failed mission to get rid of the multistate cases by electing more Republican AGs, even a majority of Republican AGs."

The 58-year-old Miller, now serving his sixth term, is the dean of state attorneys general. He is happy to recite the history of the group, recalling the easy collegiality of the earlier years when few of the AGs even knew the party affiliation of their peers. The multistate approach, according to Miller, was born during the late 1970s, when several AGs wanted to pursue a case against General Motors Corp. They were afraid the carmaker would "out-resource us," and banded together to share their strength. "We started defensively," he says, "but then we understood there were some tactical advantages to joining together as well."

During the Reagan years, many of the state attorneys general felt that the Federal Trade Commission and the U.S. Justice Department's antitrust division were too wedded to laissez-faire regulatory dogma. (Connecticut Attorney General Richard Blumenthal has called the feds of that era "toothless and clueless . . . as a matter of ideology.") The AGs also noticed that many of the types of businesses they had sued in the past in their home states, such as pharmacists and funeral home operators, had become part of national chains. So they initiated a number of successful multistate consumer protection cases.

The combined weight of the AG offices, which range in staff size from about two dozen lawyers in South Dakota to more than 1,000 in California, was enough to take on even the most sophisticated corporations. Advances in technology—notably e-mail and conference calling—made it easier for state lawyers in disparate capitals to spread and coordinate their efforts.

By the end of 2000, various groups of AGs could boast of a long list of multimillion-dollar settlements. They had won $56 million in antitrust money from toy makers and retailer Toys "R" Us, and $16 million worth of settlements with Reebok and Keds to answer price-fixing complaints. They had forced Publishers Clearing House to pay $18 million to 24 states. They settled on favorable terms with retailers and consumer credit firms that had collected on debts discharged in bankruptcy and with pharmaceutical firms over complaints about the effectiveness of medicines and improper payments to pharmacists.

The pace has not slowed down since then. In the past few months alone, the AGs have claimed victory and $51 million in a case against Ford Motor Co. over SUV safety. They have settled two cases against Bristol-Myers Squibb, collecting a $155 million payoff, after claiming the company had blocked the introduction of generic alternatives to its drugs. Last year's litigation season brought the huge Household Finance settlement and Spitzer's series of agreements with Merrill Lynch and other Wall Street securities firms. Household will refund money to mortgage borrowers who were misled into paying extra charges, buying extra insurance or accepting unfair interest rates. The Wall Street cases turned on brokers recommending the stocks of companies their firms were doing business with (and issuing misleadingly cheery research about).

The granddaddy of all the AG successes, of course, is the crusade against the tobacco companies. When this case got underway in 1994, says Mississippi Attorney General Mike Moore, "I was alone. No one had a clue it was going on." But within four years, 19 other states had filed their own lawsuits. This led, after a period of delay in which Congress wrestled unsuccessfully with the issue, to the series of settlements with states initially estimated to be worth $246 billion over 25 years.

A few weeks ago, after Moore had announced he would not be seeking reelection this year, a group of contributors at a RAGA fundraiser in Washington lustily cheered. Moore calls that reaction "unseemly," but the more appropriate word might be "naïve." Moore may have started the ball rolling, but there are now at least a dozen attorneys general equally enthusiastic about launching anti-corporate lawsuits. And as critics continually point out, the attorneys general aren't a legislative body. They don't need a majority vote to proceed.

"If you assume over the next couple of cycles that this becomes a mature political office, meaning national interests are participating on both sides," says Sommer of the MWW Group, "you're never going to have more than 30 of one party and less than 20 of the other. You're always going to have plenty of AGs who are going to sign on to litigation."

> "There has been this tremendous redistribution of legal power away from Washington, and who better than states' attorneys general to step into the void to ensure that the rule of law is enforced?"
>
> New York Attorney General Eliot Spitzer

PURSUING POWER

Until recently, there has been no political cost imposed on an attorney general joining a multistate settlement—even if he didn't approve of bringing the case initially. The money is there on the table. Most AGs feel they wouldn't be doing their jobs if they didn't take it. Virginia's Kilgore, now the point man in the Republican drive to restrain AG activism, says that his decision to sign on to the Household settlement was easy: It represented $16 million for Virginia consumers.

The reality is that where there is money to be had from the work of others, virtually every state AG will come on board, regardless of ideology. "While they're getting a lot of funding from corporations to elect Republicans," says Lisa Madigan, the newly elected Democratic attorney general of Illinois, "the fact is that Republicans are participating in settlements. Essentially, you've got Republicans working both sides of the streets."

Democrats delight in pointing out such apparent contradictions. At an AGs meeting in Washington in March, Alabama Republican Bill Pryor introduced a constituent who runs a program designed to curb violence against women. Pryor is one of the leading conservative voices against AG excesses, but the Alabama program is funded by money from a multistate case against the women's footwear company Nine West—money that Pryor didn't mind accepting. California Democrat Bill Lockyer sarcastically commended Pryor "for his enthusiastic participation in the Nine West case. It made your outstanding initiative possible." Amidst the laughter of his colleagues, Pryor could say nothing but "thank you."

Free money aside, there is additional pressure on even reluctant attorneys general to join a multistate settlement. In many instances, the company involved in a case wants them to: The more AGs sign on to a settlement, the more protection the company has from future liability. Sometimes, a firm will demand as part of the settlement that states representing 80 percent of its customer base sign on before the agreement takes effect. Or that California and New York come on board, so it doesn't have to worry about suits from the big states down the road.

Pryor sees the wave of anti-corporate activism receding a bit now because Democratic AGs are fighting the Bush administration on issues such as environmental policy, leaving less time for private litigation than they had in the Clinton years. And he sees RAGA and its campaign assistance to be a further force that will restrain AG activism in the future.

But whatever the partisan or ideological makeup of the 50 AG offices around the country might be, it seems unlikely that a majority of them will want to renounce their influence now that they have attained it. Around the same time that RAGA was being formed, Spitzer, whose Wall Street investigations have largely been a one-man show, declared to a conservative audience that "there has been this tremendous redistribution of legal power away from Washington, and who better than state attorneys general to step into the void to ensure that the rule of law is enforced?"

In the long run, that is a proposition that attorneys general of all stripes are likely to find attractive, regardless of where their campaign money came from. "Like every officeholder, they want to enhance the importance of their office," concedes James Wootten, former president of the U.S. Chamber Institute for Legal Reform and a critic of the activists. "The trend will probably continue."

34

That Clean-All-Over Feeling

Alan Greenblatt

Maine's reformers believe they are washing the special interest money out of state politics. But critics say they are just laundering it.

From *Governing*, July 2002.

Jonathan Carter is a longtime believer in campaign finance reform. When he ran for governor of Maine in 1994, on the Green Party ticket, he refused all contributions from corporations and political action committees, and accepted no more than $100 from any individual donor. That campaign, Carter says, was a "statement," designed not to win but to publicize his eco-friendly views. He got 6.4 percent of the vote.

Carter is the Green Party nominee for governor again this year, and he's still turning down PAC money and large individual contributions. But this time, he's out to do more than just make a statement. He thinks he can win. And there's a reason for that: Under Maine's "Clean Elections" law, enacted by the voters in 1996, he will receive checks from the taxpayers totalling $900,000.

Carter has already starting using his cash windfall to bring in more experienced advisers, and has expanded his platform to emphasize issues beyond environmental health. He will have the funds necessary to spread his campaign through paid advertising all over the state. "Win or lose," he boasts, "we will get our message to every single household in the state."

He can do that because Maine has become the national capital of campaign finance reform. Anyone who wishes to pursue any state office there is granted enough free money to run a credible campaign, as long as he receives a sufficient number of $5 contributions upfront to show his serious intent. More than half of this year's candidates for the legislature are renouncing private funding and going for the public money.

The major-party nominees for governor, Democrat John Baldacci and Republican Peter Cianchette, are turning down the public subsidies and raising money the old-fashioned way. But Cianchette's primary opponent, Jim Libby, went the public route and was given $314,000 on the basis of only $13,000 in small individual contributions. Libby drew 33 percent of the primary vote.

For many of the publicly funded candidates, it is an exciting new opportunity. "I think it's a very freeing feeling," says state Representative Marilyn Canavan, who sits on the heavily lobbied House Banking Committee and helped draft the law as head of the state ethics commission. "It means I can make decisions that are right for the people of Maine, and not be concerned in the least whether any campaign contributions are forthcoming."

But whether Maine has really succeeded in lessening the role of special interests in state politics is a more complicated question. Because there are no restrictions on what the parties can spend—even on behalf of "clean candidates"—there are those who see the new law as likely to attract more special interest money, not less. Among those skeptics is the governor, Angus King. The clean elections law, he says, "has a gigantic loophole that really bothers me. You're running as a clean candidate, but the party can spend a million dollars on your behalf. To me, that undermines the whole premise. What you've really done is add a layer of public money to the old system."

The argument in favor of clean elections is that they allow candidates more time to meet with constituents instead of raising money, while liberating them from the pernicious influence of big-money contributors who will want something in return. The reality is that aggressive fundraising is continuing in Maine even as most candidates receive state funding. "Because candidates are not coming after us," says Joe Pietroski of the Maine Bankers Association, "political parties are very much after us for financial support."

Beverly Daggett, Democratic leader in the state Senate, sued to block the clean elections law, but nevertheless has "no reservations about taking the money" for her own campaigns. "It means any money I raise can go into the leadership or caucus PAC," she points out, "or anywhere else I decide I want it to go." Her Republican Senate counterpart, Rick Bennett, also opposed the law initially, but has used it as a recruiting tool and encouraged members of his caucus to accept public financing. Bennett had $280,000 in PAC funding to spend during the 2000 election cycle, and will likely raise a similar amount for this year's races.

Bennett's PAC was a heavy financial player in a special Senate election in March that demonstrated some of the major weaknesses of the new system. The three leading candidates for the Portland-based seat all ran "clean," but because the election was so close and so important—it stood to break a partisan tie in the chamber and was ultimately decided by just 10 votes—it attracted more than $100,000 in independent expenditures, far more than the candidates spent themselves.

Democrat Michael Brennan, the ultimate winner, thinks his race was an anomaly, the subject of such intense interest both because Senate control was at stake and because there weren't any other campaigns taking place at the same time. But the regular primaries and general election seem to be attracting interest-group spending of a similar magnitude. The Alliance for Maine's Future, a PAC funded in large part by the Maine Chamber of Commerce and paper and construction companies, quickly raised $93,000 this spring to support candidates in Democratic primaries in June in Waterville and Skowhegan. Maine is facing one of its periodic legislative battles over workers' compensation, and the PAC was trying to defeat two Democrats who have been leading allies of organized labor.

Some specialists see all these developments as evidence that the whole idea of cleaning up election funding is misguided. "The Maine system sooner or later will once again demonstrate the folly of most campaign finance reform," predicts Larry J. Sabato, a campaign finance expert at the University of Virginia. "There is no way to stop the flow of interested money, and there will always be constitutional ways around the restrictions enacted into law."

None of those objections have detracted, however, from the law's growing popularity. The Clean Elections Act went into effect in 2000, and in the first year of operation, half the state Senate and 30 percent of the House won election "running clean." This year, the number of candidates using public money is expected to double, and take in a majority of all candidates.

Candidates like to complain that qualifying for public money is complicated and paperwork-intensive, but the basic idea is simple. Candidates must spend no more than $100 of their own money getting their campaigns off the ground. They then must collect a set amount of $5 contributions from individuals—50 for legislative races and 2,500 in the case of candidates for governor. That entitles them to as much as $18,000 if they are running for the Senate, $4,700 if they are running for the House and $1.2 million for a gubernatorial contest—assuming they win the nomination and remain active through the entire cycle.

Those may sound like tiny amounts compared with what is spent in larger states around the country. But Maine has a small population and a low-key political system with a tradition of informal personal campaigning. A budget of $18,000 comes closer to full funding of a state Senate election than it would almost anywhere else in the country.

In addition, the clean elections initiative has imposed stricter limits on the amounts individuals, corporations and PACs can give to candidates who opt for private fundraising. Where individuals could once give $1,000 to a candidate, and PACs and corporations could give $5,000, now all contributors are limited to no more than $250 per election.

All of this makes Maine's experiment the most extensive in the country up to now. But Arizona's may soon approach it. That state's voters approved a ballot initiative along similar lines in 1998, and in 2000, 59 candidates ran with public money. Two candidates for state corporation commissioner used public money and won.

The number of publicly funded candidates was considerably smaller in Arizona than in Maine two years ago, but that could change this year: By some estimates, as many as 70 percent of the 250 eligible candidates on the ballot in Arizona in 2002, including at least one in each of nine statewide contests, could go the public route. There also is a push to extend public funding to judicial candidates.

Arizona's population and districts are bigger than Maine's, so candidates there have to coax $5 contributions from more people. But they enjoy a bigger payoff as well. Legislative candidates receive $27,000 per cycle, while gubernatorial hopefuls get more than $1 million.

In most other states, recent efforts to give public financing a true test have run into problems. Massachusetts has yet to see its first publicly funded state campaign, even though voters approved pubic financing in 1998, because a hostile legislature, led by House Speaker Thomas Finneran, has refused to appropriate the money. Earlier this year, public finance advocates went to court and won the right to auction off state property to pay for implementation of the law, but only token amounts have been raised so far. (Their plans to sell furniture from the offices of Finneran and a pair of his allies were blocked.) Green Party gubernatorial candidate Jill Stein has qualified for even more money than Jonathan Carter—$3.4 million—but because of the legislative dispute, she'll never receive that amount. Finneran has launched an effort to repeal the law altogether.

Public campaign financing has also lost support in Kentucky. Governor Paul Patton and the legislature failed to reach an agreement on a budget this spring, largely because Republican legislators refused to fund public financing for gubernatorial candidates next year. Kentucky has a system under which candidates for governor who raise enough money can receive funds from the state that match the private dollars, as long as they agree to spending limits. Many Republicans feel that even this modest pubic funding system cost them the governor's mansion last time around. Both parties have taken their case directly to voters via radio spots.

A number of other states have enacted partial public finance laws of one sort or another during the past three decades, and some have achieved modest success. Candidates in Minnesota, for instance, tend to abide by spending limits and receive some public financing in return.

More commonly, however, public financing has been a failure, largely for one reason: The money available—usually from voluntary tax checkoff schemes—is insufficient to pay for the campaigns it is supposed to cover. Wisconsin, for example, became a pioneer when it enacted a public financing law 25 years ago. But spending limits have not been raised since 1986, and participation in the voluntary tax checkoff has fallen below 10 percent. That means that the amount of public financing grants has dropped to the point where no serious legislative or gubernatorial candidates are willing to choose them instead of taking private contributions.

State Senate candidates, for instance, can now receive $8,000 in public funds toward an overall spending limit of $34,500. That's peanuts when candidates are spending upwards of $150,000, and when million-dollar Senate races are no longer a rarity. The result is that Wisconsin's public financing system has been moribund for a decade.

Maine's law was carefully written to avoid the Wisconsin problem. Each office-seeker who takes public money gets an amount based on an aggregate average of campaign spending during the previous cycle. This year, all Senate candidates who go the public route will receive $18,000 for their general election campaigns, up from $12,000 last time. The increase is due in large part to one candidate, W. Tom Sawyer, who two years ago spent $153,064 on a Senate contest in a district in Bangor—five times as much as any other successful Senate candidate and close to 10 times the average amount spent to win a seat.

Meanwhile, the Maine legislature has appropriated more than enough money to cover the deficiencies of the tax checkoff. In 2000, this appropriated amount came to $865,000. In 2002, it is expected to rise to $2.5 million because of the increasing number of participating candidates and the expense of the race for governor. This has generated only occasional objections from legislators on the basis of cost.

There are, however, plenty of people in Maine political circles who argue that public financing remains a solution in search of a problem. In the cycle leading up to passage of the clean elections initiative, the average successful candidate for the Maine House spent less than $4,200. A significant number of privately funded candidates went far above this amount, but they didn't do particularly well: Half of the 10 highest-spending candidates for both the House and Senate lost.

> "I think part of the intent of the public in passing the law was to take money out of politics. It ain't gonna happen."
>
> Ed McLauglin, president of the Maine Chamber of Commerce's political wing

The state's tradition of inexpensive elections was something that proponents of the public finance initiative were able to use to their advantage. Commercials supporting the initiative featured timeworn images of fat money-men smoking cigars. They sought to create the impression that the law was needed to preserve the state's old-fashioned political culture—that without some form of public financing, Maine could turn into another Massachusetts or New Jersey.

That may have been a little far-fetched to begin with. Maine is a state where many voters still are uncomfortable with the idea of negative advertising, let alone back rooms or political bosses. But it seems clear that, whatever the presence of special interests may have been under the old system, they have not gone away.

The state's lobbyists and pressure groups are adapting to the law, changing the way they interact with candidates seeking office. Rather than treating candidates like United Way charities, writing out checks and declaring themselves done, interest groups are recruiting candidates themselves, and then running issue ads, which do not fall under the clean elections law limits. "People are changing strategies to do the same things they've always done," says Ed McLaughlin, president of the Maine Chamber of Commerce's political wing. "I expect as time goes by and people get savvy about what they can and cannot do, you're going to see more money come into campaigns. I think part of the intent of the public in passing this law was to take money out of politics. It ain't gonna happen."

35 Addicted to Corruption

William Fulton and Paul Shigley

San Bernardino has been crooked for years. It will take years to clean it up.

From *Governing*, November 2002.

One day early this summer, more than 700 people filled a hotel ballroom in downtown San Bernardino, California, 60 miles east of Los Angeles. Few events attract much of a crowd to downtown San Bernardino, a district with so little vitality that city officials are seriously considering replacing blocks of it with a series of reservoirs and canals. But on this seasonably warm day, a sellout crowd had paid $35 to attend the annual "State of the County" luncheon.

The state of the county wasn't very good. It hasn't been good in years, not because San Bernardino lacks natural advantages or economic potential, but because the government is a perennial mess. In the past four years, 13 public officials and private businesspeople have pleaded guilty to bribery charges. Two more are awaiting trial. The county has filed civil suits for corruption against nearly two dozen of its citizens, winning $15 million in cash settlements and another $7 million in judgments still unpaid.

The elected leaders who were present at the annual luncheon didn't dwell on any of this. Supervisor Fred Aguiar referred briefly to the civil suits by promising that "as far as the remaining defendants are concerned, the county is ready to go to trial." Supervisor Bill Postmus tried to make the best of it all in his invocation: "Thank you for taking us out of the difficult times that we've had in the past, Lord."

But it's far from clear that the difficult times are over. They have been going on—or at least have been common knowledge—since August 1998, when County Administrative Officer James Hlawek revealed that he was under investigation by the FBI and resigned. The announcement was stunning. The mild-mannered Hlawek was viewed as a straight arrow, and certainly a contrast to his predecessor, Harry Mays, a flamboyant, personable executive who made no apologies for playing fast and loose with conflict-of-interest regulations. As it turned out, however, Hlawek had hidden a prior felony in Arizona—and was being investigated on allegations of taking bribes from none other than Mays himself.

Over time, it became clear that Mays, Hlawek and other top elected and appointed officials in San Bernardino County had been operating a vast "pay-to-play" scheme. Sole-source contracts were available for the right price—contracts worth hundreds of millions of dollars for everything from bond underwriting to landfill operations. The procurement process included trips around the globe, campaign donations, promises of future employment and plain old cash. This wasn't a case of a few rogue officials or even a nest of wrongdoers. It was an entire system—a small-scale modern equivalent of the Tweed Ring that looted New York City in the 19th century. San Bernardino County wasn't just plagued by corruption—it was practically addicted to it.

In the years since then, several county officials, including some newly elected supervisors, have assumed the role of reformers. They have undertaken internal investigations, tightened contracting and conflict-of-interest rules, and plunged ahead with their civil suits. But even as the downtown meeting took place this summer, one of the five sitting supervisors, veteran Gerald Eaves, was continuing in office despite his indictment for taking bribes to approve billboards along Interstate 10.

After all the scandals, residents of the county are entitled to ask themselves a few simple questions. They know they live in the nation's geographically largest county. Is it possible they also live in the most corrupt?

More fundamentally, how does any local government get into trouble of this magnitude? And how does it climb out?

GROWING PAINS

California is not exactly corruption territory, especially on the local front. Thanks to the Progressive movement almost a century ago, the state has no local political machines of the East Coast or Rust Belt variety. Local government is officially nonpartisan—party involvement in local campaigns can lead to fines and sanctions—and county supervisors are usually chosen in springtime primary elections. Local politics is not free of the typical corrupting influence of campaign contributions—but out-and-out graft is rare.

Yet, as the San Bernardino story reveals, the corruption stew can bubble up anywhere the ingredients are present. In this case, the ingredients were a vast county in the midst of rapid growth, an inattentive population of commuters focused on the distant locations where they work, and a good-old-boy network ready to exploit the opportunity.

At 20,160 square miles, San Bernardino County covers more territory than any county in the continental United States. It is larger than Massachusetts, Connecticut and Rhode Island combined. Most of the land is in the Mojave Desert, including Joshua Tree National Park and military bases so large and remote that no one notices when the military conducts large-scale battle simulations with live ammunition. Most of the 1.7 million residents are in the far southwestern corner, at the edge of the Los Angeles basin.

Those people live in a spectacular natural setting—a sun-drenched valley bordered on three sides by rugged mountains as high as 10,000 feet. However, the location and topography have their drawbacks. The heat can be oppressive, and air pollution generated many miles away, along the coast, blows eastward toward San Bernardino, then hovers, trapped by the mountains. Hence, the San Bernardino-Riverside metropolitan area has the worst air quality in the country, and the snow-capped peaks are often obscured.

Like the rest of metropolitan Southern California, the

San Bernardino County Fast Facts

Geographic area: 20,160 square miles (about 90% desert)
Mean travel time to work: 31 minutes
U.S. mean travel time to work: 25.5 minutes
Year incorporated: 1853
County budget FY2002: $2.5 billion

Population 2001: 1,766,237
% Population growth since 1980: 92%
Ethnic breakdown (2000):

- White 58.9%
- Black 9.1%
- Hispanic 39.2%
- Asian 4.7%
- Other 28.3%

Source: U.S. Census Bureau, San Bernardino County

urbanized corner of San Bernardino County grew rapidly in the years after World War II. But while much of the Los Angeles region grew more affluent, San Bernardino's towns remained rooted in the working class. A huge Kaiser Steel factory, Norton Air Force Base, several large railroad yards and maintenance facilities helped provide a stable job base for decades. With the blue-collar job base and proximity to ever-encroaching Los Angeles, the county grew from just 160,000 people in 1940 to 1.4 million in 1990.

But between 1983 and 1994, Kaiser closed, railroads consolidated and pulled out, and the Air Force decommissioned Norton. As a result, the 1990s were particularly tough for San Bernardino County. During the first half of the decade, unemployment was in the 9 percent to 10 percent range. The city of San Bernardino was among the nation's leaders in the foreclosure of VA mortgages.

There are clusters of new jobs in San Bernardino County, especially in the logistics industry. Ontario International Airport, extensive rail lines and several interstate freeways make the area ideal for shipping and warehouse operations. In general, however, those jobs do not pay as well as the manufacturing and military-related jobs that vanished.

Even so, the county's population grew by 20 percent in the 1990s—nearly 300,000 people. Most of the new residents were drawn not by local job opportunities but by inexpensive housing. The working-class communities of San Bernardino County offer new houses for about half as much as cities to the west, closer to L.A. Southern California author and urban theorist Mike Davis calls places such as San Bernardino "the new dormitories for Southern California's burgeoning workforces."

BACKROOM DEALS

Until at least the 1960s, San Bernardino County essentially operated as a collection of small towns. Over time, inevitably, the size and scope of county government—and county contracts—grew dramatically. But local politics remained largely unchanged, says James Mulvihill, chairman of the geography and environmental studies department at California State University, San Bernardino. Long-time family and business connections remained as important as ever. Those who took care of a candidate were taken care of once the candidate got into office. "You can call it an old-boys network," says Mulvihill, "but it means something to voters if you grew up in San Bernardino."

Mulvihill and others suspect that quid pro quos have been standard in San Bernardino county government for decades. Supervisor Dennis Hansberger, who served two terms during the 1970s before returning to office in 1996, thinks that the corruption mess dates to the late 1970s—just as the county's population was approaching 1 million. By that time, Hansberger says, the county had started attracting intensely political supervisors "who tended to want to pursue their own interests without looking more broadly at the interests of the county government. They began to play fast and loose with county policies, and no one stopped them. I think most of their early excursions were minor, but . . . in the '80s it began to grow even more."

Backroom deals and sole-source contracts actually became county policy when Mays, who began his county career as a "Boys Ranch" probation counselor in 1966, reached the corner office in 1986. After his return to the Board of Supervisors in 1996, Hansberger recalls, then-deputy Hlawek told him, "It's our practice not to have dissension in the board room. And Harry's rule was, if we don't have agreement, it's not ready to be on the agenda."

In early 1997, there was a scandal involving a proposal to develop a giant garbage dump in the desert. Investigation centered on the dealings of two private companies that were at war over the proposal, but a grand jury indicted the county planning director, who eventually pleaded no contest to stealing a public document. A planning commissioner was later ousted for conflicts of interest.

Shortly thereafter, federal authorities began to take notice. It is widely assumed in San Bernardino (although the U.S. Attorney's Office in Los Angeles will not confirm it) that a low-level county employee tipped off federal authorities because the employee could no longer stand to see county leaders manipulate the system for their own personal benefit. A few county officials seemed to be spending more time in New York City or overseas than in San Bernardino, and these officials made no secret of the fact that they were not paying for the trips. Mays, who retired in 1994 to pursue business interests, still seemed to be calling many of the shots.

The federal investigation took time. It was not until October 1999 that federal authorities issued their first indictments. Named were Mays; Hlawek; County Treasurer-Tax Collector Thomas O'Donnell; county investment officer Sol Levin; Kenneth James Walsh, a vice president of Norcal Waste Systems Inc., which operated a county-owned landfill; and two private consultants. All seven eventually pleaded guilty to bribery, and six went to prison. Mays' two-year sentence was the longest. Hlawek cooperated with federal investigators and is due to be sentenced in November.

According to federal authorities, Mays went straight from the county payroll to a consulting job with Norcal, which paid him at least $3.5 million. Mays kicked back about $200,000 to Hlawek, who ensured Norcal received a no-bid landfill contract worth tens of millions of dollars annually. Mays also kicked back about $1 million to Walsh, who kept Mays on the company payroll.

In a second round, federal prosecutors indicted Supervisor Eaves, two businessmen, and four public officials from Colton, the town adjoining the city of San Bernardino, alleging that all but one were involved in bribery schemes for billboards along I-10. Eaves was also indicted under state law on 17 misdemeanor counts of accepting improper gifts and two counts of lying to the grand jury. He pleaded no contest to four counts of using his position to influence government decisions in which he had a financial interest and three counts of failing to report gifts. The court ordered him to pay the county $20,000 and forbid him from running for office again. Eaves' attorney called the plea bargain "an honorable close to a sordid, politically motivated ordeal," but Eaves himself continued to argue that prosecutors had exaggerated the importance of "minor ethical lapses" and paperwork problems.

LOOKING THE OTHER WAY

Why did things go so wrong in San Bernardino County? And why did top county officials believe they could openly flaunt ethical standards and the law?

People inside and outside of local government say public apathy deserves at least some of the blame. "We're talking about gratuities for services rendered," says Mulvihill, who ran unsuccessfully for city council in San Bernardino as a reformer in the 1990s. "It was basically a very simple form of corruption. It has existed for so long that people didn't even think about it."

Will Randolph, who served as county administrative officer in the aftermath of the scandals, from 1999 to 2001, agrees. "There were lots of warning signs early on that, had the public demanded action, some of this could have been headed off," he says. For example, Mays used to purchase houses—once, even an airplane—at county tax auctions. There were newspaper stories and even a civil grand jury report on Mays' practices, which may not have been illegal but which were at least in an ethical gray area. Yet no one stopped Mays.

Randolph brought in Michael Josephson, a Los Angeles-based ethics consultant, who interviewed top administrators and found that the situation had been brewing for years. "While relatively few people were engaged in corruption, a lot of people were willing to look the other way," Josephson said. "You didn't go very far in that organization if you rocked the boat. . . . There was absolutely a fear of retaliation."

Equally clueless were the newer residents, those who had moved in from the more sophisticated political environs of Los Angeles and Orange counties. They also looked the other way. In particular, they looked west, spending so much time commuting to distant jobs that they had neither time nor energy to connect to local government.

Compounding the situation was a lack of coverage by the local press. From 1992 to 1996, the *San Bernardino County Sun* did not assign a reporter to county government full-time. When the San Bernardino paper pulled out, competing, financially strapped papers—such as the *Inland Valley Daily Bulletin* in Ontario—felt comfortable doing the same. They knew they were not going to get scooped. It was in the absence of any media scrutiny at all that the county handed out its rich, sole-source contracts, including the landfill agreement with Norcal. "Unfortunately," says Supervisor Hansberger, "the media, being in the condition they are in . . . do not keep the public as informed as they deserve to be."

It was Hansberger who, shortly after taking office in December 1996, first began asking questions about the county's contracting procedures. But his voice remained the sole dissent until Aguiar, a former state assemblyman, took office in December 1998. By that time, the FBI investigation was public knowledge.

In 1999, as the news grew steadily worse, the supervisors hired Randolph, a respected executive who had been chief investigative officer in Fresno County. "I knew it was a distressed situation, but nobody knew the extent of it at the time," he recalls. One of Randolph's first tasks was figuring out whom to trust. He met with the FBI and U.S. Attorney's Office, he says, but "they didn't tell me anything."

So Randolph brought in the investigative arm of Arthur Andersen Inc.—which had a good reputation at the time—and the Los Angeles legal firm of Gumport, Reitman & Montgomery, to conduct an internal investigation and, eventually, pursue two civil lawsuits to try and get some of the stolen money back. "No matter where the trail led us to, and who it led us to, we were going to pursue it," Aguiar says. "We investigated every contract, every deal."

The following year, the county sued three of its former officials—Hlawek, Treasurer-Tax Collector O'Donnell and investment officer Levin—as well as Peter Morrison, a vice president with Salomon Smith Barney, and Jeff Jackson, an agent for the New England Adjustable Rate Government Fund. The county alleged that from 1992 through 1998, Morrison and Jackson supplied the county officials with trips all over the U.S. and Europe, bought them expensive meals and entertainment tickets, and paid cash bribes. In exchange, the county claimed, the public officials directed hundreds of millions of dollars of investments and bond activities to the financial companies.

The county filed a separate lawsuit over the scheme behind the Norcal garbage contract. And it sought to escape from $33 million worth of contracts to lease real estate owned by Mays.

More than half of the defendants have settled—Salomon Smith Barney for $7.75 million, New England Adjustable Rate Government Fund (now called CDC Nvest) for $750,000, Norcal for $6.5 million, O'Donnell and Levin for $3 million apiece. Hlawek agreed to pay $300,000 to settle some of the claims, but he, Mays and others remain defendants in the civil litigation.

UNFINISHED BUSINESS

Besides the lawsuits, the county has overhauled its contracting and leasing procedures, revised its investment policies, adopted the ICMA Code of Ethics, established a fraud hotline, hired a county ethics officer, improved background screening for job candidates, updated employee training, and shown the door to about 25 department heads and administrators. Current County Administrator John Michaelson said he feels free to make recommendations with which supervisors might disagree. "There's an honest debate," he insists, "that now happens in the light of day."

Still, questions remain. Randolph figures he got "maybe half way" with the reforms on his agenda when he departed in June 2001. "I left," he laments, "because the whole board got into this them-against-us. So the whole team I built with this board's blessing became the whipping boys."

Josephson, the ethics instructor, has expressed doubts that county officials are ready to make the necessary commitment to put the mess behind them for good. "They started the process," he says, "but they didn't finish it. To make these ethics programs work, they need to be incorporated into the entire organization. There was a big kill-the-messenger situation there."

Of course, the messenger has been delivering bad news for years. With a sitting supervisor recently indicted by the state attorney general, the bad news is unlikely to go away anytime soon. Eaves remains in office, participating in county business and refusing to go down without a fight. He contends the grounds for the case against him—that a billboard developer bribed Eaves by giving the supervisor, his family and his chief of staff 10 trips to the Stardust Hotel in Las Vegas—are flimsy. "Eaves himself does not even like going to Las Vegas," one defense motion contends.

"It's a continual distraction for us," Aguiar says of the Eaves indictment. "I don't think the county will be able to take the final step until the issue is resolved one way or the other."

Of course, the first step to recovery is admitting there is a problem. San Bernardino County's current leaders have done that. But like any recovering addict, the county will need some outside vigilance to stay clean. Right now, federal prosecutors and the press are providing that vigilance. At some point, though, the legal proceedings will end, and the story will drop from the headlines. When that happens, officials' voluntary adherence to the system will become even more important.

"These problems," says Josephson, "are not intractable. But they require a sustained commitment. . . . You've got to try to motivate the public to care."

For years, a public that was more concerned about long-distance commuting than about local politics allowed scoundrels to watch the till. Despite the outrage of the moment, there is no solid evidence that the fundamental problem of an apathetic electorate has been solved. An indicted supervisor—ordered by a court not to run again—remains in office, a graphic reminder that the fight against local corruption, like the fight to overcome any addiction, is a long, painful and uneven process.

36

The Soft-Money Crackdown

Alan Greenblatt

There's a lot that state political parties still don't know about the new campaign finance law. They need to learn fast.

Mitch Daniels is the leading Republican candidate for governor of Indiana, and he has spent the winter doing the things all such candidates do: attending Lincoln Day dinners (more than three dozen at last count), showing off his made-in-Indiana RV and extolling his own virtues and those of President George W. Bush.

The link with the president is a natural connection for him to make. The 54-year-old Daniels has had a long career in government and in the pharmaceutical business, but he is best known for his stint as Bush's budget director, a post he gave up last year to run for the top job back home. Bush's operatives helped clear the GOP field for Daniels, and the president himself has already made an early campaign appearance for him.

And Daniels, in return, praises Bush to the skies. "Providence was smiling on the United States of America," he told nearly 300 party faithful at a Lincoln dinner in Shelby County, "on that night when George Bush finally became president of the United States." Nearly all Republican regulars agree that sticking close to Bush will be a big help in November. "Around here, Bush is a shoo-in," says Rob Nolley, a Shelbyville city councilman. "Daniels' experience working for him is a big deal."

But Daniels' stamp of approval from the White House has suddenly become a lot harder for him to show off. On the day of the Shelbyville dinner, the Federal Election Commission ruled that Bush cannot appear in endorsement ads proclaiming his fondness for Daniels—or any other Republican—unless Bush's campaign pays for the ad itself. Under the new rules, if Daniels pays for or approves a TV spot that features Bush or even mentions his name, he will tech-

From *Governing*, March 2004.

nically be making an illegal donation to the Bush campaign. "Absurd is not strong enough a word," Daniels fumes. "If anything we contemplate is really proscribed by that law, it ought to be amended immediately."

The statute Daniels refers to derisively as "that law" is the Bipartisan Campaign Reform Act, known more widely as McCain-Feingold, after its two sponsors in the U.S. Senate. The law was passed by Congress in 2002 and was, for the most part, upheld by the Supreme Court last December. Political professionals are generally familiar with its effects on fundraising by federal candidates and its restrictions on advertising by outside interest groups. But state and local officeholders and party officials are only beginning to sort through the effects the law will have on parties and anyone running for office at the lower levels of the American political system.

Those effects will be profound. All the nuts-and-bolts party work that takes place within 120 days of a federal election—general or primary—such as identifying voters, registering them or bringing them to the polls, has been reclassified as "federal election activity." It is subject to federal regulation and must be paid for with so-called hard money (donations that are limited in amount and require federal disclosure). It doesn't matter whether a local party seeks merely to support its local sheriff. If there is a federal candidate on the ballot, the party's contacts with voters are considered federal activity and subject to the new regulations. "State and local parties can't get around the law by avoiding the mention of a federal candidate's name," warns Donald Simon, counsel to Common Cause and a leading campaign finance lawyer.

"You could interpret this law so broadly that if I tell people to 'vote for the Republican team,' that could trigger federal disclosure and reporting requirements," says Indiana state Representative Mike Murphy, the newly-installed chairman of the Marion County (Indianapolis) Republican Party. "The whole psyche of how people identify with political parties would be damaged if state and local candidates have to put up a Chinese wall between themselves and federal candidates."

CRIMINAL OFFENSES

It's not only going to be harder for state and local parties to help federal candidates—it's going to be difficult for them to promote state and local candidates in federal election years. The law creates new categories of money and makes it much more complicated for parties at various levels—local, state and national—to transfer money among themselves. In California, for example, the Republican Party contracts with its 58 county central committees to handle the work of registering voters. The state party has to explain to the county organizations that it can no longer reimburse them for those costs—or, if it does, the local party becomes ineligible for receiving other types of financial help from the state or national party, according to Chuck Bell, an attorney for the California GOP.

"The unfortunate consequence of the law, at least in the short term, is that it strains our relationship with the county party committees," says Bell. Even if the county parties manage to raise adequate operating money on their own, they will have to file complex monthly forms with the FEC if they spend just $5,000 a year on registering voters or calling them on Election Day to remind them to turn out. These rules may not be easy to enforce, but there are criminal penalties for violation, and few party officials will want to risk going to jail in order to test the boundaries of the law.

Over the past year, former party officials have been setting up quasi-party organizations known as 527s, after a section of the U.S. tax code. There are legions of these groups, including traditional names such as the Republican Governors' Association and new ones called America Coming Together (pro-Democrat) and Americans for a Better Country (pro-Republican). The 527s were planned as a way to skirt McCain-Feingold's restrictions on parties by spending hundreds of millions of dollars during this campaign year.

But the FEC ruled in February that the restrictions on "federal election activity" during even-numbered years apply to 527s as well as parties. So there appears to be no chance that the 527s will supersede the parties entirely. "I would rather see parties get money rather than outside groups," says Sarah Morehouse, a University of Connecticut political scientist, "because I see the parties as having the ability to broker interests or moderate interests, rather than groups that are single interests and have one ax to grind and can give a lot of money to their candidates."

American political parties are nothing if not adaptable. Once the dominant force in American politics—deciding who would get to run for what office and with how much support—they have found a new role as support organs, offering consulting and fundraising services to self-selected aspirants. Now, with those functions under legal restriction, the parties may be forced into still another role: as clearinghouses of legal advice for avoiding the law's many minefields. "The bottom line," says Wayne Hamilton, a senior adviser to the Texas GOP, "is we tell our local parties to stay completely away from any type of federal activity unless they have the money to hire attorneys that specialize in FEC regulation and federal campaign laws."

Many state parties are currently hosting seminars for local party officials, trying to help them understand the shifting world created by the new law. "It doesn't seem plausible that Congress could regulate bumper stickers for local sheriffs," says state Representative Luke Messer, executive director of the Indiana GOP. "One of the unfortunate consequences of this law is that it weakens parties."

MACHINE POLITICS

Indiana, more than most states, has a powerful party tradition. The Marion County (Indianapolis) Republicans, in particular, operated a formidable political machine, coordinating thousands of volunteers, dominating local offices, running up the score for statewide candidates and providing Richard M. Nixon the solace of knowing there was one big city where he remained popular even during the latter years of his presidency. As state Senator Lawrence Borst recalls in his memoir of 40 years in Indiana politics, the Marion County party used to screen and recruit candidates from county treasurer (still a rich source of patronage jobs) all the way up to the U.S. Senate. The local GOP was instrumental in creating a unified city-county government, which gave Republicans a 30-year lock on the Indianapolis mayor's office—a lock that was broken only four years ago by Democrats, aided by the fact that thousands of Republicans had moved beyond Marion to outer suburban counties such as Shelby, Hendricks and Hamilton.

> "It doesn't seem plausible that Congress could regulate bumper stickers for local sheriffs. One of the unfortunate consequences of this law is that it weakens parties."
>
> State Representative Luke Messer

It wasn't until the 1970s that Indiana did away with the practice of nominating candidates by party convention, rather than open primary. It wasn't until the 1980s that it abolished the custom of entrusting the parties with the lucrative job of running the county vehicle license bureaus. Even now, Indiana's parties receive funds from the sale of vanity license plates—about $750,000 a year for each party, much of which trickles down to county organizations. That may "not be enough money to wad a pop gun," as former Marion County GOP Chairman John Sweezy says, but having three-quarters of a million dollars to start with, even in non-election years, has established a steady income stream that has allowed some party officials to make six-figure salaries and has created more stable careers in politics than are possible in places where parties close up shop in odd-numbered years.

Even in an era of candidate-centered politics, there's been plenty of work for the parties in Indiana to do. During the last gubernatorial campaign, the state Democratic Party and its incumbent, Governor Frank O'Bannon, split the political chores. O'Bannon's team took care of the big money activities, such as polling and media buys. The state party handled direct mail, absentee ballot applications, phone banks, bumper stickers, posters and yard signs. It was a formula that worked very well.

But it cannot be easily repeated this year. Under McCain-Feingold, party activities that once could be split on a prorated basis between federal and state accounts will now have to be paid for entirely with federally regulated dollars (dollars that can come only from individuals in limited amounts). Local parties and candidates for state offices, who can raise large amounts from corporations and unions, have not been in the habit of soliciting strictly limited individual donations or having to account for them. "What will be the reaction of governors and state legislators when they realize state parties can't use funds the way they used to for get out the vote, voter identification and voter mobilization?" asks

Benjamin Ginsberg, counsel to the Bush-Cheney campaign and numerous state parties.

Those who believe in the McCain-Feingold approach think the critics are exaggerating the problem. Even under the strictures of the new law, parties will still raise and spend more for candidates this year than any of the outside groups that have sprung up in response to the changing rules. "Party operatives tend to have a worldview that very little regulation is good but even less regulation is better," says Simon, the Common Cause counsel. "The new law doesn't say to them that they can't do any of these activities or work with federal candidates. The law just regulates what kind of money they can use for these activities."

What they can't use is the funding known ubiquitously as "soft money"—contributions that until now have been largely unregulated and could be collected in unlimited amounts from corporations, unions and wealthy individual donors. Under the old system, state parties became conduits for soft money that was spent, sometimes surreptitiously, to support candidates at the federal level. Prior to McCain-Feingold, the rule was that state parties could use soft money for anything that qualified as "party-building activities." But the soft-money exemption grew into an enormous loophole, stretched to the point where national parties were using state parties as conduits for millions of soft-money dollars spent mostly to pay for TV ads.

During the 2000 and 2002 election cycles, the two major national parties gave $472 million in soft money to state parties around the country. In 2002, according to Anthony Corrado, a campaign finance scholar at the Brookings Institution, state parties spent only about $52 million on genuine party-building expenses such as voter registration, buttons and yard signs. Most of the rest went to produce and broadcast advertisements—ads that were essentially immune to regulation or accountability for their cost or content.

LEVIN BUCKS

In cracking down on the abuse of soft money, the authors of McCain-Feingold didn't intend to weaken state parties. They actually tried to help the parties in a couple of ways. One was to double the amount of money they could receive in hard-dollar contributions. Secondly, they created a new category of contributions: the so-called Levin funds. If state law permits, state and local parties can raise Levin funds (named for their Senate sponsor, Carl Levin of Michigan) in chunks of up to $10,000 per year from individuals, PACs, corporations and unions. Levin dollars can be used only for certain expenses related to federal election activity. They can't be used for ads or other communications with the public, and they come with numerous restrictions that lawyers will make a lot of money explaining to parties in the coming months.

Despite the complications, not everybody—even within state party organizations—thinks the parties will necessarily suffer as a result of the new law. As a state senator in 1998, George Jepsen sponsored Connecticut's first-in-the-nation state ban on soft money. "Short of public financing," he says, "if you're looking for ways to restore some sanity to the process, a ban on soft money sort of jumps out at you." Now that Jepsen is chairman of the state Democratic Party, he has to live with that ban. But he says it hasn't been so bad: His fundraising was up by more than a third in 2003, compared with 2001. His party has hired a full-time field director and is providing professional services such as enhanced voter files to town committees and candidates.

In the past couple of years, Connecticut Democrats have made major inroads into traditionally Republican territory, including the affluent suburbs of Fairfield County. Democratic mayors and first selectmen now preside over 70 percent of Connecticut's population. Jepsen attributes these gains at least in part to the Democrats' ability to adjust to the new rules and take advantage of them. "We're turning the party," he says, "from an organ that really just convened conventions and stamped people on the foreheads as Democratic candidates, into a party that actively provides services and reaches out to constituencies."

BAYH-IN

When it comes to national politics, Indiana is a reliably Republican state. Not only does it support the GOP candidate for president every four years but because of its early poll-closing time, it is nearly always the first state to be colored Republican red on network TV maps. Still, Hoosier Republicans have lost the governorship four times in a row, in large part because of Evan Bayh, the popular moderate Democrat who captured the statehouse in 1988 and 1992, then passed it along to his lieutenant governor, Frank O'Bannon, who won in 1996 and 2000. (O'Bannon died last year and his replacement, Joe Kernan, will be the Democratic nominee against Mitch Daniels.)

Bayh's strength not only boosted O'Bannon into the governor's mansion but also has helped Democrats control the state House of Representatives for all but two of the past 16 years. Bayh is in the U.S. Senate now, and he continues to maintain favorability ratings around 70 percent. Indiana Democrats running for lesser offices routinely associate themselves with him to get elected. "Why wouldn't you want to hitch your wagon to somebody like that?" asks Dan Parker, executive director of the state Democratic Party.

But because of McCain-Feingold, that is not so easy anymore. The new law imposes restrictions on using the images of federal candidates, so Bayh probably won't be featured on any of the party's posters in 2004. Merely including the senator's name on an invitation to a party event, Parker says, now requires a disclosure so long and complicated that some traditional donors mistakenly think they're not allowed to give money to the party at all.

Nothing frustrates Parker more than the prospect of losing Bayh's presence in state and local campaigns. Last November, for example, the senator agreed to appear in an ad endorsing Jonathan Weinzapfel, the Democratic nominee for mayor of Evansville. But Bayh knew that McCain-Feingold had changed the rules, so he asked for an advisory opinion from the FEC on whether it was permissible for him to appear on TV on behalf of a local candidate.

In the end, the ad was approved because Bayh wouldn't be on any ballot for more than 120 days (the period of time before a federal election during which most of the new restrictions apply). Candidates who want to use Bayh's image this year—or Republicans such as Daniels who want to feature Bush—can do so only between May 5 (the day after the state's primaries) and July 4, when the 120-day period before the November election opens up.

And even during the brief window in which the ads are legal, any federal office-holder who appears in them can't mention his job title or talk about himself in any way. "I was happy to abide by the new law," Bayh says. "It did, however, make a traditional, innocuous activity more cumbersome and expensive."

As candidates and party officials sort through McCain-Feingold's permutations, many worst-case scenarios are being trotted out. Campaigns for Congress might become legally segregated from state and local officials in ways that could cripple intraparty communication. Zealous local prosecutors may seize on violations for use as political weapons. Campaign consultants worry about having to incur the expense of producing ads far in advance, as Weinzapfel did, to allow the FEC to rule on them—thereby telegraphing strategy to their opponents in the process. Some states are even talking about moving their state elections to odd-numbered years in order to avoid the law's encumbrances.

In the end, none of these things may happen. Bayh is confident that, as the campaign season wears on, the law's complexities will get sorted out. The decision in his case, after all, set the precedent for the new restrictions on ads featuring President Bush. As the FEC's thinking becomes clear, there will be less need for parties and candidates to consult with lawyers on every move they make. Rules that are now unsettling may soon become second nature.

But the most certain outcome of the law, which was designed to limit the influence of money in politics, is still likely to be a perverse one. There will be more money raised than ever—not only by the new 527 groups but also by parties and candidates at different levels of government who previously worked together but now can't rely on each other to make sure the party's message is getting out. "We can't share plans, and we can't coordinate the way we used to," says Don Morabito, executive director of the Pennsylvania Democratic Party. "We're either going to be duplicating our efforts in significant areas, or we might be ignoring important areas. We may be wasting resources or not doing what we need to do."

37 Sugar Daddy Government

John Buntin

A new generation of billionaires is remaking American cities. The cities are better off; the democratic process sometimes suffers.

From *Governing*, June 2004.

A dozen blocks north of downtown Seattle, the neighborhood adjoining Lake Union is in the midst of transformation. Alongside the car dealerships, sign stores and furniture markets that line Westlake Avenue, there's a new biomedical research laboratory, a bioinformatics facility for Merck, the drug company, and new labs for the University of Washington. All told, more than 3 million square feet of new development is underway in a little pocket of the city.

This is happening in the midst of Seattle's worst recession in 30 years. So it's no wonder that local officials look to the laboratories and biotech businesses as a form of economic salvation. Mayor Greg Nickels says it's as important to the city "as the day Bill Boeing started to build airplanes."

The official name of this neighborhood is South Lake Union. But some residents have another name for it: Allentown. That's because it started as the private vision of one man, Paul Allen, the co-founder of Microsoft. Thanks to Allen's wealth (about $21 billion, according to *Forbes* magazine), the development of South Lake Union has been able to proceed regardless of business cycles.

It's not his only project in Seattle. Over the course of the past seven years, Allen has orchestrated the construction of a new football stadium, redeveloped the old train station, financed two museums (a shrine to rock-and-roll and a science fiction museum), refurbished a classic movie palace and contributed generously to new libraries at the University of Washington and downtown. In the process, he has emerged as Seattle's most important civic figure—more important than anyone in elected office. Allen's idiosyncratic vision and passion for development are literally reshaping the city.

There is only one Paul Allen. But there are billionaires doing roughly similar things, if on a generally smaller scale, in quite a few cities around the country these days. Some, such as New York Mayor Michael Bloomberg, have used their wealth to win power the old-fashioned way—by getting elected. Others find running for office unnecessary, even irrelevant. Instead, with major cities starved for funds, they are simply using their private fortunes and the skills that made them rich to change their hometowns.

In Madison, Wisconsin, businessman Jerry Frautschi's Overture Foundation is spending $100 million to transform the dated Civic Center into the hub of a thriving arts district. The oil-rich Bass brothers have refashioned once-decrepit downtown Fort Worth into Texas' liveliest urban center. Nor are the wealthy limiting their activities to economic development. In Los Angeles, Eli Broad, a businessman who had the good sense to establish two Fortune 500 companies, has become not just the city's most generous benefactor but its most powerful private citizen, deeply involved in controversial issues that range across the policy spectrum. Not since midcentury, when David and Nelson Rockefeller operated in New York, the Chandler family ruled Los Angeles and Amon Carter rode herd on Fort Worth, have wealthy individuals held such sway and had such impact on the official apparatus of government.

For mayors and civic activists accustomed to the negative effects of corporate consolidation and the loss of local business leaders, the appearance of a new generation of activist-tycoons sometimes seems like a godsend. "The fact they are out there enables the city government to think boldly," says David Brewster, executive director of the Seattle arts group Town Hall, "because the bold thought will appeal and the bold thought might be funded. We all walk around with much bigger ideas in our head."

Not everyone is so sanguine, however. The same qualities that make someone successful in business—decisiveness, self-confidence, the relentless pursuit of a distinctive vision—can be a recipe for conflict in the public realm. For politicians who cross their paths or for citizens who reject their visions, power-wielding billionaires can be frightening. "No matter how benevolent the actor may be," insists John Fox, the head of a group called the Seattle Displacement Coalition, "it is inherently undemocratic."

AFTER THE VAULT

There is nothing new about rich people being involved in urban planning. To a great extent, it is the way planning has traditionally been done. But it used to be done largely through organizations. In Boston, there was "The Vault," an informal but powerful group named after the bank meeting room where the city's business elite met to plot downtown developments. Los Angeles had the "Committee of 25." In Seattle, it was the Rainier Club, in Cleveland, the Union Club. The names were different, but the purposes were much the same: These were the associations of local decision makers, and they wielded enormous—if often hidden—clout behind the scenes of formal city government.

Then came the upheavals of the late 1960s and early '70s. By the end of that time, private corporate power in most (although not all) American cities was in retreat. Seattle was typical: Its city council enacted a flurry of reforms designed to open meetings and development proposals to public scrutiny and limit the role of private wealth in politics.

To much of the electorate, and to many local officials, this was good news—a sign that influence at the community level was finally being democratized. But cities soon discovered that an anemic business community could be worse than the old overbearing ones. As local retailers and hometown banks disappeared, replaced by national chains, local corporate leadership withered. Even the biggest cities were not immune from these trends. By the late 1990s, Los Angeles, the nation's second-largest city, was virtually devoid of Fortune 500 home offices. "You've got to look hard to find a major corporation headquartered here," says L.A. School Superintendent Roy Romer. "It's hard to call in a key group and say, 'You represent the structure and leadership of the community, let's get this done together . . .'"

But the same processes that were displacing local companies were creating vast new fortunes for entrepreneurs shrewd enough to harness them—people such as Paul Allen, Michael Bloomberg and Eli Broad. The relationship of these new business tycoons to their hometowns was very different from that of the old business elites. The wealth of the old business leaders had often been tied directly to the health of their hometowns. The new tycoons are in business around the world; the precise economic condition of Seattle or Los Angeles isn't crucial to their fortunes, even though they may live there. And they are more loners than joiners. When they invest their money in the city, it's a personal choice—a way to pursue an individual passion. That offers both opportunity and danger.

MAN OF MYSTERY

Paul Allen is something of a mystery even in his hometown. "It's hard to get much of a fix on him," says David Brewster. "He doesn't grant interviews. There's this kind of, 'Why are you so reclusive?' But on the positive side, people feel he is what you might call an original."

Allen is 51 years old. He and Bill Gates first met as high school students in suburban Seattle. Both were computer hobbyists, and they soon found they shared the dream of making a living writing commercial software. Eventually, they both dropped out of college (Allen from Washington State, Gates from Harvard) to join forces and start a company called Microsoft. Soon thereafter, Allen purchased the rights to the operating system that would become DOS. When IBM selected DOS to run its first consumer PCs, Microsoft's explosive growth began.

A battle with cancer forced Allen to drop out of Microsoft in 1983, but he held on to his Microsoft stock. As a result, by the early '90s he was one of the world's richest men. He invested in high-tech start-ups, bought Ticketmaster and the Portland Trail Blazers basketball team, and in 1995 stepped into local politics by supporting a plan to transform South Lake Union, a gritty commercial neighborhood with a smattering of low-income housing, into a grand urban park.

Allen came late to this effort, but after he purchased 11 acres of neighborhood land for what was called the "Commons" project, he became closely identified with the effort. Opponents denounced it as a ploy to "yuppify" Seattle, and Allen soon emerged as a central figure in Seattle's nastiest class battle in many years. Despite the project's unanimous support from the city council, the electorate rejected it twice.

After the Commons defeat, Allen was left with 11 acres of undesirable land. But his public involvement escalated. In 1997, he bought the Seattle Seahawks football team, demolished its stadium, the Kingdome, and bankrolled a referendum campaign that persuaded state taxpayers to finance a new facility. He started buying even more property in South Lake Union. It soon became clear that he had a new vision for the neighborhood: He wanted to transform it into a mixed-use, environmentally sustainable biotech center. In 2002, he found an unexpected ally in Greg Nickels, Seattle's newly elected mayor.

In many ways, it was an unlikely partnership. During the mayoral campaign, most of the city's "cyber-riche," including Paul Allen himself, had sided with Nickels' opponent, incumbent Paul Schell. Nickels, a former King County councilman, had relied on labor unions and neighborhood activists for most of his support. Nickels and Allen were not exactly buddies; they had met a handful of times, and then only at social functions or sporting events. Yet soon after taking office, Nickels decided to embrace Allen's vision for South Lake Union.

After talking with researchers at the University of Washington, the mayor concluded that the next big thing was biotech—and that South Lake Union was the place to do it. There was just one problem. South Lake Union was a grungy, low-income neighborhood cut off from the rest of the city by two freeways. Nickels proposed spending nearly $500 million in state and local funds to upgrade the area's infrastructure and make South Lake Union into a desirable neighborhood.

Nickels knew that one of the effects of such massive investment would be to further enrich Paul Allen, who owns about 40 percent of South Lake Union through his Vulcan development company. However, the mayor argued that Seattle and the state of Washington stood to benefit even more. A study commissioned by the city's Office of Policy and Management estimated that developing South Lake Union could generate as many as 23,000 new jobs and $1.3 billion in new revenues for the state and city. A third of those jobs would come in the field of biotechnology.

"I was elected eight weeks to the day after September 11," Nickels says. "Boeing was laying off thousands of people, the hospitality industry was on its knees. We have since then been in the top five in unemployment as a state and our part of the state is particularly hard hit. So the question I was facing was how to build a strong economic future."

LINGERING DOUBTS

Not everyone accepts the job-creation forecasts for South Lake Union as solid.

Local critics argue that Nickels is asking for a big public investment in pursuit of an uncertain payoff. "The projections for growth are highly speculative and rest on assumptions that Seattle will capture this inordinate share of national biotech market," says John Fox. "We could take a fraction of what we are spending"—about $30,000 per job—"and generate more jobs."

Councilman Nick Licata, Allen's toughest questioner on the council, talks in similar terms. "I think in some ways Mayor Nickels is more under the influence of Paul Allen than Paul Allen is under Mayor Nickels," he says.

Others focus on the close connection between the city administration and Vulcan, Allen's development company. "They have extraordinary access to this government right now," says Peter Steinbrueck, the head of the city council's urban development and planning committee. "I haven't seen this administration raise a single objection to anything that Vulcan has proposed. Sometimes it comes out as not Vulcan's plan but the city's or the mayor's, but much of it behind the scenes is really being directed by Vulcan." In short, there is growing fear that Allen is changing Seattle from a city where neighborhoods, activists and elected officials set the vision into a place where an unelected but immensely wealthy individual does. "It inherently works to distort policymaking and planning," John Fox complains, "to reflect the vision of the individual as opposed to the many."

BROAD AGENDA

Other cities exhibit similar ambivalence toward their current billionaire benefactors. Los Angeles is feeling it about Eli Broad, the city's second-richest man, who led the homebuilders Kauffman and Broad (now KB Homes) and the annuity giant Sun America. Broad, 71, is a native New Yorker, the son of staunchly Democratic lower-middle-class parents who, in his words, "was raised on this rhetoric of the poor workers and the big bad bosses."

While Broad made much of his fortune building suburban tract houses, he has also made a major effort to strengthen central Los Angeles, arguing that "no city in world history has been great without a center." In the late '70s, he took the lead in creating the Los Angeles Museum of Contemporary Art. More recently, he stepped in to rescue the faltering downtown Disney Concert Hall project, and adjudicated a longstanding dispute between the city and Los Angeles County over development plans for Grand Avenue, a downtown boulevard that Broad is determined to transform into Los Angeles' Champs-Elysées.

Meanwhile, Broad has used his money to alter the course of city electoral politics. Two years ago, when communities in the San Fernando Valley considered seceding from Los Angeles, he attempted to reconcile the warring camps. When that effort failed, he contributed handsomely to a successful media campaign aimed at defeating the secession movement in a referendum.

At the same time, he has emerged as an often-controversial power behind the scenes in the city's school policy decisions. In 1999, Broad helped engineer a takeover of the L.A. school board. Along with Mayor Richard Riordan, he created a new school pressure group, the Coalition for Kids, and contributed more than $200,000 to its slate of candidates. The Coalition's slate swept into office, defeating three incumbents. Two years later, Broad and Riordan pressured one board member to scale down a teacher salary increase, and then, when she refused, contributed to a candidate who ousted her in the next election. Broad is said to have dangled $10 million before the president of Occidental College in an unsuccessful effort to persuade him to run against another school board member.

All this involvement in local politics has generated a backlash, notwithstanding the general good feeling about Broad's charitable efforts. Broad has become a target for criticism not only from teachers' unions but also from the *Los Angeles Times*, which has published accusations that Broad profited from school board construction decisions and improperly lobbied the school board to build yet another Broad project: a fancy new arts high school downtown.

SUNDANCE ADVENTURES

To the extent that Eli Broad's involvement in civic affairs is a problem, however, it's a problem many other cities would love to have. In an era in which cities compete fiercely to attract new residents among the "creative class," large donations to the arts or to downtown redevelopment can be community-defining events. That certainly has been the case in Fort Worth, where the billionaire Bass brothers have spent most of the past 20 years putting their personal stamp on the city's central core.

Heirs to the estate of legendary oilman Sid Richardson, the brothers hold the largest family fortune in

Texas. Since the early 1980s, they have been committed to using some of it to bring the center of Fort Worth back to the glory days they remembered as children, when they had gone downtown to visit their Uncle Sid.

Perhaps the most committed was Ed Bass, who had studied architecture at Yale and was determined to transform downtown into a vibrant, mixed-used area. In 1983, when Ed Bass opened a nightclub in downtown Fort Worth, with an apartment for himself on top, the area was in serious decline. "The curbs were just crumbling," says Bill Boecker, who now oversees development on the 40 blocks of Bass property downtown. "Storefronts boarded up as far as you can see." There was nothing to indicate that downtown Forth Worth would escape the fate of other declining urban centers.

Bass selected an area of low-slung buildings around Main Street and named it Sundance Square, in honor of the outlaw who had frequented the area at the turn of the century. When a natural gas explosion damaged four city blocks in 1986, Ed Bass bought much of the bombed-out property, built luxury apartments, and persuaded a theater chain to put a Cineplex downtown. To run Sundance Square, the Basses brought in a manager from the Rouse Company, developers of Boston's Quincy Market and many other urban commercial projects. To ensure the safety of their developments, they created their own private police force, reportedly the fourth largest in Tarrant County. Some locals called it, jokingly, the Basstapo.

STRAINED RELATIONS

Even when activist billionaires steer clear of local politics, their dealings with civic leaders can be fraught with difficulty. In Cleveland, Peter Lewis, chairman of the Progressive Insurance Co., has repeatedly clashed with local officials and with the hometown establishment. In the mid-1980s, Lewis approached then-Mayor George Voinovich about relocating the company's corporate headquarters to a Frank Gehry-designed skyscraper downtown. Lewis' idea wasn't exactly embraced by the establishment. At the party to unveil his plan, the head of the city's most powerful law firm turned to Lewis and asked him where he worked.

To Lewis, it was a vivid demonstration of his outsider status, a sign that the insular Cleveland establishment wasn't interested in him. The deal eventually fell apart under conditions both sides still refuse to discuss, depriving Cleveland of a landmark building. Stung by this defeat, Lewis decided to focus his philanthropic activities on Case Western Reserve University and nearby University Circle, only to watch with dismay as, he says, the university mismanaged a $36 million gift. In 2001, an angry Lewis denounced the school, describing it as "a diseased university that is collapsing and sucking Cleveland into a hole with it." To protest the establishment's supposed stranglehold over the city, Lewis suspended all of his local giving.

The moratorium remained in effect until last fall, when Lewis invited cultural institutions in University Circle to request funding for plans that would remake the area into a multi-use, "must-experience" 24/7 neighborhood. In the meantime, however, New York and other cities benefited from large gifts that might otherwise have gone to Cleveland.

Lewis may be more eccentric than any of his fellow billionaire activists. He's brutally candid about saying what's on his mind. At age 48 (he is now 70), Lewis announced he was getting divorced because he would no longer go along with the pretense of monogamy. He admits to enjoying marijuana and has bankrolled ballot initiatives across the country to legalize the use of marijuana for medical purposes. But he continues to insist on what Jennifer Frutschy, his philanthropic adviser, calls "the challenge of excellence and always doing better than what was there before."

Peter Lewis shares with Allen, Broad and the Bass brothers a zeal to break with established institutional processes—to create, as Broad puts it, "new things that don't exist, rather than presiding over the status quo." Lewis' admirers applaud him for giving Cleveland's political establishment a kick in the pants, just as Allen's supporters applaud the Microsoft tycoon for prodding city leaders to think in more ambitious terms.

If the new generation of politically active billionaires is a threat to liberal democratic values, not every liberal seems to realize it. "These guys are probably more creative partners to work with than the traditional local bank executive or chamber of commerce president," says historian Walt Crowley, the founder of historylink.org and a person known throughout Seattle for his left-leaning views. "They're definitely more fun."

Crowley should know. Paul Allen is historylink.org's most generous private donor.

38

How to Win Friends and Repair a City

Rob Gurwitt

Atlanta needs all the help it can get. Luckily, it has a mayor who knows where to get it.

Last fall, the president of the Georgia Senate, Eric Johnson, published a letter in the Atlanta Journal-Constitution. It was polite, as public rebukes go, but just barely.

The subject was Atlanta's sewers, or, more precisely, Atlanta's desperate need for help in fixing its sewers. After four decades of deferred maintenance and a federal consent decree that city officials had ignored for years, the bill had come due. Under its new mayor, Shirley Franklin, Atlanta was embarking on a $3 billion overhaul, but it was also staring at astronomical water and sewer rate increases for residents. The new rates promised much hardship for Atlanta's large population of poor people—who in a few years might be paying a total of $100 a month—and for its businesses, especially hotels, which in this convention-dependent city could be paying $100,000 a month by 2008. Not surprisingly, Franklin wanted help from the state and the federal government in defraying the cost.

Johnson's letter was his way of saying "forget it." Atlanta had repeatedly shrugged off its responsibilities, he said, and now had to pay the price. "I will fight any effort to shift the costs of Atlanta's sewer repairs onto the taxpayers of our state," Johnson wrote. "And I will not participate in any effort to ask that America's taxpayers share in your costs, either. . . . Atlanta is already costing Georgia's taxpayers plenty. I will not ask them for any more."

As unsympathetic as the letter might have been, its symbolism was even more barbed: a white Republican from Savannah lecturing the black Democratic mayor of a majority-black city on its spendthrift ways. It's not hard to imagine a disastrous chain of events: fury in political circles, an angry press conference at City Hall and shattered relations between the state and its capital city.

From *Governing,* April 2004.

And that makes what actually happened all the more interesting. Franklin and Johnson had a private meeting. Shortly afterward, the Republican governor, Sonny Perdue, stepped forward with a commitment to put together a $500 million loan package. Then the GOP-controlled Senate agreed to Atlanta's request that it be allowed to vote on a sales tax increase to defray the repair costs. That bill's sponsor was Eric Johnson himself. A *Journal-Constitution* reporter called these events "the biggest pre-Christmas happy hour since Tiny Tim and Scrooge patched things up."

Actually, a lot of people are getting along surprisingly well with the city of Atlanta and its mayor these days. Since taking office in January 2002, Franklin has engineered a remarkable turnaround in the city's credibility and public demeanor. She is on friendly terms with the state's leaders. She has plunged into regional efforts to deal with metropolitan transportation, economic development and watershed dilemmas. She meets regularly with officials from the fast-growing suburban counties that surround her jurisdiction. And she has cajoled members of Atlanta's powerful corporate community into serving on task forces that deal with everything from expanding the city's park system to revising its ethics code to exploring the problems of the homeless. "She and I talk every week," says Sam Williams, president of the Metro Atlanta Chamber of Commerce. "If my phone rings at 7 in the morning, I know it's Shirley."

All this bonhomie is in large part the result of Franklin's political candor, nuts-and-bolts understanding of what makes her city tick and willingness to tackle Atlanta's problems head-on. "Before her," says Eric Johnson, "Atlanta hadn't been taking leadership, they were viewed as corrupt, no one trusted them. I think she has the highest integrity personally, but she has also gone out of her way to make everybody know there's a new atmosphere."

Yet what makes the 58-year-old Franklin one of America's most intriguing mayors isn't just her persona, it's her determination to master the trickiest balancing act in urban politics today. Franklin has decided that making progress on her city's challenges means working with everyone from the governor to suburban county commissioners to regional business leaders and nonprofit executives—as she says, "I'm looking for friends for Atlanta." At the same time, she admits it's far easier to enlist their help if the city can show it's willing to take responsibility for straightening out its own messes.

As reasonable as this may sound, it's a daunting task. To build the trust she needs among state officials and business leaders, Franklin has to bolster the political will within the city to make hard choices The state sewer deal, for instance, could not have been put together without the stunning rate increases Atlanta has asked residents and businesses to pay. Yet to sustain political support for such burdens, Franklin needs to show measurable progress in improving their lives—which she can only do with the help of people who want to see her city step up to the plate first. Franklin has juggled these demands with aplomb so far; the trick will be to continue doing so as the cost of putting Atlanta on a solid footing takes an ever bigger bite out of citizens' wallets.

CHANGING DIRECTION

There was a time, of course, when a big-city mayor in search of "friends" generally looked in only one direction: toward Washington. Chasing federal largesse for everything from highways and sewers to anti-poverty funding was a way of life. In 1982, an uproar ensued when E. S. Savas, an aide to President Reagan, drafted a report taking cities to task for relying too heavily on federal programs. Support from Washington, Savas concluded, had transformed mayors "from leaders of self-reliant cities [into] wily stalkers of federal funds. All too often the promise of such guarantees has created a crippling dependency rather than initiative and independence." The report generated such a storm of protest that Reagan publicly distanced himself from it. He also, however, began the process of cutting and reshaping federal aid.

By the 1990s, it was becoming increasingly clear that pinning a city's fortunes on substantial money from Washington was a fool's game, and a different attitude began to take hold among many mayors: the sense that in effect Savas had been right, and they could do just fine on their own.

Milwaukee Mayor John O. Norquist argued that federal policies had actually hurt cities more than they had helped, and he pulled out of the U.S. Conference of Mayors, which he believed paid too much attention to Washington. "You can't build a city on pity," Norquist insisted. Meanwhile, in New York, Rudolph Giuliani was demonstrating that a mayor who focused on issues such as safety and clean streets could create a sense of dynamism and give urban life a chance to reassert itself.

In a sense, Franklin is amalgamating the two approaches, except that rather than looking to the federal government for help, she's looking everywhere else. This is a strategy that big-city mayors across the country may have little choice but to adopt, whether they recognize it or not.

In part, it's a simple function of money. Atlanta is hardly the only city facing extraordinary infrastructure costs, as local governments in every region confront deferred maintenance on bridges, roads and transit systems and federal environmental mandates on sewers. Indianapolis, Cleveland and Providence are all raising water and sewer rates as they struggle to come up with the hundreds of millions, if not billions, of dollars they each need to bring their sewer systems into compliance with environmental regulations.

So, too, with the costs of meeting demands for better public schools and for boosting homeland security—federal mandates may be plentiful, but federal money is not—and with the costs of improving parks, neighborhoods and other amenities that urban fortunes depend on these days. Finding the resources to meet all those needs demands creativity and an ability to build partnerships at every turn.

At the same time, it's more evident than it used to be that cities' fortunes are tied inextricably to the fortunes of the communities around them. Their economies are linked, their watersheds acknowledge no political boundaries, they inherit one another's air-quality problems, their residents' cars jam one another's streets. This is hardly news, but metropolitan political leaders haven't exactly built a strong track record of taking it to heart.

"For too long, the various counties and cities in the metro region spent all their time on their own governance issues and insufficient time on how their actions affected their neighbors," says Sam Olins, chairman of the commission government in Cobb County, the huge suburban jurisdiction to Atlanta's northwest. "This

Atlanta and Its Environs

City of Atlanta: Mayor and 15-member council

- Area in square miles _____ 132
- Population _____ 423,400
- Average household income _____ $51,328

Metro Atlanta: 28 counties and 110 municipalities

- Area in square miles _____ 6,208
- Population _____ 4,262,584
- Average household income _____ $58,568

Sources: Metro Atlanta Chamber of Commerce, *Atlanta Journal-Constitution*

doesn't take a degree in public administration. It just takes common sense."

OUT OF THE RED

That may be, but in the years before Franklin took office, there wasn't a great deal of common sense on display in Atlanta City Hall. Franklin's predecessor, Bill Campbell, was smart, articulate and impressive in person, but his two terms were also calamitous for the reputation of city government. In addition to possessing an argumentative and thin-skinned nature, Campbell paid attention to the wrong details: He micro-managed personnel decisions but ignored major budget issues. He got into constant spats with the business community, disregarded the city's regional profile and engendered a deep pool of ill will toward Atlanta among politicians around the state.

By the time Franklin took over, the city was on the fiscal ropes, although not many people knew it. One of the new mayor's first moves was to bring in several teams of consultants—some of them paid for by the Metro Chamber of Commerce—to get a handle on finances and to help reorganize the human resources, procurement and information technology systems. A group from Bain & Co., working pro bono on the city's finances, discovered that, instead of the $21 million surplus Campbell's last budget had shown, the city was actually deep in the red.

"It was a very intense process," says Franklin, "with a dozen people doing a 20-year analysis of the city's budget, revenues, expenditures. In the previous years, it had spent well over its revenue. So while the city was holding property taxes low, in fact we were spending ourselves into a hole." Franklin's team eventually announced a gap of $82 million for 2002—"because at some point you just had to settle on a figure," Franklin says—although it probably amounted to more than $90 million, or over a fifth of operating expenditures.

Franklin's response was to tell residents that in order for things to be fixed they were going to have to share the pain. She persuaded the city council to raise property taxes, cut nearly 1,000 jobs from the city payroll and, in announcing a series of other budget cuts, began by slicing her own salary. Since then, she has set out to overhaul everything from yard waste collection to the municipal courts and corrections systems.

Through all of this, Franklin has mastered the political art of appearing to be non-political. It is an art she learned over two decades as an aide to previous Atlanta mayors. Franklin was commissioner for cultural affairs under Maynard Jackson in the 1970s, then chief administrator for Jackson and his successor, Andrew Young, in the 1980s. Later, she spent five years helping to organize Atlanta's 1996 Olympic Games. In each job, she managed to maintain credibility among widely disparate interests and factions. She also benefited from a tendency of those in power to underestimate her.

"I always thought she was little and cute, but I'd say 'Beware!' that first impression," warns longtime Atlanta political figure Michael Lomax, who is now head of the United Negro College Fund. "She's a powerful intellect, a tough personality and a person of extraordinary integrity. She's become formidable in her mature years."

Franklin insists that in forging coalitions with unexpected partners, she is merely responding to what voters told her they wanted during the 2001 campaign. "They wanted a mayor," she says, "who could relate to the state leadership and relate to the region." But Franklin is also responding to reality: Without allies, it would be difficult to solve any of Atlanta's significant problems. "There is no issue the city faces that can be solved alone," says Bill Bolling, a longtime civic leader.

MEETING THE CRITICS

There's no better example than the sewer crisis, which has forced the active involvement of an astounding array of players. At heart, the problem dates to several decades of infrastructure neglect, but the immediate catalyst was a pair of consent decrees, in 1997 and 1998, which the city agreed to after it was sued for violating the federal Clean Water Act. As is true in many other cities, the century-old sewer system in Atlanta combines sewage from households and businesses with runoff from the streets, and it has a tendency to overflow during heavy rainstorms, dumping raw sewage into the South and Chattahoochee rivers.

The consent decrees imposed deadlines for fixing the system, but very little had been done when Franklin took office, even though failure to meet the deadlines carried with it the threat of fines, contempt of court citations, and the very real possibility of a ban on new sewer hookups, which would effectively halt all development in Atlanta. Franklin created a task force, headed by Georgia Tech President Wayne Clough, to look at the city's options, then based the $3 billion overhaul plan on its work.

The challenge, of course, was how to pay for it. With the state and federal governments in fiscal distress, it became clear that help from those quarters would be limited, and the city's water and sewer rates would have to rise dramatically, if only to forestall court action. At the same time, the resulting rate increases were unsustainable for either the city's businesses or its residents, and the only way for the city to roll them back even in part was to get help from somewhere on the outside to underwrite the repairs.

For much of 2003, nothing seemed to be happening. A majority on the city council, worried about constituent anger, refused to pass the rate increase that Franklin was proposing. Governor Perdue and Senate leader Johnson ruled out any state grants, while other Republicans at the state capitol suggested that Atlanta ought to sell its international airport and use the proceeds for sewer repairs. Perdue did eventually offer a $100 million loan, but Franklin rejected it. "Though a generous offer compared to the zero we'd gotten before," she says, "$100 million wasn't going to significantly help the people or the ratepayers." And the Fulton County Commission, which had to approve any sales tax increase for Atlanta, voted against one three times.

Behind the scenes, however, progress was being made on two fronts. The Metro Chamber of Commerce, worried by the prospect of Atlanta failing to fix its sewers and appalled at the possibility that a federal court would shut down development, created a task force on the problem, headed by Lee Thomas, president of Georgia Pacific and EPA administrator under Reagan from 1985 to '89. And Franklin hired a lobbyist to represent the city at the state capitol: Linda Hamrick, an influential white Republican who was a friend of Eric Johnson's and a board member of the state's Christian Coalition.

The key breakthrough came after Johnson sent his letter to the newspaper, rebuking Franklin and the city's demands for money. Hamrick called to tell him he really ought to sit down with Franklin, that they would actually like one another. Johnson called Franklin, and she accepted his offer. "Her attitude is if people say nasty things about you, apparently they don't understand, so you better meet with them," says the Chamber's Sam Williams.

What had rankled Johnson most was that Franklin sent out a letter to close to 200,000 Atlantans recommending that they get in touch with everyone from President George W. Bush to state legislators asking for financial help for the city. "His complaint," Franklin recalls, "was that I didn't give him a heads up—I should have called him. I explained that the element of surprise was part of our plan, but I appreciated that he didn't like it. Then I said that just because it was part of our plan didn't make it right. So he and I began to talk about what it was we really needed."

Meanwhile, Lee Thomas was serving as a broker between Franklin and Governor Perdue. Once the governor had been convinced that the state had to act somehow, he settled on amending a loan program for localities so that Atlanta could qualify for the $500 million Franklin had been hoping for, albeit over a 10-year period. Senator Johnson, for his part, agreed to help Atlanta make an end-run around the Fulton County Commission and vote on its own local-option sales tax. And in January, the city council finally agreed to pass Franklin's rate increases.

"Once the governor said, 'I understand this is a Georgia problem and I'll step into it,' Lee Thomas explains, "he communicated with legislators to say, 'We have to step up.' But they had to see the city was going to pass the rate increase. At the same time, the governor coming in was probably the big thing in helping us with the city council." For her part, Franklin happily gives credit for the arrangement to everyone else. "All I did," she told local business leaders in January, "was hold on by my fingernails until everybody else realized I was about to fall off a cliff."

RICHER AND POORER

With the sewer crisis largely behind her—"to say it's been smooth sailing is an overstatement," she confides, "but at least we're not bailing water"—Franklin has turned her attention to the broader issues facing Atlanta. Close to a quarter of the city's population lives below the poverty line, and although there are signs of gentrification dotted throughout the city's southern (read African-American) neighborhoods, there are still many places that look as though no one with any influence has paid attention to them for years. The city's overall population has been growing larger, wealthier and whiter. Demographic forecasts predict a metro region increase of 2 million people over the next 25 years, but not everyone is confident this will benefit the inner-city black community. Atlanta seems fated to endure a whole new round of stresses as it figures out how to apportion the benefits of its growth.

For a mayor who entered office facing a budget deficit, infrastructure crisis and economic downturn, Franklin provoked little overt opposition during her first year. But frustration is beginning to surface. The mayor's willingness to take uncomfortable measures to improve the city's image among outside power-brokers has raised questions in the poorer neighborhoods. Although the property tax increase, the water and sewer rate increases and a recent rise in property values haven't yet generated angry protests, they are becoming political issues. "She made a lot of people unhappy with some of the decisions she made," says Sandra Robertson, a longtime anti-poverty activist who runs the Georgia Coalition on Hunger, which sits in a depressed neighborhood in south Atlanta. Robertson is quick to add, however, that Franklin still enjoys not only her support but that of the people with whom her agency works.

For her part, Franklin has begun to talk about wealth-and-poverty issues. She has asked a cross-section of the community to advise her on homelessness, and on how the city ought to pursue a living wage for its residents. While the specifics haven't taken shape yet, she insists that they will. "The city of Atlanta's interactions with people of low income around issues of poverty are [limited to] law enforcement," she says. "That's how we interact with them. Well, we've got to shift that model." She is also looking for advice on persuading companies that fled to the suburbs to return to the city.

These are long-term strategies, and whether they'll pay off in time to forestall unrest among key portions of Franklin's constituency is anyone's guess. "The problem she faces is that Atlanta is a poor city," says Robertson. "It has this image as a prospering, glitter city, but it is a poor city. She does not have a large tax base to support the government. And then, there's a very strong, organized corporate community she has to deal with. So far, she's gotten a bye from the citizens, but it's not everlasting. Shirley is going to have to handle that, and that's why I keep her in my prayers."

39
Capital Gains

Jonathan Walters

The District of Columbia, once the nation's poster child for managerial incompetence, is staging a comeback.

In most places, local ordinances require citizens to mow their lawns regularly. But in the District of Columbia, from the late 1980s to the late 1990s, the city government itself was notorious for failing to cut the grass in public parks and playgrounds—to the point that residents in some neighborhoods paid private contractors to do the work.

Although waist-high weeds in summer and unplowed streets in winter were among the most visible signs of municipal mismanagement, they were actually the least of Washington, D.C.'s problems. During its decade of dysfunction, the city was popularly known as the "murder capital of the U.S.," it had no integrated information technology system, five major agencies were operating under court-ordered receivership and its accumulated fund balance was $518 million in the red.

The tax and revenue department was so disorganized that Julia Friedman, the current deputy chief financial officer, described paying taxes in D.C. as "a system of voluntary contributions." There was no methodical record of who had paid their taxes and who hadn't. Business and personal tax returns were simply thrown into bins in storage rooms filled with unsorted forms, some of them with checks still attached. "The motto in D.C. was, 'We will cash no check before its time,'" quips Natwar M. Gandhi, the city's current chief financial officer and a 20-year veteran of the General Accounting Office, where he spent the bulk of his years auditing the IRS.

In the past several years, however, the city has fought its way back from the administrative abyss. The transformation has been engineered by a wide spectrum of people and institutions, including elected and appointed officials and volunteers, private-sector con-

From *Governing,* August 2002.

tractors and a Congress confident that infusions of new money given to competent managers would be money well spent. If any one person deserves credit for its turnaround, though, it is Mayor Anthony A. Williams.

A career government bureaucrat who had built a solid, if unheralded, record as a deputy state comptroller for Connecticut and chief financial officer for the U.S. Department of Agriculture, Williams became the District's CFO in 1995. Williams was hired by then-Mayor Marion Barry, but only the federally appointed control board that had been set up to oversee D.C.'s finances could fire him. That arrangement gave Williams an unprecedented level of autonomy, although few expected him to take full advantage of it; many observers sized him up as a mere fiscal technician unlikely to have much success in a city famous for defying change while chewing up outsiders.

But if Williams was a bean counter, he was a bean counter with an attitude and some ambition. He went to work quickly, firing 165 people in the tax department and replacing them with his own handpicked staff to restore order to the District's revenue-collection process. At the same time, Williams fought to get control of the city's budget, publicly sparring with Barry over spending plans. Not content to rule by control board-backed fiat, Williams also started riding the community speaking circuit, explaining to anyone who would listen his plans for municipal fiscal recovery.

As it turns out, there was political method to Williams's peripatetic communications strategy. In 1998—pushed, he says, by a coalition of community groups—the CFO-from-nowhere ran for mayor and won in a landslide, replacing the flamboyant and controversial Barry, whom many people (including many members of Congress) blamed for the District's woes.

Williams took charge promising what he had promised as CFO: to focus on performance and results. He was so serious about it that he had the equivalent of municipal baseball cards made up for all his department directors. On the front were the directors' pictures; on the back were the core performance measures by which each of them would be judged. Annual contracts with his department heads spelled out expected results. He also pledged to get the city on a performance-based budget footing, in keeping with a 1994 congressional directive that the District begin to track fundamental performance measures and to link performance to spending.

Seven years since his arrival—and now almost a full term into his tenure as mayor—there is no doubt about Williams's influence when it comes to turning the city back in the right direction. Today, D.C.'s tax system is considered world-class, the city has balanced its budget five years in a row (which triggered the dissolution of the financial control board last fall), all departments also are back under local control and public parks are now carefully manicured every other week by city-employed contractors, who methodically rotate through the city's grasslands.

But as Williams looks to a second term—he seems a shoo-in for reelection, despite an embarrassing flap over thousands of fraudulent signatures on his nominating petitions—the challenges he now faces are considerably more ingrained than those he's addressed so far. The District's infamously inept Department of Motor Vehicles, for example—which had begun to show concrete signs of getting better in recent years—is back in the headlines. Earlier this summer, the DMV's introduction of a new computer system was a disaster, creating almost immediate reversion to the days of long waits and testy employees.

D.C. Data

Budget, FY 2002

$5,290,222,000

General Fund Revenue

Income taxes	38%
Property taxes	21%
Sales taxes	21%
Non-tax and other revenue	9%
Gross receipts taxes	7%
Other tax revenue	4%

City Government Employees

1992 _____ 51,200
(876 per 10,000 residents)
2001 _____ 35,900
(628 per 10,000 residents)

Sources: D.C. Office of the Chief Financial Officer and U.S. Bureau of Labor Statistics

Likewise, agencies such as children and family services and mental health still have a long way to go before they're operating at the same level of simpler-to-fix departments such as parks or public works. The city's chronically under-performing schools, meanwhile, have undergone nothing like the kind of turnaround engineered in taxation and information technology. On the internal management side, the city's personnel department still operates on a paper basis, although a rollover to computers is expected next year.

And scrutiny of Williams's performance is likely to be much tougher than during his first term. "Because city service delivery was pretty much in the toilet for so long, we applaud mere competence," says Kevin Chavous, a nine-year veteran of the D.C. City Council, who ran against Williams in the 1998 Democratic primary. "We think it's an achievement because the trash is being picked up. I think we need to go beyond those things and look at rebuilding depressed communities, instituting fundamental change in public education and developing up-to-date approaches in public safety. We're not there yet in terms of those things."

In particular, Williams will be judged on his neighborhood economic development efforts. Critics charge that he has been a "downtown" mayor, neglecting the city's outlying areas in favor of the center city. Williams counters that the city has invested in its neighborhoods, most notably in the long-neglected Far East Side, cordoned off from the rest of the District by the Anacostia River. "We have invested a billion dollars east of the river" for projects ranging from housing to retail, he notes.

"Things have gotten better," says John Frye, a member of the Deanwood Advisory Neighborhood Commission in the city's notoriously impoverished Ward 7. He credits Williams for improved streets and sidewalks and for agreeing to shut down some of the trash transfer stations that had been scattered throughout low-income neighborhoods. But lots of work still needs to be done on things such as towing abandoned cars and dealing with derelict houses. "It's a slow process," says Frye, "but you can see improvements."

Williams doesn't deny that there are areas of the city that still need lots of help. He says he's using a strategy of placing city offices in key sectors around the District as a way to stimulate economic activity in those neighborhoods. Chavous thinks Williams needs to more aggressively strong-arm developers who've made money downtown and force them to begin investing in tougher areas.

The downtown-versus-neighborhood investment debate certainly is not unique to D.C. And sorting out the political economics of local community development corporations is a job that could stymie even the General Accounting Office. But what frustrates Williams is that he frequently doesn't get credit for what he has done—with a few highly visible exceptions such as rat eradication. A recent *Washington Post* article, for example, notes that the District wound up leading the greater Washington region in job creation in 2001, beating out the economic powerhouses of Montgomery County, Maryland, to the north and Fairfax County, Virginia, to the south.

It turned out to be a one-day story that didn't seem to stick to the mayor. Nor, it seems, have some of the more fundamental social improvements that have occurred on Williams's watch. Homicides, for example, are down by more than a third (although on a per capita basis, the homicide rate is still high, and clearance rates are uneven). The District's deplorable infant mortality rate, which had approached third-world proportions, has been cut almost in half.

By contrast, Williams's decision last summer to close down inpatient services at the city's ailing D.C. General Hospital—and to lay off 1,400 people in the process—stuck to him like hot tar. When he closed down D.C. General, which served mostly the African-American neighborhoods in the northeast and southeast quadrants of the city, he was vilified—even though the hospital was best known for its bad care and was spending twice as much as it was taking in, and even though he put in its place a system of community health centers and contracts with other hospitals to cover residents.

Indeed, the battle over D.C. General was a defining moment in the mayor's political standing in the District, and it highlights the city's thorny and deep-rooted racial politics. The city is divided—almost literally—between white and black, with most of the District's 190,000 white residents living in the affluent northwest quadrant and most of the city's 300,000 black residents living in the poorer northeast and southeast quadrants.

To whites, closing the hospital was an example of the mayor making a difficult policy decision crucial to the city's long-range fiscal health. To many black residents, it was powerful evidence of indifference on the part of the mayor—who is African American—toward the city's black population and neighborhoods.

According to a recent *Washington Post* poll, Williams' approval rating among African Americans fell from 72 to 54 percent in the past two years. His standing among white residents over the same span remained at an astronomical 83 percent. At the same time, and somewhat paradoxically, the approval rating of city services among blacks and whites was the highest recorded in the seven-year history of the poll question, at 69 percent.

Another possible explanation for the mayor's unpopularity among blacks is his attitude toward District government hiring. Marion Barry had honed patronage to a bad art, building the District's payroll to nearly 50,000 people by the end of his second term in 1990, or almost one employee for every 11 residents—a ratio completely out of line with other big cities. Since then, the employment rolls have been pared back to about 33,000.

The size of the District's workforce and the cost of government, generally, have long been dicey issues. D.C. has more employees and spends more per capita than any other city in the country. For example, its per capita spending on fire protection is $200, compared with the U.S. average of $78. Police protection spending is $604 per capita, compared with the U.S. average of $196.

One good reason for the District's high per capita spending is that it provides services that in other cities would be handled by a county or state. Nevertheless, both close and casual observers of District government report a still-too-bloated workforce, still too-generously sprinkled with employees for whom performance and results don't seem to be a high priority.

While Williams has had some trouble filling some top spots in D.C. government, virtually everybody agrees that the mayor has put together a stellar upper-management team, consisting of outsiders—such as John Koskinen, a former deputy director of the U.S. Office of Management and Budget, as city administrator; Suzanne Peck, formerly head of IT for Sallie Mae, as CIO and Neil Albert, a New Yorker with experience in both financial management and parks administration, as director of the parks department—and long-time insiders—such as Leslie Hotaling, a 14-year veteran, who now runs public works.

What's worrisome is what's going on below those top managers. When city and state governments were going through the serious and painful budget and personnel contractions of the late 1980s and early '90s, D.C. was still staffing up. The studies of span-of-control ratios and clerical-to-professional-staff ratios that drove personnel management in other places over that time period still haven't hit the District. In spite of having cut its employee rolls by an impressive 30 percent, those working in and around the District government report an overabundance of clerical staff—a group that seems to spend more time and energy fighting over who won't do some job or another than they do concentrating on transforming the District into a model of efficiency, critics say.

When fingers are pointed, they all seem to swing back to Marion Barry. But Chavous, for one, doesn't buy the criticism. "The administration has come to paint all these people with the same brush," he says. "Yes, some of the people need to go, but with a lot of them, their talents are being ignored. It's assumed that if you were hired under the Barry administration then you're a bum, and that's not fair."

But even some of the District's department heads who have tried to tap such talents and instill a performance ethic in their workforce admit to some discouragement. When asked about the relative commitment of his parks workforce, Neil Albert says, "It hasn't changed as much as I'd like."

Williams bristles a bit when asked about the attitude of the city workforce. It's management's job to either motivate employees to get with the pro-

> "It's one thing to achieve change in Sunnyvale, California. It's quite another to do it in the complicated, brutal, Byzantine political environment of Washington, D.C."
>
> Anthony Williams, Mayor of Washington, D.C.

gram or move them out, he says. On that score, one of his early personnel initiatives was to create an entirely at-will "management supervisory service" for all mid-level managers and higher. Those managers, Williams says, need to be held accountable by department directors for the performance of employees below them.

As for the bloated payroll, Williams—and others—point out that besides having to provide services normally performed by a county or state, Washington experiences both chronic and acute special demands. Those range from large political demonstrations that drain policing, transportation and public works resources, to dealing with the impact of the huge daily infusion of Maryland and Virginia residents who work in the city.

But the issue of the D.C. workforce can't be so easily dismissed. While more visible issues such as finance, community development, public safety—and even potholes—may be briskly debated citywide, ultimately the question of whether D.C.'s still-nascent turnaround will be sustained depends on how committed city employees are to making the place work efficiently.

It's a question that D.C. Council Chairman Pro Tem Jack Evans says he's been wrestling with for years. "Something like 72 percent of the District's workforce lives outside the city," says Evans, one of the longest-serving of the city's 13-member council. "And so it's a workforce that sort of flies below the radar. I don't want to say this about all employees, because we have some good ones, but you have so many who if the job doesn't get done, it doesn't hurt them because they don't live here."

Evans has additional concerns about the District's efficiency. "The city doesn't regularly benchmark against other places," he says. "And to the extent that it does, the information always comes back that we spend more dollars to perform a like service than any other jurisdiction in the country."

While Williams might not be overjoyed about those kinds of questions around city performance, he is quick to argue that they mark huge progress. Getting D.C. from a point where it couldn't do anything right to one where the discussion is now focused on things such as performance measurement, benchmarking and efficiency means, he says, that "the city and its expectations have fundamentally changed and changed for the better."

For Williams, that's not a bad first-term legacy, particularly for an outsider in a place such as the District of Columbia. "It's one thing to achieve change in Sunnyvale, California," he says. "It's quite another to do it in the complicated, brutal, Byzantine political environment of Washington, D.C."

40
Huge Turnover in Hard Times

Alan Greenblatt

A bumper crop of new state leaders will move in next January. Some may soon wonder why they wanted the job.

"These are challenging days to be a governor," Virginia's Mark Warner said recently, halfway through his first year in office. It's hard to imagine anyone disagreeing with him. A year ago, Warner was the Democratic gubernatorial nominee, running on a platform of making schools better and bringing "the bounty of the information age" to every corner of his state. But even as he spoke, the bounty itself was slipping away. By the time he took office this past January, Virginia was facing a deficit of $3.8 billion. Warner was forced to slash higher education funding and, he ruefully notes, many of the high-tech executives whose help he was counting on to revive the state's rural areas were struggling to stay in business themselves.

Next year's crop of incoming governors will have one advantage over Warner: They won't be caught by surprise. All of them will know what they are about to inherit. But they may find it a little depressing, nevertheless. Virtually all states are facing deficits next year that could be even worse than this year's record shortfalls. The relatively easy one-time spending cuts and funding shifts have already been made, and the rainy day and tobacco trust funds are all but spent. Now come the hard choices. "It's no longer just a question of where else you can cut," says Warner. "It's really going to go into questions of what are the functions state government should perform."

The people who will be asking and answering those questions will be, for the most part, new to the game. There are 36 elections for governor this year. At least 20 of them are certain to result in new officeholders because of term limits or voluntary retirement. It is the largest number of open governorships in 40 years. On top of this, at least a half-dozen incumbents face serious challenges. The

From *Governing*, October 2002.

bottom line is that there are likely to be more governors starting out fresh in January than at any point in recent times.

What the new gubernatorial voices will be clamoring for is far from certain. Whether Democrat or Republican, they will barely have time to sweep up after their inaugural balls before they have to begin patching billion-dollar deficits. How they go about doing that, at a time when tax revenues are plummeting, Medicaid costs are soaring and education remains one of the sacred cows of American politics, will set the tone of state governance for the decade ahead.

The new governors will have plenty of first-term company in the legislatures they will be seeking to influence, with as much as 25 percent average turnover in the legislative ranks. Term limits continue to wreak their effects: This year's election will result in a 50 percent turnover in the Missouri House, for example, and a 75 percent change in membership of the Michigan Senate. Quite a few legislatures are likely to change partisan coloration as well. In an average election year, about a dozen legislative chambers around the country switch control. If anything, the odds this year favor more upheaval than usual.

Democrats, whose decades-long dominance of state legislatures eroded seriously during the 1990s, now have only the slimmest lead in the number of seats they hold nationwide. If history is a guide, Democrats should be able to rebuild their numbers a bit this year. The president's party has suffered a net loss of legislative seats in every midterm election going back 60 years, according to the National Conference of State Legislatures. But in the current situation, history may be misleading. Republicans were well positioned to dominate last year's redistricting process in several of the larger states, and by and large they did so. Even if Democrats increase their overall numbers among the nation's 7,400 state legislators, Republicans should be able to preserve or even enhance their control of legislative chambers.

In particular, Republicans have reason to be

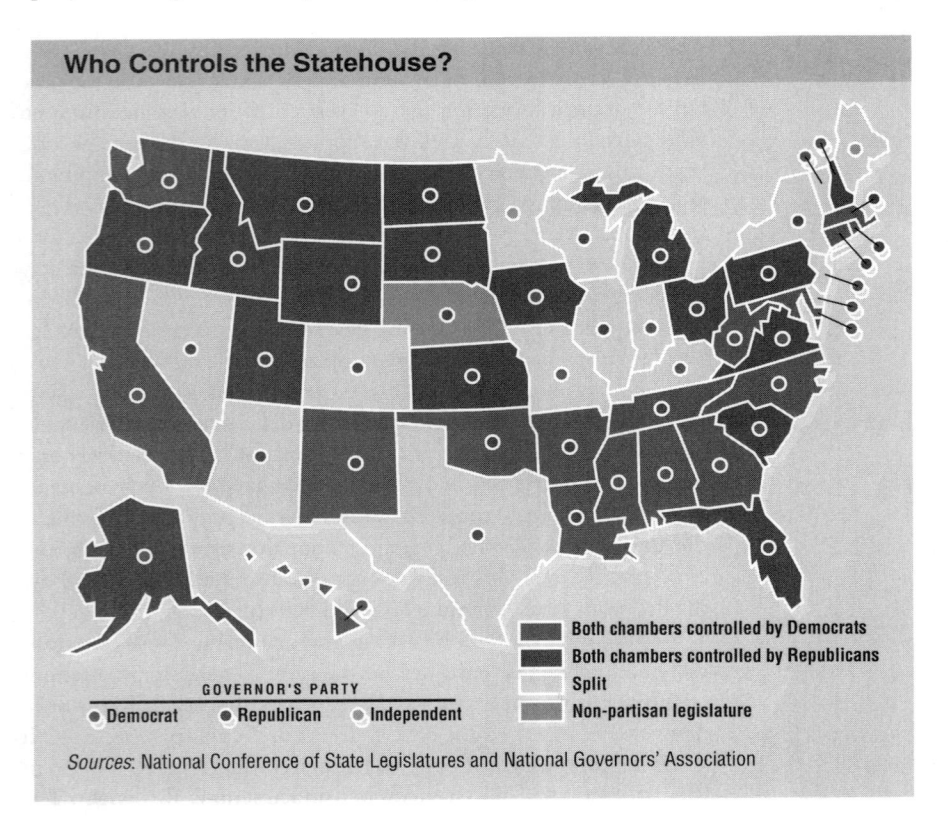

> *"Whether Democrat or Republican, [new governors] will barely have time to sweep up after their inaugural balls before they have to begin patching billion-dollar deficits."*

Who Controls the Statehouse?

- Both chambers controlled by Democrats
- Both chambers controlled by Republicans
- Split
- Non-partisan legislature

GOVERNOR'S PARTY
- Democrat
- Republican
- Independent

Sources: National Conference of State Legislatures and National Governors' Association

optimistic about surging into House majorities in North Carolina, Oklahoma and Texas. Democratic control seems shaky in the Vermont House, and Democrats were lucky to pull into a tie two years ago in the Arizona Senate, while both narrowly Democratic chambers are up for grabs in Washington State. The few solid hopes for Democratic takeovers lie in the Illinois Senate, the Minnesota House and the two chambers in Oregon.

But even as they continue building muscle in legislatures, Republicans are almost certain to lose ground at the gubernatorial level. They currently lead Democrats 27 to 21, with two independents, but it's hard to construct any plausible scenario under which they could hold those numbers.

Democrats not only have momentum on their side, having won 12 of the last 15 gubernatorial elections, but they are defending far less turf than Republicans, who must protect the governor's mansion in 23 states with just 11 incumbent candidates (including two unelected incumbents, in Wisconsin and Texas).

Whatever the individual results, 2002 will mark the end of an era in American gubernatorial politics—a relatively brief but important era in which Republican governors took advantage of their numbers to lobby Washington for a devolution of power to the state level. It was an era dominated by GOP voices such as those of John Engler in Michigan, Tommy Thompson of Wisconsin and Tom Ridge of Pennsylvania, governors who had the ear of the congressional leadership and, most recently, of the president. And tangible changes in the state-federal relationship took place as a result.

Many Republicans are hopeful that, even with the departure of these stars, the GOP case for devolution will still be a persuasive one in Washington. "It's like a basketball team," says Connecticut Governor John Rowland, first elected in 1994 and now seeking a third term. "You've lost a lot of starters but you're moving people up from off the bench." Even with an effective corps of new spokesmen, however, Republican governors will have to make their arguments without the benefit of majority status.

To start with, Democrats are favored in the contest for the biggest gubernatorial prize of all: California. Democratic incumbent Gray Davis, although weakened by a $24 billion deficit and by last year's electricity deregulation debacle, drew a stumbling opponent in businessman-novice Bill Simon. "Governor Davis is beatable," says one national Republican strategist. "Whether we have the candidate to beat him remains to be seen."

Meanwhile, Democratic candidates hold a substantial edge in states that have long had Republican governors but have been voting Democratic for other offices: Illinois, Michigan, New Mexico, Pennsylvania, Rhode Island and Wisconsin. Democrats are competitive—or even leading—in several other states where they have not won recently, such as Kansas, South Dakota and Tennessee.

Incumbent Democratic governors are nervous in Alabama, Iowa and South Carolina, and a Republican is likely to be elected in Hawaii for the first time since 1959. GOP candidates have an excellent chance to win governorships that Democrats are vacating in Alaska and New Hampshire. But the bottom line is that Republicans simply have to defend too much ground this year, and have too few seasoned incumbents to defend it all effectively. All in all, it's likely to be a happy night for Democrats on the gubernatorial front November 5.

How happy they will be come November 6, though, is another story. Most of the Democrats running for governor this year are counting on the party's traditional messages on education, the economy and health to resonate with anxious voters. And they may. But with the

Leaving Already?

Legislators forced out by term limits in 2002

Ariz.	House–9 of 60	Senate–6 of 30
Ark.	House–14 of 100	Senate–11 of 35
Calif.	Assembly–20 of 80	Senate–7 of 40
Colo.	House–7 of 65	Senate–5 of 35
Fla.	House–14 of 120	Senate–12 of 40
Maine	House–28 of 151	Senate–8 of 35
Mich.	House–23 of 110	Senate–27 of 38
Mo.	House–73 of 163	Senate–12 of 34
Mont.	House–7 of 100	Senate–15 of 50
Ohio	House–9 of 99	Senate–4 of 33
S.D.	House–7 of 70	Senate–4 of 35

Total–322 members*

* This number is down from 330 (January 2002) due to mid-term resignations by eight termed-out legislators in three states

Source: National Conference of State Legislatures

decline of state revenues, Democrats can no more realistically proffer large-scale spending programs than the GOP can deliver on big state tax cuts. For all the talk about core domestic issues and the Democratic desire to blame both state budget shortfalls and business scandals on Republicans, Democrats have not been putting forward ambitious plans, excepting the now perennial promises to supply senior citizens with prescription drugs.

The grandest plans afoot this election year, as is typically the case, have taken the shape of ballot initiatives and referenda. There are a couple of truly ambitious ones, such as a measure to abolish the income tax in Massachusetts and one to provide pre-kindergarten care to every 4-year-old in Florida. But those are rare exceptions. November's ballots will include relatively few ballot measures nationwide, including fewer than 50 initiatives—representing the lowest number since 1986 and a 40 percent decline from just two years ago. "Lawmakers have added increased regulation to make the process more difficult for people to use," complains M. Dane Waters, president of the Initiatives and Referendum Institute.

But Waters admits that another inhibiting factor for initiative writers has been uncertainty in many states about the makeup of next year's gubernatorial leadership, about the changes that will reorder legislative power, and perhaps most important, about trying to sell any major initiatives at a time of serious economic stagnation. "Post-September 11, everyone's concerned about the government not having enough money," Waters says, "so some people have decided to hold off."

Index

Abbott v. Burke, 26
Abdi, Nuradin, 120
Abramson, Jerry, 8, 10–11, 12
Accenture, 45
Act 47 (Ohio), 32
Advantage Capital Partners, 35, 36, 37
AFSCME 79, 53, 55, 56
Aguiar, Fred, 152, 155, 156
AIDS, 99
Air pollution, 131, 132–133
Akron, Ohio, and homeland security, 116–117
Albert, Neil, 175
Alexandria, Virginia, 23
Alfred P. Sloan Foundation, 72
Allen, Paul, 162, 163, 164–165
Allen, Ray, 94
Allen, Tina, 101, 103
Alliance for Maine's Future, 149
Ambramcheck, Frank, 44
America Coming Together, 158
American Federation of State, County and Municipal Employees Council 79. *See* AFSCME 79
Americans for a Better Country, 158
America's Army (computer game), 72
Anacostia River, 18
Anderson, Gary, 45–46
Angelides, Phil, 131, 132
Anthem Blue Cross Blue Shield of Maine, 103
Arizona
 campaign finance reform, 150
 Government Information Technology Agency, 62
 party in power, 179
Arkansas
 education funding, 26
 state venture-capital program, 37
Armstrong, Dave, 10
Armstrong, Michael, 41
Arthur Andersen Inc., 156
Association of Counties poll on public health services, 100
Atlanta, Georgia, 167–171
Atlanta *Journal-Constitution* on state-city agreement to fix city sewers, 167–168
Attorneys general, 77, 144–147
Autry, Alan, 135–138

Bain & Co., 169
Baker, Nancy Kassebaum, 27
Baldacci, John, 101, 148
Baltimore City Council, 2, 6
Baltimore *Sun* on city council, 2
Barrales, Ruben, 138
Barry, Marion, 173, 175
Bass, Ed, 165–166
Bass brothers, 163, 165
Baum, Kevin, 42
Bayh, Evan, 160, 161
Beaulac, Mike, 65, 66
Beaumont, Constance, 111, 113
Bell, Chuck, 158
Benjamin, George, 98

181

182 INDEX

Bennett, Rick, 149
Berg, Alicia Mazur, 85
Bertoletti, Barbara, 20
Best Beginnings program (Seattle), 99
Billionaire funding of cities, 162–166
Biorn-Hansen, Sonja, 73, 74
Bipartisan Campaign Reform Act. *See* McCain-Feingold
Blagojevich, Rod, 51
Bloomberg, Michael, 118, 163
Blue Hill, Maine, 101–103
Blumenthal, Richard, 145
Bobb, Robert, 43
Boecker, Bill, 166
Bohannon, Mark, 132
Bolling, Bill, 170
Borst, Lawrence, 159
Bosley, Freeman, Jr., 4
Boston
    city planning by "The Vault," 163
    homicide rates, 87–92
    Police Department, 89, 91–92
    Public Health Commission, 98
    WBUR-radio and game to choose gubernatorial candidate, 69
    zoning, 84
Botkin, Mary, 51
Bowen, Debra, 61, 62, 63, 77
Bowman, Shayne, 70
Boxer, Barbara, 136
Bratton, William, 40, 88, 89, 92
BreakAway Games Ltd., 71
Brennan, Michael, 149
Bresette, Patrick, 45
Brewster, David, 163, 164
Bristol-Myers Squibb, 146
Broad, Eli, 163, 165
Brodsky, Richard, 18, 20
Brooklyn Supreme Court, 69
Brown, Jerry, 43
Brown v. Board of Education, 25
Bruno, Joseph, 18
Budget
    Atlanta, 169
    city deficit and tax structure, 29–32
    deficits and game-playing, 68–72
    HUD, 142
    pension funds and, 50
    state vs. local, 125–129
Buffalo, New York, 9

Bullock, Scott, 104
Bullock, Terry L., 24, 25, 26, 27, 28
Bureau of Justice Statistics, 91
Burton, John, 129
Bush, George W.
    Kyoto accord and, 131
    No Child Left Behind Act and, 106
    stem cell research and, 131
    2004 election campaign, 157
Bush, Jeb, 47, 52–56

Cable franchises, 137
CAFR. *See* Comprehensive Annual Financial Report
Calabro, Dominic, 56
Calhoun, Brian, 9
California
    Air Resources Board, 133
    campaign finance reform and, 158
    Department of Information Technology, 59
    e-mail and spam regulation, 77–78
    hiring IT personnel for state agencies, 59
    home rule, 127, 128
    IT use and policy in government, 61–62, 63
    national issues handled by, 130–134
    on-line budget game, 69
    party in power, 179
    public health services, 97
    state legislature, 14
    state vs. local budgets, 125–129
CalPERS, 131, 132
CalSTRS, 131
Campaign finance reform, 148–151, 157–161
Campaign for Fiscal Equity v. State of New York, 26
Campbell, Bill, 169
Canal Corp. (New York), 17, 18, 20
Canal Park Stadium (Akron, Ohio), 116
Canavan, Marilyn, 149
Can-Spam Act, 76, 78
CAPCOs (certified capital companies), 33–38
Cape Verdean gang, 89
CARB (California Air Resources Board), 133
Caro, Robert, 16
Carson, Keith, 128
Carter, Jonathan, 148, 150
Case Western Reserve University, 166
Cash Management Improvement Act of 1990, 117, 119
CDC. *See* U.S. Centers for Disease Control and Prevention
Ceasefire program, 90
Center for Efficient Government (Florida), 47

INDEX 183

Centers for Disease Control and Prevention. *See* U.S. Centers for Disease Control and Prevention
Central Cities Council (National League of Cities), 3
Certified capital companies (CAPCOs), 33–38
CGI-AMS consulting firm, 65
Chaddick, Harry, 84
Chaney, Carolyn, 136
Chavous, Kevin, 174, 175
Chicago
    homeland security, 118
    lobbyist in Washington to represent, 136
    zoning issues, 83–86
Christensen, Doug, 106
Christoffersen, Chris, 38
Cianchette, Peter, 148
Cisneros, Henry, 140, 141, 142
City councils, 1–6, 70
City planning, 83–86, 163
Civic Progress, 4
Civil service overhaul, 52–56
Clark, Margaret, 128
Clean Elections Act (Maine), 148–150
Clean Water Act, 74, 170
Cleveland
    billionaire's leadership role in, 166
    Union Club, 163
    University Circle development, 166
Clough, Wayne, 170
Coalition for Kids, 165
Cobb, Charles E., Jr., 55
Coburn, Andrew, 102
Coffman, Mike, 38
Cohn, Carl A., 40
Collins, Susan, 118
Colorado
    CAPCO program, 34, 35–37, 38
    clean water regulation, 75
    public health services, 98
Columbia Falls Public Schools v. State of Montana, 26
Committee for Education Equality v. State of Missouri, 26
Commuter taxes, 32
Comprehensive Annual Financial Report (CAFR), 21, 23
Compstat (NYPD), 88, 89, 90, 92
Computer games, usefulness in governance, 68–72
Computers. *See* Technology
Connecticut
    clean water regulation, 74–75
    sentencing and parole, 94
    state venture-capital program, 37

Consumer protection, 144–147
Contra Costa County, California, 50
Convergys Corp., 47
Conway, Joe, 18
Corby, Michael, 122, 123
Corcoran, Tony, 49, 51
Cordon, Bruce, 74
Coronavirus, 97
Corporate governance, 20, 131
Corrado, Anthony, 160
Corruption, 140, 152–156. *See also* Ethics
Cortez, Eli, 59
Council of 100, 55
Council of Educational Facilities Planners International, 113
Counter-Terrorism Coordinating Council (South Carolina), 120
Cox, Christopher, 117–119
Cox, Mike, 145
CPS Human Resources Services, 42
Creager, Kurt, 138, 139, 141, 143
Crew, Rudy, 40
Crime prevention
    homicide rates, 87–92
    sentencing and, 93–95
Crosby, Peter, 36
Crowley, Walt, 166
Cummins, Diane, 129
Cuomo, Andrew, 138–142
Cutler, Lynn, 136
Cybersecurity, 121–124

Daggett, Beverly, 149
DaimlerChrysler, 133
Daley, Richard M., 84
D'Amato, Alphonse, 18
Daniels, Mitch, 157, 158, 160
Davenhall, Bill, 98
Davis, Gray, 59, 128, 132, 133, 179
Davis, John, 46
Davis, Mike, 154
D.C. General Hospital, 174
Dean, Doug, 34
Deficits. *See* Budget
Delaware
    computer systems security, 121, 124
    e-mail and spam regulation, 78
    River Port Authority, 17
Delehanty, Dolores, 11

Deloitte Consulting, 45
Democrat governors, 177–180
Demolition of historic buildings, 5
Denver, Colorado, 8
Detroit city council, 2
DHS. *See* Homeland Security, Department of
Diallo, Amadou, 89
DiIulio, John, 91
Dillinger, Terry, 81
Dinkins, David, 88, 89
Dirigo program for universal health care (Maine), 101–104
Disease tracking by "syndromic surveillance," 98
District of Columbia
    CAPCO program, 34
    mayoral leadership, 172–176
    Motor Vehicle Department, 81, 173
    redevelopment planning, 18
Dresslar, Tom, 77
Drug abuse
    public housing funding for drug treatment, 139
    sentencing for drug offenses, 93–94
Duchin, Jeffrey, 98
Duggan, Kevin, 42
Duncan Associates, 85
Dunford, Robert, 91
Dunlap, Ed, 115
Duquesne University (Pittsburgh), 30

Easley, Mike, 126
Eason, Bob, 58
Eaton, Pauline, 111
Eaves, Gerald, 153, 155, 156
Eckert Seamans, 32
The Economist on marginalization of California, 131
Edmonds, Carolyn, 100
Education
    Elementary and Secondary Education Act of 1965, 107
    funding, 24–28, 107
    Improving America's Schools Act of 1994, 108
    integration of state and local information, 67
    litigation over constitutionality of funding, 25
    school construction and sprawl, 110–115
    standardized testing and federal mandates, 105–109
Edwards, Michael, 114
Egan, Conrad, 142
Ehrlich, Robert L., Jr., 93, 95
Elections for governors (2002), 177–180
Elementary and Secondary Education Act of 1965, 107
Ellis, Lena, 23

E-mail
    protection of government systems, 121–124
    spam regulation, 76–78
Engler, John, 179
Enhanced Colorado Issuer, 37
Enstrom, Michael, 66–67
Environmental issues. *See* Pollution
EPA. *See* U.S. Environmental Protection Agency
Erie Canal, 17
Erie County, New York, 9
Ethics
    attorney general suits, 144–147
    Brooklyn Supreme Court, 69
    campaign finance reform, 148–151, 157–161
    kickbacks and corruption, 152–156
Evans, Jack, 176
Evans, Paul, 89, 90, 91
Everett-Church, Ray, 77
Exchange Network, 65, 66

Farrell, Michael, 92
Faster and Smarter Funding for First Responders Act (proposed legislation), 118
FBI investigation of San Bernardino, California government, 152–156
Federal Communications Commission, 137
Federal Election Commission (FEC), 157, 158, 161
Federal First Responder/Critical Infrastructure program, 117
Federal Highway Administration, 23
Federalism
    local governments and federal funding, 135–138
    national issues handled by state government, 130–134
    public housing and HUD policy, 139–143
    state vs. local budgets, 125–129
Federal Trade Commission, 78, 145
Federation Inc., 37
Fellman, Ken, 137
Ferguson, David, 54
Feuding
    by city councilmen, 2–3
    by state legislators, 14
Filler, Josh, 119
Finance. *See* Campaign finance reform; Funding
Finneran, Thomas, 150
Firefighters, pay cuts for, 32
527 organizations, 158
Fix Your Commute (computer game), 70
Flaherty, Tom, 29, 32

INDEX

Florida
   CAPCO program, 34, 35
   civil service overhaul, 52–56
   outsourcing of government functions, 47–48
   Public Employee Relations Commission, 55
Florida Council of 100, 55
Florida State University, 56
Florida TaxWatch, 56
Food and Drug Administration (FDA), 36
Ford Foundation, 14
Ford Motor Co., 146
Fortuna, Diana, 19
Fort Worth, Texas, 165–166
Foster, Kathryn, 17
Fountain, Jay, 23
Fox, James Alan, 91
Fox, Joe, 47
Fox, John, 163, 165
France, Stan, 122
Francois, Kurt, 87
Franklin, Shirley, 167–171
Frautschi, Jerry, 163
Frederickson, George, 40
Fresno, California, 9, 135–136, 138
Friedman, Julia, 172
Frutschy, Jennifer, 166
Frye, John, 174
Fulton County Commission, 170, 171
Funck, Steve, 23
Funding
   billionaire funding of cities, 162–166
   education, 24–28, 107
   GASB Statement 34, 21–23
   homeland security, 116–120, 137
   local governments seeking federal funding, 135–138
   public health, 97–99
   state budgets' relationship with local funding, 125–129
   venture-capital schemes, 33–38

Galion, Ohio, 111
Games to simulate policy making and management, 68–72
Games-to-Teach (computer games), 71
Gandhi, Natwar M., 172
Gangs and crime prevention, 89–90
Gardner, Jim, 70
Gartner consulting firm, 58, 59
GASB Statement 34, 21–23
Gates, Bill, 164
General Motors Corp., 133, 145

Georgia
   CAPCO program, 34
   civil service overhaul, 55, 56
Georgia Coalition on Hunger, 171
Gephardt, Richard, 4
Giambra, Joel, 9
Gilligan, John J., 27
Gilmore, Jim, 82
Gingrich, Newt, 140
Ginsberg, Benjamin, 159
Giuliani, Rudolph, 88, 89, 92, 168
Glazer, Elizabeth, 90
Glendale, Ohio, 113
Glendening, Parris N., 115
Goldberger, Paul, 19
Goodyear Tire & Rubber Co., 116
Gould, Rod, 40, 43
Gould, Roxanne, 134
Governmental Accounting Standards Board (GASB) Statement 34, 21–23
Government Information Technology Agency, 62
Grand Theft Auto (computer game), 70
Granholm, Jennifer, 112
Greater Binghamton, New York, 17
Greater Louisville, Inc., 8, 10, 11
Green, Ken, 111
Greenhouse gases, 131, 132–133
Green Party, 148, 150
Gubernatorial leadership, 177–180
Gumport, Reitman & Montgomery, 156
Gun control, 139

Hagert, Celia, 45
Hagood, Ben, 115
Hamill, Pete, 88
Hamilton, Wayne, 159
Hamrick, Linda, 170
Hancock v. Driscoll, 26
Hansberger, Dennis, 154, 155
Hartford, Connecticut, city council, 2
Health care
   integration of state and local information, 66–67
   outsourcing of inmate health care, 46
   public health services, 96–100
Health insurance, 101–104
Heard, Robert, 37
Heavy Lifting: The Job of the American Legislature (Rosenthal), 15
Heckel, Jason, 76

Herald (Everett, Washington) games on policy making and management, 70
Herenton, Willie, 9
Herrald, Mike, 8, 12
Hevesi, Alan, 16, 18, 20
Hickenlooper, John, 41
Hickok, Eugene, 107–108
Higdon, Steve, 8, 10
Hiring freeze, 59
Historic buildings, 5
Hlawek, James, 152–153, 154–155, 156
Hoadley, Jack, 102
Hoke County Board of Education v. State of North Carolina, 25
Holahan, John, 102
Holland & Knight, 136
Homeland security
  drivers' license issuance and, 81
  funding, 116–120, 137
  protection of government networks against hackers, 121–124
Homeland Security, Department of (DHS), 117, 118, 122
Homeland Security Appropriations bill of 2005 (proposed legislation), 119
Homeland Security Grant Enhancement Act (proposed legislation), 118
Home rule in California, 127, 128
Homicide rates, 87–92
Horner, Blair, 19
Hotaling, Leslie, 175
Household Finance, 144, 146
Housing and Urban Development (HUD), 137, 139–143
Houston, Paul, 40, 43
Howard, Philip K., 55
HUD. *See* Housing and Urban Development
Hughes, Mark Alan, 2
Human resources. *See also* Pension funds
  city deficit's effect on compensation package, 32
  civil service overhaul, 52–56
  District of Columbia, 175–176
  IT personnel, 57–59
  outsourcing, 44–48
Hunter, Bob, 41
Hunter, Molly A., 25
Hutton, Claudia, 20

Ibarra, Mickey, 138
ICA (Intergovernmental Cooperation Authority), 31
ICMA. *See* International City/County Management Association
Idaho clean water regulation, 75

Identity theft, 130, 133
Illinois
  party in power, 179
  pension funds, 50–51
Improving America's Schools Act of 1994, 108
Incident Commander (computer game), 71
Incorporation of cities, 7
Indiana and campaign finance reform, 157–161
Indianapolis
  city expansion, 8
  crime prevention, 90
Industrial Exhibit Authority (New York), 17
Ingersoll-Rand, 131
Institute for New Media Studies (University of Minnesota), 70
Intelligence for Education, Inc., 112
Intergovernmental Cooperation Authority (ICA), 31
International City/County Management Association (ICMA), 41
  Code of Ethics, 156
Intervale Posse (Boston street gang), 90
Iowa
  Department of Motor Vehicles, 80, 82
  IT use and policy in government, 62
  party in power, 179
  state venture-capital program, 37
ISAC (Multi-State Information Sharing and Analysis Center), 123
Ischemia Technologies, 36, 37
Isenberg, Phil, 133
Islip Resource Recovery Authority (New York), 17
IT. *See* Technology

Jackson, Gregory, 61
Jackson, Jeff, 156
Jackson, Maynard, 170
Jackson, Rebecca, 10
Jefferson County, Kentucky, 7–12, 118
Jenkins, William O., 120
Jennings, Ed, 63
Jepsen, George, 160
J-Lab (University of Maryland), 70
Joanis, Steven, 36
John Hancock, 35
Johnson, Eric, 167–168, 170, 171
Johnson, Lyndon, 107
Jones, David, 137
Jones, Mike, 4
Josephson, Michael, 155, 156
Joyce, Paul, 92

Judd, Dennis, 3, 6
Junk status of municipal bonds, 32
Justice Department, 72, 145

Kansas
  Department of Health, 98
  drug crime sentencing, 94
  homeland security funding, 120
  litigation over constitutionality of school funding, 25, 27–28
  party in power, 179
  systems security, 123
Kansas City, Missouri
  city council, 5
  hiring IT personnel for city agencies, 59
Kansas Club for Growth, 28
Kassebaum, Bill, 27, 28
Kauffman and Broad (KB Homes), 165
Keds, 146
Kelley, Steve, 61, 62, 63
Kemp, Jack, 140–141
Kennedy, David, 90
Kentucky campaign finance reform, 150
Kentucky Derby, 64
Kern, Richard, 94, 95
Kernan, Joe, 160
Kerr, Rhoda Mae, 39
Kettlewell, Larry, 121–122, 123
Kickbacks, 152–156
Kiley, Robert, 40
Kilgore, Jerry, 145, 146
King, Angus, 149
King, Jason, 81
King, Joe, 31, 32
Kirst, Michael, 107
Klang, James, 75
Kline, Phill, 145
Klonsky, Michael, 113
Kocheisen, Carol, 137
Kolodney, Steve, 65
Koskinen, John, 175
Kotrlik, Alice, 36
KPMG audit report on Pittsburgh's financial situation, 32
Kress, Sandy, 106–107, 108
Kulongoski, Ted, 51
Kus, Ed, 84–85, 86

Lake, Linda, 99
Lake View School District, No. 25 v. Huckabee, 26
Lakeview zoning issues (Chicago), 83–85

Landon, Alf, 27
Lavigna, Bob, 42
Law Enforcement Alliance of America, 145
Lawson, Al, Jr., 56
Le, Van, 67
Leadership
  billionaires' role in cities, 162–166
  mayoral, 167–176
  party in power, 177–180
League of California Cities, 125
League of Wisconsin Municipalities, 127
Leavitt, Mike, 61
Lee, Bob, 38
Levin, Carl, 160
Levin, Sol, 155, 156
Levin funds, 160
Lewis, David, 58, 59
Lewis, Peter, 166
Libbey, Pat, 100
Libby, Jim, 149
Licata, Nick, 3, 165
Lieberman, Bill, 31
Lindseth, Al, 26, 27, 28
Linn, Henry, 110, 113
Lipper, George, 34
Liu, Michael, 142, 143
Lloyd, Alan, 133
Lobbying by cities, 136–138
Locke, Gary, 82
Lockyer, Bill, 77, 132, 147
Lomax, Michael, 170
London Underground, 40
Los Angeles
  billionaire's leadership role in, 163
  city council, 3, 5
  Committee of 25, 163
  flight of big business from, 163
  homeland security, 118
  lobbyist in Washington to represent, 136
  Museum of Contemporary Art, 165
  Unified School District, 114
Los Angeles Times and criticism of Broad, 165
Losen, Daniel, 109
Louisiana and homeland security funding, 120
Louisville, Kentucky
  merger with county government, 7–12
  "special events situation awareness" software used by, 64–65
Louisville *Courier-Journal* and proposed Louisville-Jefferson County merger, 11

INDEX

Louisville-Jefferson Metro Government, 8
Lower Manhattan Development Corp., 19
Luken, Charlie, 137

Mackenzie, Jake, 126, 128
Madigan, Lisa, 147
Madison, Wisconsin, 163
Madrid, Mike, 125
Magnolia Venture fund (Mississippi), 37
Maine
    campaign finance reform, 148–151
    health insurance, 101–104
    on-line budget game, 69
    state venture-capital program, 37
Malanga, Steve, 17, 20
Maple, Jack, 88, 90
Marion County (Indianapolis) Republicans, 159
Marstiller, Simone, 56
Martin, Dean, 60, 61, 62, 63
Martinez, Mel, 139, 140, 141, 143
Martinez, Ray, 80, 82
Maryland
    clean water regulation, 75
    public health services, 98
    school planning priorities, 115
    sentencing reform, 93, 95
    state venture-capital program, 37
Massachusetts
    campaign finance reform, 150
    education funding, 26
    hiring IT personnel for state agencies, 58–59
    on-line budget game, 69
    state venture-capital program, 37
MassBalance (computer game), 70
Massie, Elfreda, 40
Mathis, Bill, 108
Maximus, 45
Maxwell, Joe, 37
Mayer, Virginia, 136
Mayoral leadership, 6, 167–176
Mays, Doug, 25, 28
Mays, Harry, 152, 153, 154–155, 156
McCain-Feingold, 158–161
McCallum, Scott, 126–127
McConnell, Jim, 114
McCormack, Pat, 80
McDermott International, 131
McGreevey, Jim, 126

McKenzie, Chris, 126
McLaughlin, Ed, 151
McLelland, Mac, 112
McMillan, Michael, 1, 2
Meck, Stuart, 84
Mellon Bank, 30
Memphis city council, 5
Menino, Thomas, 88
Merger of city and county government, 7–12
Merrill Lynch, 144, 146
Merry, Molly, 23
Messer, Luke, 159
Metro Atlanta Chamber of Commerce, 169, 170
Metropolitan Life, 35
Metropolitan Transit Authority (New York, MTA), 17, 18, 20
Michaelson, John, 156
Michigan
    clean water regulation, 75
    Department of Education, 109
    Department of Environmental Quality, 65
    education initiatives, 108–109
    party in power, 179
    school construction policy, 115
Michigan Land Use Institute, 112
Microsoft, 144, 162, 164
Middlebrook, William, 105
Miller, Harold, 30
Miller, Tom, 144, 145
Miller, Zell, 55
Milwaukee
    city council, 5, 6
    merger proposal, 9
    zoning, 84
Minneapolis
    city council, 5
    crime prevention, 90
Minnesota
    campaign finance reform, 150
    clean water regulation, 74
    Department of Motor Vehicles, 80
    IT use and policy in government, 63
    on-line budget game, 69
    state legislature, 14
Minnesota Public Radio, 70
Minnesota River, 74
Minorities and standardized testing initiatives, 105–109
Mississippi state venture-capital program, 37

INDEX

Missouri
   CAPCO program, 37
   education funding, 26
Modernizing Florida's Civil Service System: Moving from Protection to Performance (Council of 100), 55
Monongahela River, 29
Monroe, Bill, 67
Monrovia, California, 128
Montana education funding, 26
Montgomery High School (Somerset County, New Jersey), 105
Montoy v. State of Kansas, 25
Moore, Adrian, 47
Moore, Alisoun, 42
Moore, Mike, 146
Moore, Richard, 71
Morabito, Don, 161
Morehouse, Sarah, 158
Morrison, Peter, 156
Morton, David, 142
Moses, Robert, 16
Motor vehicles departments, 79–82, 173
Mount Pleasant, South Carolina, schools, 114
MTA. *See* Metropolitan Transit Authority (New York)
Multi-State Information Sharing and Analysis Center (ISAC), 123
Multnomah County, Oregon, 67
Mulvihill, James, 154, 155
Murphree Colorado Capital, 36
Murphy, Frederick, 140
Murphy, Gerard, 117–118, 119
Murphy, Mike, 158
Murphy, Tom, 29, 32
Myers, Hardy, 51

Naake, Larry, 137
NAHRO, 139, 143
National Association of Attorneys General, 77
National Association of Seed and Venture Funds, 34
National Conference of State Legislatures, 178
National Governors' Association, 37
National Institute of Medicine, 97
National League of Cities, 3, 138
National Rifle Association (NRA), 139
National School Boards Association, 26
National security. *See* Homeland security
National Trust for Historic Preservation, 111
NCLB (No Child Left Behind), 105–109

Nebraska
   education standards, 106
   Emergency Management Agency, 120
Neighborhood Transformation Initiative (Philadelphia), 3
Neimeiser, Mark, 53, 55
Neis, John, 37
Nevada and systems security measures, 124
New England Adjustable Rate Government Fund, 156
Newfarmer, Jerry, 41
New Hampshire on-line budget game, 69
New Jersey
   education funding, 26, 27
   pension funds, 51
   state vs. local budgets, 126
Newman, Margie, 5
Newman, Matthew, 129
Newtek Business Services, 35
New York
   CAPCO program, 35
   Department of Motor Vehicles, 79–80
   Dormitory Authority, 20
   education funding, 26, 27
   outsourcing of state functions, 47
   Power Authority, 19, 20
   Public Authorities Control Board, 19
   quasi-governmental authorities, 16–20
   Racing Association, 18
   Retirement System, 50
   State Bridge Authority, 18
   State Thruway Authority, 16, 17
   systems security measures, 123
New York City. *See also* World Trade Center
   city council, 5
   GASB 34 implementation, 23
   homeland security, 118
   homicide rates, 87–92
   lobbyist in Washington to represent, 136
   Police Department, 88–89, 91, 92
   Public Health Department, 98
   tracking diseases by "syndromic surveillance," 98
The New Yorker on Kiley's role in subway systems' overhaul, 40
Nexbitt, Fred, 50
Nickels, Greg, 162, 164–165
Nine West, 147
Nixon, Richard M., 159
No Child Left Behind Act, 105–109
Nolley, Rob, 157
Norcal Waste Systems Inc., 155, 156

Norquist, John O., 168
North Carolina
    clean water regulation, 75
    education funding, 26–27
    party in power, 178
    pension funds, 50
    state vs. local budgets, 126
Northwestern Mutual, 35
NRA (National Rifle Association), 139
Nunes, Devin, 136

O'Bannon, Frank, 159, 160
O'Donnell, Thomas, 154, 156
Office for Domestic Preparedness (Department of Homeland Security), 120
Office of Asset Management (Federal Highway Authority), 23
Office of Intergovernmental Affairs, 138
Office of Program Policy Analysis and Government Accountability, 47
Office of State and Local Government Coordination, 119
Ohio
    education funding, 26
    School Facilities Commission, 111
    school renovation or replacement policy, 110–111
    state venture-capital program, 37
Oklahoma
    education standards, 106
    party in power, 178–179
    state venture-capital program, 37
Olins, Sam, 169
Olson, Walter, 78
Omaha Public Schools, 114
O'Malley, Marianne, 128
O'Neill, Bob, 39
Orange County, Florida, 23
Oregon
    Clean Water Services, 73–74
    pension fund for state employees, 49, 51
    state venture-capital program, 37
Oregon Helps!, 67
Outsourcing, 44–48
Outstanding Schools Act of 1993, 26
Overcoat Development Corp. (New York), 17
Overture Foundation, 163
Owens, Bill, 38

PACs. *See* Campaign finance reform
Paige, Rod, 108

Parent, Bill, 80
Park, Peter, 41
Parker, Dan, 160, 161
Parking structures, 5
Parmer, Alyce, 54
Party affiliations of governors, 178
Pataki, George, 17, 18, 19, 20, 42
Patrick, Susan, 62
Patton, Paul, 150
Patton Boggs, 136
Pavley, Fran, 132–133
Peck, Suzanne, 175
Pedestrian Street in city planning, 85
Pelgrin, Will, 122, 123, 124
Pellegrino, Karen, 80
Pennsylvania
    party in power, 179
    state venture-capital program, 37
    tax-law changes, game to figure effect of, 69
Pension funds
    corporate governance, 131
    investment in state venture-capital programs, 34, 37
    municipal debt due to, 31
    payout planning, 49–51
Perdue, Sonny, 168, 170, 171
Peters, Mike, 2
Pew Center for Civic Journalism, 70
PHAS (public housing inspection program), 142–143
Philadelphia City Council, 2, 3
Phillips, Gregg, 48
Phillis, William, 26
PHINs (Public Health Information Networks), 66
Phoenix City Council, 5
Phoenix Project (South Carolina), 79
Pietroski, Joe, 149
Pittsburgh, Pennsylvania, 2, 29–32
Pittsburgh Post-Gazette on tax increases due to city shortfall, 32
Pittsburgh Stadium Authority, 18
Plough, Alonzo, 96, 97, 98
Plusquellic, Donald, 116, 117, 119, 120
Police and homicide rates, 87–92
Policy
    crime prevention, 87–92
    health insurance, 101–104
    public health services, 96–100
    school construction, 110–115
    sentencing, 93–95
    standardized testing and federal education mandates, 105–109

Pollution
    California regulation, 131, 132–133
    trading and clean water regulation, 73–75
Polymer Science Institute, University of Akron, 116
Port Authority of New York and New Jersey, 16, 19
Portland, Oregon, 22
Postmus, Bill, 152
Potts, Randy, 124
Privacy regulation, 130, 133
Privatizing, 44–48
Progressive Insurance Co., 166
Proposition 13 (California), 128, 129
Pryor, Bill, 147
Public employees. *See* Human resources; Pension funds
Public Financial Management, 32
Public Health Information Networks (PHINs), 66
Public health services, 96–100
Public housing inspection program (PHAS), 142–143
Public Policy Institute of California, 128
Public-sector executives, 39–42
Publishers Clearing House, 146
Purcell, Carolyn, 57, 59

Quasi-governmental authorities, 16–20

Race
    District of Columbia and, 174–175
    standardized testing initiatives and, 105–109
Radanovich, George, 138
Raftery, William, 21, 22
RAGA. *See* Republican Attorneys General Association
Rahr Malting Co., 74, 75
Randolph, Will, 155, 156
Reagan, Ronald, 168
Reebok, 146
Reese, Roberta, 22
Regulation
    e-mail and spam, 76–78
    motor vehicles departments, 79–82
    water pollution, 73–75
    zoning, 83–86
Rejeski, David, 69, 71
Rendell, Edward, 2, 69
Reno, Janet, 88
Republican Attorneys General Association (RAGA), 145, 147
Republican governors, 177–180
Republican Governors' Association, 158
RESTART program for drug problem and mental evaluation of prisoners, 95

Retirees and state pension funds, 49–51
Richmond, Virginia, city council, 5
Ridge, Tom, 117–119, 137, 179
Rigby, Robert, 140
Riley, Trish, 101, 102, 104
Riordan, Richard, 165
Rivers, Eugene, 91
Roberts, Jim, 30
Robertson, Sandra, 171
Robert Wood Johnson Foundation, 99
Roddey, Jim, 31
Romer, Roy, 114, 163
Romney, Mitt, 117
Roper, Gail, 59
Rosborg, Jim, 106
Rosenthal, Alan, 14–15
Rotherham, Andrew, 107
Rove, Karl, 108
Rowland, John, 179
Ruppel, Warren, 23
Rustem, Bill, 112, 115
Rydell, Charlene, 103
Ryder, John, 9

Saar, Mary Ann, 95
Sabato, Larry J., 149
Sacramento, California, 130–134
St. John, Christopher, 102, 103
St. Louis, Missouri, 1–6
St. Louis Board of Aldermen, 3–6
Sales, Sandra, 59
Sales taxes, 128
Salomon Smith Barney, 156
San Bernardino, California, 152–156
Sandoval, Brian, 145
Sanford, Mark, 46, 79, 112
San Francisco city council, 5
SARS (severe acute respiratory syndrome), 96, 97, 99–100
Savas, E. S., 168
Savors, Rick, 111
Sawyer, W. Tom, 151
Schaffer, Jan, 70
Schary, Claire, 75
Schell, Paul, 164
Schoharie County, New York, 122
School construction, 110–115
Schools. *See* Education
Schwarzenegger, Arnold, 14

INDEX

Seattle
    billionaire's leadership role in, 162, 164
    public health services, 96–100
    Rainier Club, 163
Sebelius, Kathleen, 27
Sebelius, Keith, 27
Security issues. *See* Homeland security
Selecky, Mary, 99
Sentencing, 93–95
Serious Games Initiative (Woodrow Wilson Center), 69, 71
Service First, 52–56
Sewer repair, 167–168, 170–171
Shively, Kentucky, 7
Shosteck, Eron, 132
Shreve, David, 106, 108
Shrewsbury, Jim, 2, 3, 4, 5–6
Sichterman, Nicholas, 101, 103
Silicon Valley, California, 8, 33, 133, 134
Silver, Sheldon, 18
SimCity (computer game), 70
Simitian, Joe, 134
Simon, Bill, 47, 48, 179
Simon, Donald, 158, 159
Simon, Leonard, 135, 136, 138
Sinkler, Michelle, 113, 114
Skoler, Michael, 70
Slap, Albert, 113
Slay, Francis, 4
Small businesses and health insurance, 102–103
Smallpox-vaccination program, 97
"Smart Growth" (Maryland initiative on school sprawl), 115
Smith, Eric, 40
Smith, Irene, 3
Social services
    integration of state and local information, 67
    outsourcing functions of, 44–48
    reduction in federal funding, 68
Soft money. *See* Campaign finance reform
Software. *See* Technology
The Sometimes Governments (Ford Foundation), 14
Sommer, Bob, 144, 146
Sorkin, David, 77
South Carolina
    Counter-Terrorism Coordinating Council, 120
    Department of Motor Vehicles, 79, 80, 82
    education funding, 27
    outsourcing of inmate health care, 46
    party in power, 179
    school construction policy, 112–113, 115

South Carolina Coastal Conservation League, 112–113
South Lake Union, Seattle, 162, 164
Spammers, 76–78
"Special events situation awareness" software, 64–65
Spitzer, Eliot, 17, 18, 20, 132, 144, 146, 147
Spokane, Washington, schools, 114
Sports stadiums, 4, 18
Squire, Kurt, 71
St. John, Christopher, 102, 103
Stadiums. *See* Sports stadiums
Standardized testing and federal mandates, 105–109
Standard & Poor's, 143
Starkey, Elayne, 121, 124
Starr, Paul, 70
State constitutions and education clauses, 27
State Domestic Preparedness program, 117
State legislatures
    national issues handled by, 130–134
    party in power, 178–179
    structure of, 13–15
    technology and, 60–63
Steele, Linda, 23
Stegman, Michael, 141
Stein, Jill, 150
Stein, Lana, 4
Steinberg, Darell, 129
Steinbrueck, Peter, 165
Stem cell research, 131
Stephens, Fred, 82
Stewart, Billy, 90
Stonehenge Capital Corp., 35
StorePerform Technologies, 37
Street, John, 2
Structure of government
    city councils, 1–6
    merger of city and county government, 7–12
    quasi-governmental authorities, 16–20
    state legislatures, 13–15
Summers, Bill, 7
Summerset residential project (Pittsburgh), 29, 31
Sun America, 165
Sweezy, John, 159
Szaley, Steve, 126

Tanner, Kevin, 57, 58
Taxation and city budget deficit, 29–32
Tax credits for state venture-capital programs, 35, 37
Taylor, William L., 106

INDEX

Technology
    computer games, usefulness in governance, 68–72
    disease tracking by "syndromic surveillance," 98
    e-mail and spam regulation, 76–78
    identity theft via, 130, 133
    integration of state and local information, 64–67
    IT personnel, 57–59
    motor vehicles departments, 80–81, 173
    protection of government networks against hackers, 121–124
    public health services and, 98
    "special events situation awareness" software, 64–65
    state legislatures and, 60–63
Teeter, Dorothy, 98
10 Point Coalition, 89
Term limits in state legislatures, 179
Terrorism
    homeland security funding, 116–120
    protection of government networks against hackers, 121–124
Terry, Fred, 126
Texas
    CAPCO program, 34
    Department of Information Resources, 57
    drug crime sentencing, 94
    Education Agency, 67
    education funding, 26
    Health and Human Services Commission, 45
    on-line budget game, 69
    outsourcing functions of state agencies, 44–45, 48
    party in power, 179
Thomas, Lee, 170, 171
Thompson, Dan, 127
Thompson, Tommy, 179
Three Rivers Stadium (Pittsburgh), 18
Thunder Over Louisville air show, 64
Tillett, Deborah, 72
Time magazine on NYC crime rate, 88
Tobacco suits, 146
Topeka Capital-Journal's game on city council members, 69–70
Topeka City Council Survivor (computer game), 69
Torlakson, Tom, 128
Toys "R" Us, 146
Trading and clean water regulation, 73–75
Travelers, 35
Tualatin River (Oregon), 73–74
Tuberculosis (TB), 99
Tyco International, 131

Udin, Sala, 30, 31
Udow, Marianne, 109
Underwood, Julie, 25
United Parcel Service, 10
Universal health care, 101–104
Unruh, Jesse, 14
Up from Zero (Goldberger), 19
Urban Area Security Initiative, 118
Urban Development Corp. (New York), 19
Urban Institute, 91
Urban Renewal Act of 1949, 4
U.S. Census Bureau, 11, 17, 18, 153
U.S. Centers for Disease Control and Prevention, 64, 97
U.S. Chamber of Commerce, 145
U.S. Conference of Mayors, 3, 117, 135, 137, 168
U.S. Department of Education, 105
U.S. Department of Health and Human Services, 72
U.S. Environmental Protection Agency (EPA), 65, 66, 74, 138
U.S. Food and Drug Administration (FDA), 36
U.S. Housing and Urban Development. *See* Housing and Urban Development (HUD)
U.S. Small Business Association, 77
Utah
    education standards, 106
    IT use and policy in government, 61
    Office of Planning and Budget, 68
Utah Budget Simulator (computer game), 68–69

Valuation of infrastructure, 21–23
Van Daniker, Relmond, 22
Varn, Richard, 62, 63
Ventura, Jesse, 14
Venture-capital schemes, 33–38
Vermont
    education standards, 106
    party in power, 179
Villa, Matt, 5
Virginia
    clean water regulation, 75
    Department of Motor Vehicles, 82
    drug crime sentencing, 94–95
    education standards, 106
    state vs. local budgets, 126
    state venture-capital program, 37
Virtual U (computer game), 71
Voinovich, George, 166

Wage freezes for government workers, 32
Wagner, Jack, 18

Wall Street suits, 132, 144, 146
Walsh, Kenneth James, 155
Wandro, Mark, 81, 82
Ward, Lynne, 69
Wardynski, Casey, 72
Warneke, Mark, 114
Warner, Mark, 177, 178
Washington (State)
    Department of Motor Vehicles, 82
    e-mail and spam regulation, 76, 78
    IT use and policy in government, 61
    party in power, 179
    public health services, 100
Washington, D.C. *See* District of Columbia
Washington Post
    on approval rating of D.C. mayor, 175
    on D.C. job growth, 174
    on D.C. top education post, 40
Washington State Association of Counties, 100
Waterfront Renaissance (computer game), 70
Water pollution regulation, 73–75, 170
Waters, M. Dane, 180
Watkins, Tom, 109
Weber, Shari, 27
Web sites. *See* Technology
Wegener, Brian, 75
Weil, Alan, 102, 104
Weinzapfel, Jonathan, 161
West Nile virus, 97, 99
West Orange-Cove Consolidated ISD v. Neeley, 26
Wexler, Richard, 47
Whitman, Christie, 51
Why Johnny Can't Walk to School (National Trust for Historic Preservation), 111
Wiesner, Paul, 98

Wiggins, Patricia, 129
Wilhelm, Daniel, 94
Williams, Anthony A., 40, 173–176
Williams, Sam, 168, 171
Willis, Chris, 70
Wilshire Associates, 50, 51
Wilshire Group, 35
Winkley, Mary, 61
Winston-Salem crime prevention, 90
Wisconsin
    campaign finance reform, 150
    CAPCO program, 34
    Natural Resources Department, 75
    party in power, 179
    Public Health Information Network, 66
    state legislature, 14
    state vs. local budgets, 126–127
Witt, Anne, 81
Wohlgemuth, Arlene, 45, 48
Wood, Jane, 127
Wood, Rod, 41, 42, 43
Wood, Steven, 78
Woodrow Wilson International Center for Scholars, 69, 71
Wootten, James, 147
World Trade Center, 19, 69

XML, 66

Yeater, Royce, 110
Yoran, Amit, 122
Young, Andrew, 170
Young, Parry, 51
Youth Violence Strike Force (Boston), 89, 90

Zoning, 83–86